ONE WEEK LOAN

SUPERVISING OFFENDERS IN THE COMMUNITY

WELFARE AND SOCIETY
STUDIES IN WELFARE POLICY, PRACTICE AND THEORY

Series Editors:
Matthew Colton, Kevin Haines, Peter Raynor, Tim Stainton and Anthea Symonds
School of Social Sciences and International Development,
University of Wales Swansea

Welfare and Society is an exciting series from the University of Wales Swansea, School of Social Sciences and International Development in conjunction with Ashgate, concerned with all aspects of social welfare. The series publishes works of research, theory, history and practice from a wide range of contemporary applied social studies subjects such as Criminal Justice, Child Welfare, Community Care, Race and Ethnicity, Therapeutic and Intervention Techniques, Community Development and Social Policy. The series includes extended research reports of scholarly interest as well as works aimed at both the academic and professional communities.

Supervising Offenders
in the Community
A History of Probation Theory and Practice

MAURICE VANSTONE

ASHGATE

© Maurice Vanstone 2004

Published by
Ashgate Publishing Limited
Gower House
Croft Road
Aldershot
Hampshire GU11 3HR
England

Ashgate Publishing Company
Suite 420
101 Cherry Street
Burlington, VT 05401-4405
USA

Ashgate website: http://www.ashgate.com

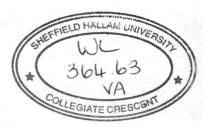

British Library Cataloguing in Publication Data
Vanstone, Maurice
    Supervising offenders in the community : a history of
    probation theory and practice. - (Welfare and society)
    1.Probation - Great Britain - History 2.Police supervision
    - Great Britain - History
    I.Title
    364.6'3'0941

Library of Congress Cataloging-in-Publication Data
Vanstone, Maurice.
    Supervising offenders in the community : a history of probation theory and practice
/ by Maurice Vanstone.
        p. cm. -- (Welfare and society)
    Includes bibliographical references and index.
    ISBN 0-7546-4190-2
    1. Probation--Great Britain--History. 2. Police supervision--Great Britain--
History. I. Title. II. Series.

    HV9345.A5V36 2004
    364.6'3'0941--dc22

                                                                    2004007432

ISBN 0 7546 4190 2

Printed and bound in Great Britain by Antony Rowe Ltd, Chippenham, Wiltshire

Contents

For Jen

Preface

The year in which the probation service has merged with the prison service to form the *National Offender Management Service* is, perhaps, an appropriate time to reflect back on the history of the practice of 'managing' offenders in the community, and to seek an understanding of the discourses and rhetoric of that practice. Such an understanding has to be based on a parallel understanding of the historical context of that practice, and that in turn involves engagement with complexities relatively unexplored by orthodox accounts of the early origins and development of the probation service. Invariably, these accounts trace the origins of the probation service to the police court missionaries and pressure for penal reform by a homogeneous movement motivated by humanity and Christian principles. While not denying these religious and humanitarian dimensions to the creation of probation, in this book it is argued that the concept of probation and its practice is best understood within a synthesis of the influences and pressures (political, social and cultural) that were dominant at the end of the 19th century and the beginning of the 20th century. Fundamental to this argument is the notion that the early history of probation is linked inextricably to the emergence of the study of individual psychology; the shift from individualism to individualisation in the application of punishment; political and societal concerns about the maintenance of social order; and the evangelical humanitarian mission. As another narrative in a long line, it does not lay claim to be the revisionist history urged by Mair (1997). More modestly, it attempts to build on the pluralistic accounts of historians like McWilliams (1983), and suggests that the point is one of emphasis; accordingly, the evolution of probation is portrayed, more appropriately, as a configuration of those different and sometimes contradictory factors.

Whilst many historians have portrayed the philanthropic tradition as the direct consequence of a new empathy for the plight of the poor and an aversion to the injustices of class relations, Ignatieff (1978) has argued convincingly that, it was in reality predicated on anxieties about the threat to social order posed by harsh responses to crime. The reformers believed that social order depended on 'popular consent', and as Ignatieff puts it, 'Howard's success in presenting the reformative ideal as a vision of humane moral reclamation has obscured its function as a legitimation for an intensification of carceral power'. It was, therefore, an essential element in the dominant elite's goal of achieving 'social order based on deferential reconciliation' (212-3).

This history, in part, aims to demonstrate how the development of probation has greater coherence within that analysis. In addition, it is argued that analyses which locate penality in the modern project - and more recently in the post-modern (Pratt 2000) - have drawn evidence from the realms of policy and legislation or what might be termed the macro level, and neglected those of practice and theory (the micro level). It is a detail, which at times confirms, but at other times, confounds the broader trends. For example, the 'nothing works' research is

Supervising Offenders in the Community

accepted generally to have been a critical factor in the demise of the rehabilitative ideal: examination of policy trends confirms this, whereas exploration of practice through the 1970s and 1980s challenges this orthodoxy in so far as practitioners continued to work towards the rehabilitation of those under their supervision. Practice and practice discourses, it is contended, are often missing from criminological theorising (at the micro-level), and this book, therefore, is an attempt to fill the gap. Nevertheless, to the extent that the exploration of those micro-level ingredients focuses on an institution over a period of years, it represents what Baker (1988) describes as a 'macro-level historical view' (269).

The book is based on a PhD thesis which in methodological terms was divided into two distinct periods, the early part of the 19th century to the mid 1940s and the second half of the 20th century. Evidence relating to the first was drawn from memoirs and other personal accounts, contemporary studies, official reports, journal articles, newspapers and other documents. In addition to those sources, evidence relating to the second included interviews with serving and retired officers (whose collective experience of practice and training spanned nearly forty years); four telephone interviews, and nine written accounts. In this adaptation and contraction of the thesis, some of those latter accounts have been excluded. Nonetheless, the book still places more emphasis on the accounts of practitioners (or the rank and file), and in this sense draws on the broad tradition of oral history.

Whilst it approaches the history of probation from a different direction, and presents 'evidence from the underside', thus challenging 'some of the assumptions and accepted judgements' of other historians (Thompson 1978: 5-7), the various sources from which the narrative is drawn each have problems of relevancy, authenticity and validity. So, the memoirs and interviews are likely to have been varnished to obscure any facts that might be discreditable to the author; the official reports represent a selective 'social perception of facts' (98); and the journal papers reflect professional expectations and aspirations. At best, they will describe what some practitioners believed they did with some people for some of the time. Most of the sources provide retrospective information, so will represent what is remembered and what is selected for recall; none represent an explanation of what happened the previous day or have the quality of immediacy. As Thompson asserts, retrospection on recent events rests 'somewhere between the actual social behaviour and the social expectations and norms of the time' (100); and retrospection on events further back maybe be shaped, unwittingly or otherwise, by subsequent changes in values and norms.

Moreover, information from the documents used, such as the Church of England Temperance Society (CETS) reports, training curricula and the National Association of Probation Officers' publications, provide near contemporaneous records of the life of the organisations and insight into perceptions within the organisations (Forster 1994). However, they reflect the image that the organisation is trying to project, may contain 'biases, gaps and flaws' (Cheetham et al.1992: 43), and therefore need to be read carefully. Their greater value lies in the fact that they help the researcher to 'look more closely at historical processes and development in organisations and can help in interpreting informants 'rewriting' of history in later verbal accounts' (Forster 1994: 148). Indeed, some of the detail may be uncovered by 'accretion measures' (May 1993: 136). May uses the analogy of the mud on someone's shoes, and what this might reveal about where they have been; and in this book for instance, the eugenicist language of some of the early practitioners may be viewed as mud on their shoes and of deductive interest. Documents, then, provide important documentary data, so for instance we know from the CETS reports not only what the police court missionaries did but also what they were expected to do and from what moral standpoint.

To summarise, then, the piecing together of this history from the underside of the probation service is part of its claim to originality. It is not a denial of the validity of previous accounts; indeed, in a number of respects it endorses it. Rather, it is an attempt to tell the full story, and in so doing accord the various characters in the story the respect of judging and evaluating them within their social and cultural context. It begins with the legend of a letter from one friend to another.

Acknowledgements

The study on which this book is based would not have been possible without the help of the following people who in their own unique way contributed to my thinking about the shape of probation history: Bob Anderson; Roy Bailey; Peter Brice; Brian Caddick; Matthew Colton; Gerry David; Mark Drakeford; Sir Michael Day; Eirlys Emery; Stan Green; Don Henley; Jan Hill; Denis Hodges; Noel Hustler; Terry Johnston; Keith Jones; Dorothy Lloyd-Owen; David MadMeson; McGuire; Brenda McWilliams; John Minkes; Bob Needham; Mike Nellis; Chris Noble; Phyllida Parsloe Philip Priestley; Joyce Rinimer; Bruce Seymour; Stephen Stanley; Rob Thomas; Jill Wheeler and Andy Willis.

For help with access to historical documents and papers I gratefuUy acknowledge the help of staff at NAPO headquarters, the British Library, the Lambeth Palace Library, the librarian at the Galleries of Justice, and Stephen White, For directing me to the Rainer Archive, thanks are due to Vie McLaren, and for help in the submission of the original thesis thanks are due to Carol Cook.

For their contribution to my thinking about probation work over more years than I care to remember, I thank all my former colleagues in the Mid Glamorgan Probation Service. Finally, special thanks are due to the late David Sutton.

Chapter 1

The Origins of the Probation Service:
the Orthodox Accounts

The letter of Frederic Rainer to his friend and vicar, Canon Ellison the chairman and co-founder of CETS, has a prominent position in most accounts of the origins of the probation service.[1] Osler (1995) refers to it as legend, and in so far as the original is apparently lost (Page 1992) and cannot therefore be authenticated, he is correct. However, quotes that seem to originate from the letter appear frequently in the literature, the most substantial of which is in an advertisement for the now defunct Rainer Foundation (no date):

> ...once a person got into trouble through drink or other cause, there seems no hope for him. Offence after offence and sentence after sentence appeared to be the inevitable lot for him or her whose foot had once slipped. Can nothing be done to stop this downward career? I hope that some practical work could (sic) be organised in the police courts, and I enclose five shillings that a fund may be started so that an agent may be appointed to attend the police courts to help the prisoners.

A paraphrase of this is repeated both in a history of the first sixty years of CETS (Church of England Temperance Society 1922), and an account of the Rainer Foundation (Kay: no date). Moreover, a report on a public meeting at Windsor Town Hall held in 1927 to commemorate the unveiling of a plaque to Frederic Rainer (and in attendance at which were his son and the son of Canon Ellison) quotes an address by the Reverend James Bell, chairman of the Advisory Board of the Police Court Mission:

> In London he [Rainer] beheld the sight of prisoners and ex-prisoners, helpless and friendless. His heart was moved with pity. He thought of his friend and vicar – Canon Ellison – who was at that time Chairman and founder of the C.E.T.S. He stated the case for prisoners and enclosed 5s. donation, begging that an agent be appointed to attend courts (*Windsor, Eton and Slough Express* 1927).

The circumstantial evidence of the sending of the letter as an historical event, therefore, is strong. However, legend or fact its true importance lies not in the part it plays in describing how the progenitors of the probation officer came about but rather in its symbolic status in orthodox histories. As argued in the introduction, those histories mostly place the origins of probation within the context of humanitarianism, good works and continual 'reformist pressure' (Bochel 1976; Jarvis 1972, 1972a,

King 1969; Minn 1950; Timasheff 1941, 1941a) or what more recently Pratt (2000a) has described as the *civilising continuum.*[2] The discourse of those histories is imbued with an acceptance of motivation based on an undiluted altruism towards the unfortunate, and its emblem is Rainer's letter.

It is not the purpose of this history to deny the humanitarian elements in the development of the probation project and subsequent probation practice; its history is incontrovertibly one of humanity and altruistic endeavour but the story is more complicated than that and the majority of histories to date are distinguished by their failure to unravel that complexity. The largely untold early history of probation draws it into a force field of social, religious and political ideologies and arguments, an exploration of which is essential to a full understanding of probation as a concept and a practice. Before taking an excursion into this relatively uncharted territory it is necessary to condense the essence of the orthodoxy to be challenged.

The Origins of Recognizance

While the essential facts contained in these accounts are consistent, there is variation in the speculations about the origin of this concept of releasing people from court without conviction on some kind of condition that they behave themselves in the future. Put together they provide a useful backdrop to our understanding of statutory probation. One commentator, in discussing the obscure beginnings of the principle of binding over, refers to an attempt to establish Athelstane, Anglo-Saxon king as the originator of probation:

> ...men should slay none younger than a fifteen winters' man [and] if his kindred will not take him nor be surety for him, then swear he as the bishop shall teach him, that he shall shun all evil, and let him be in bondage for his price. And if after that he steal, let man slay him or hang him, as they did his elders (Report of the Departmental Committee on the Treatment of Young Offenders 1927, quoted in Le Mesurier 1935: 19).

Novel though it might be Chute and Bell (1956) consider this 'one of the earliest recorded examples of the modification of rigid criminal laws' (11). Le Mesurier (the editor of the first handbook of probation) also refers to part of a verse in Chaucer's Shipman's Tale.[3] In addition, she publicises Sheldon Glueck's assertion made in 1930 that the idea of probation is much older than the work of John Augustus (the first known probation officer who lived in Boston).[4] According to him, that credit is due to the Pilgrim Fathers in so far as the Records of the Courts of Assistants of the Colony of Massachusetts reveal 'illustrations of the seventeenth century use of what looks like probation. For instance, the General Court respited the case of Mrs. Harding until the next Court, and ordered that in the meantime she be dealt with by Mr. Cotton, Mr. Wilson and the Church, to see "if she may be convinced and give satisfaction" .... John Cooper, Junior, was for some offence "committed to his father for correction"' (Glueck 1930, quoted in Le Mesurier 1935: 20-1).

Grinnell (1917) adds weight to this view in a discussion of the application of criminal justice before the adoption of the American Constitution which he characterizes as 'the bloody period of criminal administration' (595). He identifies three practises that might fairly be identified with the principles underlying probation. The first, *Benefit of Clergy* was an exemption from prosecution 'which originated in the claims of ecclesiastics to be exempt from criminal process before the secular courts [and was] subsequently extended by various English statutes [...] to commoners who could establish themselves as 'clerks' by proving that they could read' (Grinnell 1941: 73). According to Grinnell, as early as the 17th century, bishop's clerks performed the function of the modern probation officer in providing an opinion to the court on the eligibility of the prisoner's claim to *Benefit of Clergy* (Grinnell 1917: 597).[5] The practice was brought to America by colonists and survived up to the Constitution but afterwards because of concerns about its arbitrary application it was abolished by statute in 1841 (Chute and Bell 1956). The second method of alleviating severe punishments for relatively minor offences, the provision of security for good behaviour (or 'good abearance'), was a common practice throughout the New England States during the 18th century. For example, in a New Hampshire case in 1746, Justice Burns commented: 'I lately granted the good behavior against one for that he had bought Ratsbane and mingled the same with Corn and then wilfully and maliciously did cast the same among his Neighbors (sic) Fowls, whereby most of them died...' (600). The third method, Grinnell describes as the subjecting of indictments 'to the keenest technical scrutiny and granting motions to quash after verdict with the result of freeing the prisoner' (600). Thus the courts were able to introduce a degree of humanity and 'practical justice' into a harsh system. He does not argue that each necessarily represents a pure form of probation but rather his concern is with the relevance of their core principle: in his view, the subsequent probation system can be described accurately as 'a modern scientific application of the underlying principle in these methods' (601). This analysis leads him to the conclusion that whilst the recorded history of probation began in Massachusetts with the case of *Commonwealth v. Chase,* it is 'quite probable' that probation in some form was applied some time before.

In acknowledging the significance of the *Commonwealth v. Chase* case, Grinnell speculates that the judgement of the presiding judge, Peter Oxenbridge Thatcher, might be 'the earliest recorded judicial discussion of the subject of probation in its modern sense' (601).[6] The basic facts of the case are that the defendant, Jerusha Chase, had pleaded guilty to theft from a dwelling house, and the indictment was placed on file because she entered into recognizance with sureties to come before the court in the future if required. Subsequently, she was tried for an offence of theft and was acquitted; following this verdict the County Attorney filed for sentence on the original offence. Judge Thatcher established the legal concept of probation with the following words:

> But it is asked by her counsel, where an indictment has been suffered to sleep upon the files of the court for several terms, and no notice has been taken of it on the record or docket to keep it alive, whether it is competent to call it up at a future period, and to proceed upon it as a living process? But I do not understand that a prosecution like this can ever be said to be dead in law. If it should be said, however, to be hard measure to pronounce judgment after it has

been suspended for years, I answer, that the party might at any time have appeared in court, and demanded the judgment of law. It has been delayed from tenderness and humanity, and not because it ceased to be the right of government to claim judgment. By mutual consent, therefore, the judgment has been delayed till this time, and this consent takes away all error in the proceedings. (Quoted in Grinnell 1917: 602-1).[7]

Moreland (1941) seems to provide confirmation of embryonic probation in Massachusetts as argued by Grinnell when he challenges the traditional view that probation began with John Augustus, and instead asserts it 'came from the enlightened legal thought of Boston judges in the decade before him' (2). According to his version, people had been given a form of probation in Boston as early as 1830, and had been supervised by voluntary probation officers. However, Moreland emphasises the importance of Augustus in as much as he provided an exemplar of a 'treatment process, which would gain the interest, understanding and respect of the courts'. Without this, he argues, probation could not have been developed from its embryonic form in 'legal thought and practice' (2).

Like other commentators, Timasheff (1943) highlights the importance of existing institutions which historically in North America and Britain had been part of the framework of 'preventative justice'; namely, suspension of sentence, recognizance for peace and good behaviour, and the 'friendly' supervision of ex-prisoners and young offenders by benevolent people and charitable organizations. He acknowledges the use of recognizance in Massachusetts during the 17th century, and accepts that there are no recorded cases in Britain until the 19th century; nevertheless, he cites Blackstone's reference to the issuing of recognizance as a well established institution[8] to support his contention that the practice occurred in Britain a century earlier (Timasheff 1941).

In their discussion of the development of probation for juveniles Flexner and Baldwin (1914) identify the roots of child protection and correction through the 'constructive work of the court' as the power used by English Chancellors through which children were made wards of the King (or wards of the State in America) by the Chancery Court (7). The application of this power was confined to children who were neglected or destitute, and it was the juvenile courts which extended the practice to children who had offended.

Others also refer to what according to Bochel (1976: 4) is 'widely accepted as the legal origins of the probation system', namely, the medieval common law concept of recognizance (Brownlee 1998; Jarvis 1972; King 1969). However, Ayscough (1929)[9] points out that the International Prison Congresses had promoted the use of continental law as a means of imposing a conditional sentence, a procedure which was different to the English system in that it involved a conviction. Inherent in the principle of recognizance is the suspension of sentencing and conditional release, and it was this Flexner and Baldwin (1914) argue that led inevitably to the court requiring 'some record of the conduct of those so treated', thus stimulating the introduction of some form of oversight (79). Notwithstanding these arguments there is general agreement that it is in the refinement of this concept that the influence of Massachusetts is most significant, for as Mesurier (1935: 21) puts it: '[e]ven if

America borrowed from us a valuable legal instrument, we must gratefully acknowledge that it was returned to us tempered by imaginative insight and forged to new purposes'. Johnson, F. R. (1928)[10] has no doubts that probation originated in America, and proclaims that its development in Europe 'in large measure followed American antecedents' (14).

The Work of Matthew Davenport Hill and Edward Cox

Whatever the truth about these various interpretations of history the influence of John Augustus in America and the Warwickshire magistrates, Matthew Davenport Hill and Edward Cox in Britain is unchallengeable (Bochel 1976; Jarvis 1972; Page 1992). In this country in the 1820s, the Warwickshire magistrates adopted the practice of committing young people who came before them to the care of their employer following, it is suggested, imprisonment for a day. They did not use bail, recognizance, or any system by which they could follow up a case to find out if it was successful. Matthew Hill practised as a lawyer in those courts and was influenced by magistrates at Stretton – on – Dunsmoor who in 1817 established reformatories that aimed to reform juveniles through outdoor work and a family atmosphere (Bartrip 1975).[11] Later in 1841 when appointed as Recorder in Birmingham, he determined 'to try the experiment myself' (Hill 1887: 351) but he introduced what he believed to be an improvement on the Warwickshire magistrates' system by including the keeping of a register and follow-up inquiries by 'a confidential officer' (Bochel 1976: 5).[12] In addition, he made it a requirement that the parents or guardians signed a statement that they took on 'the obligation to do their best for the child' (Minn 1950: 128). Accounts such as these focus exclusively on Hill's humanitarian attitudes to juvenile offenders; but he had particular and strongly held views about the treatment of offenders which provide a broader canvas for his portrait. These will be examined later; for the moment, it is illuminating to draw on a more contemporary account of his practice. In his charge to the Grand Jury of Birmingham in 1848 it is noted that:

> for a period of seven years, beginning early in the year 1841, he had thus acted with regard to juvenile offenders:- that when there was ground for believing that the individual was not wholly corrupt – when there was reasonable hope of reformation – and when persons to act as guardians kind enough to take charge of the young convict (which at first sight would appear to present a great difficulty, but which in practice furnished little impediment to the plan), he had felt himself justified in at once handing over the young offender to their care, in the belief that there would be better hope of amendment under such guardians than in the gaol of the county (Hill 1857: 117).

Hill built checks into his system by using a confidential officer to visit whoever had agreed to act as guardian in order to investigate and collect and register details of what was happening. It is reported that during a seven year period 166 juveniles were dealt with in this way; of these 71 were deemed to have been of good conduct (and most of those were completely reformed), 40 were assessed as being doubtful, 53 as bad, and two were dead. The system appears to have been successful (the first *What Works* bandwagon and similar to modern rates), and later he applied his system to adult offenders. However, Hill's views were consistent with contemporary judgements about the purposes of punishment. He believed that pain should be 'a necessary incident to the course of life' of those sent to prison but that it 'ought not to be inflicted in a vindictive spirit as retribution for the past': rather it should retain the purpose of reforming the individual (102).

Later, as described in these accounts, Edward Cox when he was both the Recorder of Portsmouth and Chairman of the Second Court of the Middlesex Sessions from 1870 to his death in 1879 used a combination of a special inquiry officer and recognizance. He was reluctant to imprison first offenders who he argued should have the opportunity to redeem themselves, and this left him with two alternatives: either he could reprimand the offender or he could 'place him under recognisances (sic) to come up for judgement when called on, with a threat of how tremendous that punishment will be if he offends again' (Cox 1877: 37). The latter, which 'require[d] the convict to find surety for his own coming up for judgement' and was followed by discharge without punishment, 'proved entirely successful', and he had used it for a number of years (44). Before releasing a person on recognizance, Cox was concerned to ascertain through 'careful preliminary enquiry' whether they were suitable for reformatory treatment or whether they were a habitual or a professional criminal. To this end, he employed Mr. George Lockyer, an 'active intelligent (sic) officer', to make enquiries and report back to the court; in addition, he used the constable in charge of the case to inquire about the person's character and behaviour. His list of questions to which he required answers provides not only an interesting illustration of Garland's (1985) process of *individualization* in the implementation of justice but also a clear picture of their practice:

> Are there any persons in Court who know him – who can give an account of him? Can he give an account of himself? Who is he? What is he? Has he been at work lately, and with whom? Has he parents, friends, employers? Where are they to be found? Not content with his own answers, inquiry should be made out of doors (Cox 1877: 45).

In the event of evidence being given by the police that the defendant was a professional criminal the defendant was given the chance to disprove the charge by giving evidence. In unclear cases, the inquiry officer was often asked to seek new information and verify the evidence given by the defendant (White 1978). This, it is claimed, may have involved a superficial form of supervision by the officer and took Hill's idea a step closer to the modern concept of probation (Bochel 1976; White 1978). Evidence is in short supply on this point but there is some hint of Lockyer's practice in his work with girls. Cox was even more reluctant to imprison girls, and he therefore required Lockyer to search for 'a place, or a refuge, or a charitable institution, or some charitable person who will receive her'. Failing this he would put a homeless girl under the supervision of the parish officer or if she was able to provide for herself he would 'discharge her on her own recognisances' (Cox 1877: 47). His commitment to this approach with first offenders was strong: he urged other judges to follow his lead, and he professed himself to 'be more and more inclined to its adoption' (163).

Tallack (1884) refers to an experiment in Belgium whereby if a person was found drunk a policeman would take him home and the following day would return to the house with a broom and the offer of sweeping the streets for two hours or severe punishment. However, he identifies the London 'City Custom of Apprentices' as the real precursor to the probation system in Massachusetts:

> [T]he semi-private Court of the Chamberlain of London, at the Guildhall, exercises a controlling power over all apprentices in 'the City' properly so called. This tribunal affords a prompt, cheap, and excellent mode of dealing with their delinquencies, except such as may be of a graver nature; and it is much valued by the citizens (310-11).

Employers, if they had a problem with or complaint against an apprentice, for a fee of a shilling could apply for a summons for him to appear before the Chamberlain who would investigate and advise. If the apprentice's behaviour was intransigent he could be sent to a private Bridewell for two weeks, and after reflection, an apology and a promise to behave, be released. Tallack refers to it as a means of avoiding public trial and a valuable form of probation but adds that the Massachusetts' system strengthened probation by parents and guardians being 'persuaded or compelled to a better performance' (310-11).

The Church of England Temperance Society

A parallel development referred to in all accounts is the work of the Church of England Temperance Society (and its missionaries) founded originally in 1862 as the Church of England Total Abstinence Society (Harrison 1971). Teetotal work was an integral part of revivalist activities, and within that 'pledge-signing often marked an important stage in the conversion process' (171). According to Harrison, a significant increase in teetotalism occurred in the 1850s when the Reverend Stopford J. Ram, an evangelical vicar, placed an advertisement in the press calling for all abstaining clergy to make contact with him: the signing of a teetotal address by 112 clergy followed. Subsequently, the National Temperance League sent out 100,000 copies of a pamphlet entitled *Haste to the Rescuer* to the Clergy, and it was this, Harrison proposes, that led to the creation of the Society (181-183). Among other things then, the missionaries involved themselves in rescue work visiting, for example, cabstands, railway stations and lodging houses. Then, in 1872 the Society widened its objectives to encompass 'not only the promotion of temperance and the reformation of the intemperate but also the removal of the causes of intemperance' (King 1969: 2). In so doing, it immersed itself in a wider social work project underpinned by the idea that intemperance might be 'a symptom as well as a cause of evil' (3). Frederic Rainer's intervention and exhortation that the work should be focused also in the police courts, fits neatly within the conceptual framework of this analysis.

Thus with the appointment on 1st August 1876 of George Nelson [13] to the Southwark and Lambeth courts, and in the following year of William Batchelor to Bow Street and Mansion House courts (both incidentally ex-Coldstream guards who had served at Windsor), the Society demonstrated its commitment to Rainer's idea. In less than ten years, seventeen missionaries (one of whom was a woman) had been appointed in London, Rochester, Lichfield, Liverpool, Manchester, Worcester and Peterborough; in addition, six female missionaries working under the auspices of the Women's Union of the Society, had been appointed in Bristol, Cambridge, Derby, Durham and Oxford (National Police Court Mission 1950). Indeed the minutes of the London C.E.T.S's Annual Council Meeting in 1889 reflect the sustained enthusiasm of this aspect of missionary work. A Mission fund was suggested for the purpose of giving grants to match to the funds raised by the Diocese for both the appointment of police court missionaries and setting up Shelter Homes. The following resolution was passed:

> That the Council beg to suggest to the Executive the desirability of considering a plan by which they be able to promote and stimulate the appointment of Police Court Missionaries and the institution of Shelter Homes in the various diocese (Church of England Temperance Society 1889: 89).

Evidence of the effect of such support is contained within the Chairman's address to the Council of the CETS in 1889, which refers to 'the large extension of the Police Court Mission' (99).

In addition, the Mission focused on the welfare of prisoners. Such concern has a voluntary tradition that predates the work of the CETS, originating as it did at the beginning of the 19th century with the activities of a small number of Discharged Prisoners' Aid Societies (DPAS). Prior to 1862 these societies operated independently and served local county gaols; the passing of an Act of Parliament in that year for the relief of discharged prisoners was the spur for an increase in the number of societies and the beginnings of a process of centralization (NADPAS 1956). In the late 1870s, however, the Police Court Mission added its weight to the project of helping prisoners.

In one year James Mercer the police court missionary for the diocese of Liverpool made 1097 daily visits to the police courts and saw a hundred prisoners who were given a free breakfast, a 'few earnest words' or the help of one of his voluntary helpers, and invited to sign the 'pledge' (Ayscough 1923). Other areas soon followed suit. During 1884, 1,666 prisoners were dealt with and given help with accommodation, employment and emigration, and by 1894 the number of prisoners met at the gate had risen to 15,809 (Jarvis 1972) The contribution of the Mission to this area of work was not insubstantial but despite these initiatives, the main responsibility for most ordinary prisoners, both inside and outside prison, continued to be undertaken by volunteers under the auspices of the DPAS.

The American Influence

Some courts made use of the Summary Jurisdiction Act 1879 to discharge people to the informal supervision of the missionaries who along with police and industrial schools officers used bail periods to facilitate inquiries (Bochel 1976). Bochel, however, disputes the connection between these practices and probation and asserts a much closer relationship with another hero of probation histories, John Augustus. In her view, probation was undoubtedly developed in America, and even though the 'legal instrument' may have been obtained from Britain it was returned 'tempered by imaginative insight and forged to new purposes' (21). As in Britain, the origins of probation in America were closely associated with the temperance movement. Moreland (1941) asserts that it was undoubtedly the Washingtonian temperance reform movement 'which led Augustus to the police court and later to the municipal court in Boston': it was a movement underscored with a strong belief that the drunkard was capable of being saved 'through understanding, kindness and moral suasion, rather than through commitment to prison' (3-4). Soon after the Washingtonian Total Abstinence Society was set up in Boston on 25 April 1841, its members began operating in the police courts, and its first report published that year indicates that their practice preceded that of Augustus. Indeed the pioneering work of Augustus is invariably portrayed as idiosyncratic, and yet it is clear that he did not operate alone. He was originally a member of an early Temperance Society, and when the Washingtonian was established in Boston he joined: it was at this point that 'the idea flashed across his mind of saving men' (*The Christian Register*, 15 May 1847 quoted in Moreland 1941: 78).). There are indications, therefore, that he appeared in court if not as a representative of the Washingtonian Temperance Society, at least as a recognized member; moreover, other members were active in the courts with him, and for a time he had a voluntary worker, John Murray Spear, working alongside him. In addition, he was reliant on the enlightened views of the judges before whom he pleaded, one of whom, Judge Abel Cushing had a 'fixed determination to protect the rights of every prisoner who [was] brought before him, however poor or degraded' (Fenner 1856: 97). Not in doubt, however, is the fact that he was a shoemaker who 'devoted much of his time to temperance work and to anti-slavery and moral reform activities' (Jarvis 1972: 12; Fenner 1856), and was, it appears, a well known character in Boston as his obituary attests:

> The deceased was well known in this community in connection with his benevolent exertions in (sic) behalf of poor criminals, the latter years of his life being almost entirely spent in ameliorating their condition by becoming bondsman for their good behavior, and providing means and opportunities that would tend to a reformation (*Boston Herald* 22 June 1859 quoted in Moreland op. cit: 13).

From 1846, he gave up his business, supported himself with a small income and devoted himself full time to philanthropy. Moreover, he has provided a full description of the early probation system in Boston, Massachusetts (see chapter 4). Following a 'cursory' investigation, he would recommend bail and then supervise the offender before providing a report at the end of the period of bail (White 1978). Court records show that between 1842 and 1858 he stood bail for 1,946 people and in the process made himself liable for $243,235. He died aged 74 'from a general prostration due to overtaxing his powers' (Johnson, A. 1928a: 429).

As previously argued, he was not the only figure of significance in the development of probation in America. While, Spear may not have been 'the great figure' that Augustus was, he worked in the Boston courts from 1848 to 1852 and was among other things also a prison reformer, teacher, and worker with discharged prisoners. His importance, Moreland argues, rests with the fact that like Augustus he publicized probation and demonstrated its potential. The Reverend George F. Haskins who established in 1851 the first Catholic refuge for boys in New England pleaded in the Boston courts for children on trial to save them from penal institutions. The work of Rufus Cook and Miss L.P. Burnham of the Boston Children's Aid Society which began four years after the death of John Augustus, gives the Society a significant position in the history of probation and work with juvenile offenders.

Cook (known as Father Cook) was also the chaplain of the Boston prison, and he began visiting the courts and gained acceptance as an advisor who made enquiries into the circumstances of both adult and juvenile offenders (Johnson , F. R. 1928). Moreland describes Miss Burnham as 'the first career woman in the probation field [whose] work was a precedent for the position which women were later to occupy in the probation field' (17-18). Miss Burnham may well have been the first female probation officer but her significance has been lost in male storytelling.

The final stone in the foundation of the early American system was the work of Gardiner Tufts in the State Visiting Agency of the Board of State Charities of Massachusetts, established in 1869. Chapter 453 of the Acts of 1869 directed visiting agents to attend court in all cases when a child might be committed to a reformatory. Tuft organized the intervention of agents in these situations and encouraged recommendations for probation, and 'opened another chapter in probation history' (19).

The Emergence of Probation in the United Kingdom

So Bochel (1976) is only partially correct in proposing that Augustus' system with the elements of postponing of sentence, the threat of recall, selection, supervision and reporting, and the keeping of records encompasses most of the ingredients of modern probation: the system was more extensive than the work of a lone philanthropist. In so far as both the Howard Association and politicians like Howard Vincent used the American system as an exemplar in their arguments for a system of probation in this country, Bochel rightly stresses its importance but others suggest a closer link between the police court missionaries and later probation. Jarvis, while admitting that a direct, simple link is present, gives more emphasis to the role of the missionaries:

> They were the pioneers; they developed the concept of social workers working in and for the courts; they provided the rudiments of the techniques of individual concern for and a personal relationship with, offenders in the open; this is all true (9).

Howard Vincent was appointed Director of Criminal Investigation, a position which was established as a result of his report on the French detective system (White 1979). Subsequently, he set up the Convict Supervision Office at Scotland Yard from which policemen supervised those prisoners on licence or recidivists sentenced to police supervision, and it was this, White argues, that influenced heavily the development of probation in not only England but also Australia and New Zealand. In 1883, following a visit to Massachusetts, he promoted the idea of probation in his address to the annual conference of the National Association for the Promotion of Social Science. He became the Member of Parliament for Sheffield in 1885, and his commitment to the concept of probation coupled with his positive view of police supervision of offenders, led him on his first day in parliament to introduce the Probation of First Offenders Bill in 1886.[14] Initially lost when parliament was dissolved, the Bill was re-introduced in the following year. However, he failed to convince his peers of the efficacy of police supervision modelled on the ticket of leave system, and as a result the Bill came onto the statute in 1887 with no provision for supervision at all or any reference to enquiry reports; thus it was rendered 'almost superfluous' (White 1979).[15]

Nevertheless, as White indicates, his enthusiasm for probation was not diminished. In 1892, he aligned himself with the Howard Association and continued to campaign for the setting up of a legal system of probation; and in 1904 he returned to Massachusetts to re-examine the operation of the probation system. Subsequently, in a letter to *The Times*, he proposed the employment of probation officers in the courts in the United Kingdom, adding that 'the expense would be trivial compared to the good which they could do and the saving of prison expenditure'.[16]

By April 1906, according to Ayscough (1929), 'a movement was on foot for the appointment by the government of certain officers, called Probation Officers' in order that adult offenders could be reformed instead of being sent to prison (71). This movement was in the form of a deputation to the Home Secretary by the C.E.T.S, which offered itself as the organization to implement the scheme. But who else were the main players in this movement?

It is clear from most accounts that the Howard Association played a prominent role in the pressure that led up to the introduction of a probation system in 1907. Le Mesurier (1935) in stressing the importance of that contribution says, 'they have thrown the whole weight of their influence in securing the Probation of Offenders Act and subsequent amending Acts' (201). Ruggles-Brise, the Prisons Commissioner (an ally to Vincent in his advocacy of the use of police in probation supervision) is also referred to as a prominent figure in the pressure for its introduction. A *Times* leader refers to his report on a visit to America in which he 'speaks highly' of their probation system, and adds that '[a] much less risky experiment in dealing with crime is the establishment of 'probation officers' whose business it is to do systematically what informally is done with us by the police and prisoner aid societies'.[17]

Miss E.P. Hughes who had been Principal of the Cambridge Training College for Women Teachers prepared a particularly influential report. Following her visit to America in the winter of 1900-1 she described probation there as 'an attempt *to reform a prisoner outside prison*, in which a special kind of warder – the probation officer – supervises the prisoner in the prisoner's own home' (Hughes 1903: 3-4). Having delineated the advantages of the system, she suggested an experiment in London, Birmingham and Bristol 'in which probation officers (not police officers) with a religious motive, humanitarian impulse, intelligence and education, organised, funded and trained by a philanthropic society should be responsible to a judge' (14). Undoubtedly, all these visits to America are significant; however, according to Muirhead (1914) Joseph Sturge from Birmingham first drew attention to the system in Massachusetts in his evidence to the Royal Commission on Reformatory and Industrial Schools in 1883.

Probation was placed on the statute book in 1907, and as Timasheff (1949)[18] proclaims, was to become recognized throughout the world. However, whilst its importance has been emphasized (Radzinowicz 1958) concerns about the implications for civil liberties have been obscured. During the debate in its second reading Mr Cochrane of Ayrshire referred to the potential harm to young offenders if a probation officer followed them around the country; and Mr Wortley of Sheffield Hallam asked, '[w]hat deduction was to be made of liberty of the person who was placed under the control of the probation officer?' (Hansard 1907: 297). But it was also received with a confidence exemplified by the Earl of Meath's statement that '[t]here can be no doubt whatever that this Bill will prevent crime, and to a large extent empty our jails' (House of Lords 1907; 1487). However, as the letter of one correspondent to *The Times* suggests, the introduction of probation was not without its critics. John Rosh, a member of the Tower Bridge Police Court (role unspecified), in challenging the success of the 1887 Act as promulgated by the 'philanthropists' argued that it was time the Government heard a 'murmur' of opposition from outside.[19] Whatever store we might wish to place on the claims and counter claims for the potential of probation, the Act does mark the beginning of modern probation, and at the same time it brings to a close the gestation of the idea as it is portrayed in the orthodox histories. Before elaborating an alternative version, however, it is necessary to describe a further common feature of the orthodoxy, namely the value context of that gestation.

The Social and Political Context

In linking 'the humanitarian movement' to concern about the imprisonment of children, Bochel (1976) maintains, 'the Victorians, influenced by humanitarian considerations characteristic of the period, were able to waive, in the interests of possible reformation, strongly held precepts about individual responsibility' (2). It is this overriding humanitarian concern that permeates most descriptions of the progress to probation in the last eighty years of the nineteenth century. One of the most recent references, in a brief history, alludes to the prevalence of mercy over severity and worries about poverty in the motivations of reformers, although in a tantalising throwaway line typifies the Victorian age as 'a time of rising concern at the moral degeneration of the working class' (Whitfield 1998: 12).

Another commentator contrasts the near 'panic measures' implemented to deal with public disorder and crime associated with the 'uncontrolled changes of the industrial revolution' in the early part of the century with the later more enlightened, human response of people such as Elizabeth Fry (King 1969: 206). She couples the change towards 'the treatment of offenders as human beings with normal human needs' to the broader development of social work amongst the disadvantaged based as it was on the provision of a 'spiritual and moral' help designed to reclaim them as responsible members of society (206). With what may seem unwarranted certainty, King also makes a significant claim about the subjects of that provision which, it will be argued later, is a cornerstone of orthodox accounts:

> During most of the nineteenth century such help tended to be confined to the 'deserving' but in later years special efforts were made on behalf of prostitutes, drunkards and criminals, and it was amongst these that the Police Court Mission was in due course to take a pioneering place (206).

Within the parameters of her version the increasingly frequent incursions of the state into penal services was founded 'more on reason and responsibility and less on panic and revenge' (207). This premise is not without foundation: debates at the beginning of the twentieth century were infused with the tensions between these opposing approaches. In 1901, a leader in *The Times*[20] took issue with Dr. Robert Anderson, the Assistant Commissioner of the Police of London who in an article had railed against the reformers who were undermining and bringing into disrepute the criminal justice system with their misguided pity for criminals or what he termed 'these human beasts of prey'. It begins by referring to the fact that the latest report of the Criminal Investigations Department shows that crimes such as burglary had fallen in London. Then, it argues that offenders who are 'weak, shiftless, ill-fed, badly trained human beings' are more common than Anderson's 'wild beasts'; and it concludes by proposing that 'wise preventative measures' tinged with a little pity are 'likely to do infinitely more good than harshness'. Yet, some fifty years later, a principal probation officer confidently asserted to a European seminar that the birth of casework was the result of Victorian reformers united in their concern about the conditions in which the poor lived (Paskell 1952).

So, inspired and fuelled by religious zeal and motivation, the stirrings of the probation concept are located directly in the groundswell of humanitarian sensitivities that motivated many of the penal reforms of the nineteenth century (Jarvis 1972). Significantly, Le Mesurier (1935) begins her account of the movement towards probation with reference to the influence of John Howard and Elizabeth Fry in exposing the state of English prisons. That those elements existed is indisputable; the issue is the supremacy accorded to them in the orthodox accounts. This supremacy has been challenged in most contemporary accounts and it is to those that I now turn not only to explain them but also to build on them.

Several relatively recent histories broaden the conceptual framework of probation service history but stop short of a full revision (Mair 1997; May 1990, 1991, 1994; McWilliams 1983, 1985, 1986; Oldfield 2002). Oldfield argues that the techniques of the police court missionaries were welcomed in the courts because of their applicability to the 'problematisation of a particular aspect of working class life which had aroused respectable concern' (21). May (1990: 4-5) draws on what he terms Foucault's genealogical analysis to paint a picture of probation's evolution on a background of the penal and political thought of the time surrounding those concerns. Juxtaposed to this he places first, Bentham's utilitarian calculation that crime is a matter of rational choice, and second, a justice system that strove to achieve an equilibrium between deterrence and retribution in order that crime might be prevented without propelling offenders down the path of further crime. Thus probation fulfilled the need for moral training as an alternative to prison.

He continues with an outline of two schools of criminology – eugenics and environmentalists – and rehearses Garland's explanation of how the opposing theories of social determinism and environmentalism found an accommodation in their focus on the individual. This pragmatic compromise, or *soft determinism* as May calls it, leaves the issue of individual responsibility always in doubt, thus creating the need for clarification and investigation. Probation, therefore, emerges to satisfy that need, driven by a charity-based movement combining the 'reforming zeal of the evangelical spirit and a middle-class entrepreneurial philosophy' at a time when 'the philosophy of self-help and entrepreneurial spirit were paramount' (9). Then he completes his history with the structure and analysis of McWilliams to which I will return later.

Mair (1997) provides a short, conventional history of the development of probation but he criticizes the orthodox histories for their reliance on 'a somewhat old-fashioned conception of history' (1198). He alludes to a broader context by suggesting that probation came about during what might be defined as a moral panic about drink and its effects but nevertheless argues the need for a revisionist history 'which takes full account of the socio-political background' (1198); and suggests the works of Ignatieff, Rothman or Garland as offering a possible framework. Before leaving the readers' appetite wetted, he cites McWilliams and Young (see below) as the providers of analyses that will lead the way.

As Pease puts it in his memorial lecture (reproduced in the *Howard Journal*), Bill McWilliams 'described the main strands in probation thinking as being from special pleading, through diagnosis to managerial pragmatism' (Pease 1999: 5). Whilst McWilliams provides a full history of probation (1983, 1985, 1986, 1987), it is his focus on the earlier stages of the history that is of interest here; and a clue as to why his history only partly revises the dominant orthodoxy is provided by that focus. He is interested particularly in how the police court missionaries with their distinct religious philosophy and 'their transcendent task' of 'saving souls' yielded to the 'radically different philosophy of "scientific" social work', and how their work could 'be translated into a pre-occupation with the diagnosis and treatment of offenders' (McWilliams 1983: 130).

It was, according to McWilliams, the Probation of First Offenders Act 1887, combined with the use of recognizance, which widened the scope for alternatives to imprisonment. It contained a number of implications: a reduced prison population; a perception that offenders posed less of a threat to society and their offences were less serious; an increase in leniency; and the magistrates through dealing with more serious offences being drawn into debates about disparity of sentencing and the need for severity or leniency. Because the cumulative principle (the more court appearances and convictions, the greater the punishment) had led in the 1870s and 1880s to harsh and controversial sentences (McWilliams cites the case of a 75 year old woman receiving ten years penal servitude for stealing fifteen pence worth of goods), justification for leniency assumed an added urgency. Moreover, it was because the missionaries, through their representations on behalf of offenders, could provide justifications for leniency that they were welcomed in the courts.

He throws light on a Victorian landscape strewn with the human debris of harsh socio-economic conditions attended by poverty, drunkenness, prostitution and a spiralling prison population, and captures the CETS' 'individualist solutions' premised on rescuing, converting and thereby saving individual drunkards. Upon a picture that contains all the factual detail of previous histories, McWilliams superimposes his thesis that the magistrates were caught in a conflict over leniency versus harshness and that the 1879 Summary Jurisdiction Act, widening as it did the scope of their jurisdiction, created opportunities for leniency and mercy. These opportunities created a problem of selection, and '[m]ercy stood between the offender, the missionary and the sentencer, and it was mercy which made sense of the relationships' (137). Mercy is the critical issue, and it is here, by implication that he touches upon part of the neglected story of probation this historical account aims to illuminate, namely its role in the denial of mercy to the undeserving and their consequent imprisonment. According to McWilliams (1985), the missionaries through the application of common sense nostrums helped the courts decide on who should be saved by the achieving of divine grace (administered through the distinctly human process of sentencing). He is partly correct but a reading of the descriptions, by some missionaries, of their practice suggests that they understood *and valued* the moral dimension to their assessments.

The problem of how the deserving were to be admitted to divine grace is the key with which McWilliams unlocks the answer to his question about how the missionaries succumbed to science; it produced a fatal 'flaw in their ideal' which let in the social diagnosticians. Within their doctrine, divine grace could only be achieved for the drunkard if there was a melioration of the drink problem itself. This, McWilliams asserts is a stumbling block which has to be removed before the person can be open to God.[21] Implicit in its removal is that the stumbling block is determinist, and once some missionaries began to conceive of it in this way 'the Mission had no ultimate defence left against the determinist ontology of the diagnosticians' (1983: 139). He illustrates how two prominent figures in the history, Thomas Holmes and Canon J. Hasloch Potter, advocate incarceration and castration as means of solving drink problems. This significant but understated aspect of the history with its eugenic overtones will be discussed in more detail later.

The final part of his history of relevance here, relates to the change from the early period of special pleading to the period of diagnosis and assessment of suitability for supervision. He locates this change in the period from 1920 to the 1960s when a treatment based philosophy incorporating the notion that offending is 'a manifestation of psychological or psychosocial disease and, as such, susceptible to expert diagnosis and treatment' was developed (McWilliams 1985: 260). Pressure for training followed the slowly emerging dominance of the model but the stress on religious vocation survived; therefore, he indicates, when the probation service was on the verge of its era of professionalism it still clung to 'its roots in religious inspiration and missionary zeal' (271).

All the potential features of a revisionist history, then – the religious, social and political contexts, the development of psychology, and eugenics – are there in these later accounts. What is lacking is a more detailed analysis that integrates those features into a conceptually legitimate narrative. The next chapter is an attempt to achieve that goal.

Notes

[1] His obituary in *The Times 26 December 1899* states that his commitment to the temperance movement 'at that time an unpopular agitation' prevented his rise to high office in the Church of England. It refers to his work in the fight against 'the liquor traffic among the natives of Africa' and the fact that he 'had the almost unique distinction of having belonged to the chapters of three English cathedrals.

[2] In relation to this point about humanitarianism, it is interesting to reflect on Foucault's argument that it stemmed not necessarily from 'some profound humanity' but from 'a necessary regulation of the effects of power' (1977: 92).

[3] Translated by Coghill (1951) (Penguin Books) as:

> For he was bound by a recognizance
> For twenty thousand crowns he had to pay.

[4] Born in Burlington, Massachusetts in 1785, he moved subsequently to Lexington and set up a shoe manufacturing business in his own home. By 1820, he had set up business in Boston, and it was from here that he began his philanthropic activities. Usually, he is referred to as the first probation officer but Moreland (see this page) suggests that there may have been others before him.

[5] The British soldiers convicted after the Boston Massacre avoided a severe penalty through this devise. A report of the trial quoted in Grinnell (1917: 597) relates the following verdict: 'Matthew Kilroy and Hugh Montgomery, not guilty of murder but guilty of manslaughter....Kilroy and Montgomery prayed the Benefit of Clergy which was allowed to them, and thereupon they were each of them burnt in the hand in open court and discharged'.

[6] Judge Thatcher sat in the Municipal court of Boston from 1823 to 1843, and was recognised as one of the foremost expert on criminal law of his day. Grinnell argues that his judgment in this case had its origins in the history of law and treatise on punishment by among others Bentham.

[7] Jerusa Chase was sentenced to solitary confinement for 5 days and six months in the house of correction. It is interesting to note that she was sentenced for the original offence despite the fact that she was acquitted of the subsequent offence and in a modern sense was not in breach of probation. However, as Timasheff (1941) points out, forfeiture of the recognizance surety was not made invalid by acquittal.

[8] *Commentaries on the Laws of England*, edited by R. M. Kerr, 4th edition, London 1886: 264-268.

[9] General Secretary of the Church of England Temperance Society and the National Police Court Mission.

[10] Chief Probation Officer of the Recorder's Court of Detroit.

[11] Interestingly, he was influence also by a visit he made in 1848 to Mettray, an Agricultural Colony near Tour in France which boasted a reform rate of 85 percent and was based on the principle of the boys being distributed to 'family' houses within the reformatory headed by a 'father' (a tradesman) (Hill 1857).

[12] In fact, the Chief Superintendent of Police (Hill 1857).

[13] He served until 1885 when he was replaced by a Mr. A. C. Thompson (Church of England Temperance Society 1885).

[14] In the first of two letters to *The Times* on 26 July 1986 Vincent argued that the Bill was 'calculated to save hundreds from a habitual life of crime, to give back to the State many an honest citizen, and to save the pockets of the taxpayer.' In the second, he urged a sympathetic response to a proposal 'the only object of which was in certain cases to relieve

our prisons of first offenders whose reformation might be effected by means less injurious to their future prospects, and at the same time to save the public the expense of maintaining them in gaol and of repressing the war upon society of many manufactured habitual criminals.'

[15] In the final reading of the Bill Mr. Addison MP for Ashton-under-Lyme argued the case for first offenders not being made 'one of the criminal class and subjecting him or her to the contamination of the prison surroundings' (Hansard 18th February 1987: 115).

[16] Letter to *The Times* 1 December 1904.

[17] Taken from a leader in *The Times* 15 May 1899: 9.

[18] Assistant Professor of Sociology, Fordham University New York.

[19] This letter dated the 17 May 1907 was followed by a rejoinder from Howard Vincent in which he asserts that only 10 percent of those released on probation under the 1887 Act were reconvicted and that the taxpayer had been saved £300, 000 in prison expenses (*The Times* 27 May 1907).

[20] Leader, *The Times* 12 February 1901, page 9.

[21] Canon Ellison, the founder of the Church of England Temperance society made an earlier reference to this concept in a sermon delivered at St. Pauls in 1873 (*Church of England Temperance Chronicle*).

Chapter 2

The 'Crusade' Begins: the Origins of the Probation Service Revisited

In general, the partly revisionist accounts describe the purposes of probation as a response to political, religious and social concerns; a way of reducing the escalating prison population; a method for reducing crime or drunkenness; a means of saving people from damnation; and/or a way of ameliorating social and personal problems. In this chapter, an attempt is made to argue, like Young (1976), that more specifically it was embroiled in contested political, religious and cultural ideologies that defined and labelled offenders in ways that, in part at least, shaped those purposes.

The Penal Context

Probation was conceived as an idea in the context of what Garland (1985) describes as the Victorian Penal Complex but it grew up in the Modern. Shortly after Queen Victoria's birth, the system, if it can be called such, was characterized by competing pressures and tensions that were to dominate penal thinking for the next 180 years or so -- on the one hand the stirrings of pressure for reform stimulated by overcrowding in prisons, and on the other demands for austere punishments. In the 1820s reform movements and reformists such as the Quakers and Elizabeth Fry contributed to pressure that led to the Gaols Act 1823. This Act introduced separate confinement for women and men and a shift to centralized control by requiring the sending of local magistrates' annual reports to the Home Secretary. At the same time rising crime and worries about the disorder among the agricultural and urban poor led to austere methods and harsher conditions (Ignatief 1978; Priestley 1985). In a sense, this is an over simplification because as Hudson (1996) rightly points out, the prisons which developed in the 19th century were alternatives to capital punishment and transportation not community sentences, and the features of austerity referred to above later merged into a process of attempted reform through work and contemplation. This is symbolized by Pentonville Prison, opened in 1842 and based on the belief that association led to moral harm, and that separation allowed for reflection, self-examination, security and control. In 1853, transportation ended and the 1861 Whipping Act virtually abolished whipping but the use of longer periods of incarceration was extended across a range of sentences (Garland 1985).

So during the period of the late Victorian Penal System (1865–95), the tariff of sanctions covered death, penal servitude, imprisonment, reformatory school, corporal punishment (birching for juveniles), release on recognizance and the fine. There were two forms of incarceration: imprisonment of up to two years in a local prison, and penal servitude (five years minimum) plus supervision on ticket of leave. Penal Servitude, which was introduced in the 1864 Penal Servitude Act, was meant to increase deterrence but it led to incarceration in a local prison becoming the predominant sentence.[1] Only two alternatives existed, the fine (which often meant prison for non-payment) and release on recognizance (Garland 1985).

Garland argues that the main policy emphasis of the Victorian system was the prison because of its 'disciplinary potential', and what he describes as the Victorians' 'deep ideological affinity to prison' infiltrating the political institutions. Politically favoured, the existence of prison was taken for granted, and social and political discourse focused merely on improvement. The broad aim was repression of crime through a disciplined, orderly regime structured by separate cells and isolation to prevent communication and contamination; ease of surveillance; the regulation of sleep and activity (including precisely measured wooden beds); a minimum necessary diet; labour (oakum picking, the crank or treadmill); education and moral improvement; and a system of graded punishments (14-5). It was a system in which uniformity was crucial, and in which the individual was only recognized in terms of moral culpability: '[i]t was thus a system which recognised individuals, but not individuality' (14). To this extent, it fitted the basic tenets of classical criminology, the offender as a free moral agent and the offence as a matter of individual choice. In the wider framework of the penal system, offenders were given a proportional measure of retribution and deterrence combined with rehabilitation. In general, this analysis holds true. However, as the list of questions delineated by Cox (1877) as part of the process of enquiry before sentencing (see previous chapter) suggests, interest in the individual (individualization which Garland ascribes to the post 1895 period) may have occurred earlier.

One historian (Rose 1961) has argued that philanthropy revived in the second half of the 19th century: in 1865 Ruskin gave Octavia Hill her first three houses; in the following year Dr. Barnardo first came face to face with the problem of street children; and in 1869 the Charity Organisation Society was founded. These, so he contends, were indicative of a new direction in social work, which featured individualization, humanitarianism, and the development of professionalism. Very significantly, however, classification, already a fundamental element in the 1834 Poor Law was reshaped to encompass individualized treatment, and inevitably, this meant the exclusion of categories of people. As Rose puts it, '[i]t was not possible, however, to help those who would not help themselves', and there was a groundswell of opinion that those people deemed to be deserving should have their problems addressed, and 'that the "undeserving" – the vagrants, prostitutes and criminals – should be severely treated under the Poor Law and the criminal law' (15). In this way a principle was established that would inform philanthropic activity, including recognizance and later probation.

During the period from 1895 to 1914 to which Garland attributes the creative period of the Modern Penal Complex, among other things, penal servitude for children and young persons, and prison for 14 to 16 year olds (unless unruly) were abolished; and the minimum period of penal servitude was reduced from five to three years. Moreover, the new interest in the individual led to the introduction of responses based on this individualization such as detention in reformatories for the inebriate, detention for the mentally defective, probation and borstal. Prison thus moved from the prime sanction to one of last resort, reformation assumed increasing importance and offenders became objects of interest to be assessed, classified and processed (Garland 1985; Hudson 1996). As Ruggles-Brise, Chairman of the Prison Commission explains:

> each man convicted of crime is to be regarded as an individual, as a separate entity or morality, who by the application of influence, of discipline, labour, education, moral and religious, backed up on discharge by a well organised system of patronage, is capable of reinstatement in civil life (Ruggles-Brise 1911, quoted in Garland: 26).

Garland's comparison of the Victorian and Modern complexes provides an illuminating conclusion to this contextual summary. The Victorian involved a tariff of penalties, consideration of the nature of the offence, and examination of mitigating and aggravating factors. The punishment was commensurate with the judgement made about those elements. Individualism determined the offender's treatment, and the responsibility for reform was the individual's; moreover, because no knowledge was required about the offender there was no need for inquiry. The core sentence was imprisonment based on negative conformity; the enactment of the law was premised on an exclusively penal discourse; and behaviour was regulated through legal prohibition and penalty. Conversely, the Modern involved a process of assessment of the offender to determine the nature of the appropriate punishment, a disregard for the equality of legal subjects, and a focus on the characteristics of the individual (individualization). The regime with its knowledge and curative techniques based on a variety of methods of inquiry was responsible for reform. Its legal process incorporated the application of both law and human sciences to an attempt to control behaviour through normative interventions; and prison was the last resort. Accordingly, although freedom of choice and the ability to reason were attributed to the offender, it was acknowledged that his culpability might be mitigated by predetermined factors. Consequently, the relationship between the offender and the state was no longer based on a contractual obligation to punish but on a positive attempt to normalize, and in this process the state became the expert (Garland 1985).

In as much as Probation, on its journey from individualism to individualization, assimilated science and rationalism it can be seen as a part of the scientific penal project (Garland 1990). As will be seen, it was not quite like that, because probation remained embroiled in a hybrid discourse of the religious and scientific up until the 1950s but as a broad conceptualization of the process probation went through in its early years it will do.

Panics, Conflict and Charity Giving

The probation system, therefore, was developed partly in the shadow cast by the Victorian prison wall and partly in the light beyond its perimeter; without the prison, it would have been difficult for probation to assume an identity as a penal provision because prison was the main form of punishment and probation was instead of punishment. In this sense, therefore, it was always an alternative to imprisonment, and the theory and practice of probation cannot be articulated fully outside of that function. Paradoxically, to the extent that it provided a humanizing factor in the process of administering justice, it allowed for the continuation of prison: it justified the imprisonment, initially of those who were not deemed to be deserving of mercy, and subsequently of those who did not qualify for community treatment.

An appreciation of the political and public concerns about crime and how they were moulded enhances understanding of the conflicts inherent within the dynamic processes of penal development in the period leading up to probation. So the harsh punitive regime of the crank, treadmill, and bread and water diet in prisons (the Terror as characterised by Ignatief) which led to the suicide in Birmingham prison of fifteen year old Edward Andrews, whilst not undermining the faith of the reformers in the potential of the prison for effective social control, did prefigure a significant change in the criminal justice system in which the emphasis moved away from capital and corporal punishment and transportation (Ignatieff 1978: 207-8).

The latter was abolished in 1857, the flogging of adults in 1861 and public hangings in 1868. The country was on the verge of accepting what Pearson (1983) describes as 'a distinctively modern penal system that rested on the reformative and deterrent influence of the prison as its major instrument' (127). However, at this particular point concerns about street crime were escalating. Typically, (as Pearson has so convincingly demonstrated) these concerns were aroused initially by foreigners. A *Times* leader asserted that '[t]he old Spanish war-cry of "War to the Knife" is now sounding with a witness throughout the streets of London' and that discharged foreign soldiers were making the streets unsafe for 'respectable women'.[2] Later, attention focused on ticket-of-leave men. In 1855, it was reported in *The Spectator* that the Recorder of Bath, 'Mr. Jardine pronounced the ticket-of-leave system exceedingly 'dangerous' and 'the system of discharging prisoners merely because the gaols are full,' with an ill-considered selection of those to be freed' (Hill 1857: 516-7). In fact, Hill himself railed against the fact that during the panic of the winter of 1855 all the blame was put on ticket-of-leave men, and even more so in the even greater panic of 1856-7:

> Almost every discharged convict was called a ticket-of-leave man [...] The public misapprehension, both as to the disease and as to its remedy will scarcely be credible a few years hence (Hill 1857: 610).

In reality as soon as the first ticket of leave men were released in 1853 they quickly became the scapegoats for public anxiety about crime, and were lumped together with the Chartists and other political radicals as a 'potential source of danger to the state' (Ignatief 1978: 201). Garrotting, described by *The Times* as a 'new variety of crime' (Pearson 1983: 128), was frequently attributed to these released prisoners.[3] The year 1857 did see a rise in convictions for offences of violence against the person (Bartrip 1981), and although the panic of the 1850s subsided, '[t]he debate on penal servitude and the legislation of 1853 and 1857 were shaped by public perceptions of the "ticket-of-leave" man turned garrotter' (Taylor 1998: 33). Public anxiety was re-inflamed by what *The Times* described as the 'Murderous attack on Mr. Pilkington, M.P.' late at night when he was walking from the House of Commons to the Reform Club. As the victim himself put it 'from the contusions at the back of my head, that it must have been a blow that stunned me, and, from the pain round the top of the neck and immediately under the chin, my medical men conclude it was an attempt at garotting (sic)'.[4] Press coverage, in *The Times*, *Observer* and *Punch* was considerable, and although there was not necessarily an increase in this type of crime there was a familiar process of amplification of public anxiety and police reaction.[5] The structuring of a new, reformed penal system, therefore, was greeted by 'howling disapproval' (Pearson 1983), and those who were opposed to philanthropy were able to capitalise on public concern. As a consequence, although flogging had only been abolished in 1861, a Security Against Violence Bill was pushed forward to re-introduced flogging for robbery with violence, and the 'Garrotter's Act' (as it was called) came on to the statute book in 1863. It specified that any person convicted of armed robbery should in addition to the normally prescribed punishments 'receive up to 50 strokes of corporal punishment' (Bartrip 1975: 168). Moreover, as Pearson (1983) reports it was to become 'a cause celebre among successive generations of floggers' who without any evidence would cite the Act as the solution to the problem (143).

Clearly, the transition from capital punishment and transportation to the penitentiary was not an easy one. To begin with, a loss of faith in the reformative capacity of Pentonville emerged in the same decade it opened. This was expressed in meetings in 1856 and 1857 organised by Henry Mayhew,[6] and in a series of protests from 1853 to 1858 by ticket of leave men and prisoners about their stigmatisation and the long terms of imprisonment that replaced transportation (Ignatief 1978).

The significance of these events to the later emergence of probation is threefold: firstly, it serves to show that the process of reformation during the Victorian period was underpinned by a complex political struggle between competing forces; second, as Ignatief argues, it shows that the state changed its social control strategy to one of identifying, supervising and neutralizing the dangerous; and third, it exposes the growing concern about criminals as a product of degeneracy. Ironically, as it will be argued in more detail later, that concern was to unify political, social and religious forces that in ordinary circumstances were on opposing sides in the debate about offenders and what to do with them. The symbol of the garrotter as a physical threat to the well being of each individual was to be supplanted by the symbol of the degenerate criminal as a threat to the nation as a whole. As Taylor (1998) puts it, to some '[t]he habitual criminal was one manifestation of the racial degeneration that was taking place in the towns and cities of late Victorian England' (51). Of course, this view of the offender was not unchallenged, and environmentalists continued to put their case. In 1856 the *Economist* argued that 'the less there were amongst them [the lower classes] of poverty and pauperism – the less there would be of crime in the community…how desirable it is, in order to diminish crime, that the multitude should be as rich as possible' (quoted in Taylor: 55). It is clear that the political and social elites were not unified in their views about the causes of crime or the response required, and the clearest attempt to position the development of probation in the midst of the conflicts between and within these elites (and in a class analysis) is that of Young (1976). In terms of the modification of the Service's history it is only partly complete but it demands detailed attention as an essential launch pad for the fuller re-telling that follows.

Young challenges the core elements of the orthodox histories of social work and probation. He defines them as reforming zeal formed by evangelical spirit; compassion for the disadvantaged tinged with an awareness of their sinfulness; charitable spirit translated into reformist legislation; charity based social work; social work (and therefore probation) as part of the natural development of good government and symbolic of the reform movement; and clear uncontested goals of welfare. This version of probation history is linked, therefore, to the inexorable, onward march of progress, and 'infused with an ideological optimism' and 'biased, misplaced hagiology' (48) that pre-determines the features of that history – what Pratt (2000) describes as the civilising process.

Young is concerned with 'the silences as well as the utterances', and according to his thesis, the origins of probation are embroiled in the sometimes conflicting ideological explanations for social problems by humanitarians, and the 'directed social action', namely charity giving, predicated on those stances. This analysis makes sense of the earlier argument of this study, that Rainer's letter became a potent symbol of 'the middle class as the prime historical agent involved in charity giving' (48). However, those stances tell a more intricate story.

He argues that these histories assume middle class reformers to be a homogeneous group with a shared commitment to charitable works and reform of the prison system emanating from their concern about the conditions in which the poor lived their lives; in short, they shared an evangelical-entrepreneurial ideology. The reality, however, is that there were a number of heterogeneous groups each with different attitudes to, and views about charity (see Hill on charity above).

Moreover, at about the time the first police court missionary was appointed charity was primarily in the hands of professionals who were part of a highly centralized system in the shape of the Charity Organisation Society. 'Scientific charity' was organised to diminish 'demoralisation of character' and pauperism, and to combat indiscriminate charity, which was deemed to exacerbate the very problems it was intended to reduce (49). Interestingly (and this is a theme to be examined in detail below), although it was some 35 years before the Eugenics Society was to be established, the concerns about a version of degeneracy are evident.

In the 1860s, 'indiscriminate almsgivers' (typically shopkeepers and small-scale industrialists who saw pauperism as a particular kind of social problem) dominated the provision of charity; and these new middle class people were viewed with disdain by both the established and professional middle class. Tellingly, Young describes a situation of conflict rather than harmony, of ideological difference rather than a shared philosophy, and he accuses traditional historians of overlooking 'the considerable dynamics of the social relationships involved' (51), and producing a selective history. Within the parameters of this selective history, then, the social significance of charity is defined in terms of the altruistic attempts of the middle class to provide the working class with the opportunity to improve itself both materially and emotionally: this was based on principles of self-help and independence in an open and fluid society. It was akin to what others have called the 'unilateral gift relationship' (Corden 1980), and it was intended to allow everyone a share in a competitive ethic founded on individualism. Charity's purpose, therefore, was to confirm the rightness of a middle class view of society, and maintain its dominance. Those who failed to take the opportunities presented to them were classified as moral failures, thus bolstering the notion that people had problems because of individual failings and not because of economic or political reasons. Young goes on to argue that historians have underestimated this dimension, and thereby promulgated the view that the motives for charity giving were cocooned in individuals whose employment status was a sufficient indicator of a shared and particular ideology. The motivations of police court missionaries, for example, would be assumed to be humanitarian and not part of any social or political structure.

Therefore the basic premise of Young's argument is that the development of probation cannot be separated from class conflict and its relationship to social order. As part of the apparatus of charity giving, it was another means of controlling particular sections of the working class. More specifically, the police court missionaries by tapping in to traditional religious views highlighted the difference within the working class between the deserving and the undeserving. In this way they contributed to the acceptance of moral individualism as a truth as opposed to an ideology.

Young's account, as will be shown, has silences as well but echoes of this last point can be seen in words from the Report of the Departmental Committee on the Probation of Offenders Act:

> Probation should not be regarded as yet another means by which poor people of indifferent character can obtain charitable relief. The methods adopted by Mr. Wheatley, to whose care large numbers of cases are committed from the London Quarter Sessions, seem to us to be open to objection, for his evidence gave the impression that he regarded the personal influence of the Probation Officer upon the probationer as quite secondary to relief in money or in goods (1909: 8).

In fairness to Young, he identifies the study of the relationship between the classes only as a starting point for a fuller understanding of the early history of probation, and therefore acknowledges the silences of his own account. The filling of those silences requires analysis of a configuration involving the development of the psychology of the individual, the emergence of eugenics, the role of religion, and social and political concerns about social degeneracy. However, this configuration assumes a particular relevance when viewed against the backdrop of the shift from individualism to individualization referred to earlier. An interesting starting point for a more detailed examination of that shift is the work of Saleilles (1911).[7]

From Individualism to Individualization: the Rise of Psychiatry

In general terms, Saleilles describes the anatomy of the individualization of punishment by reference to the progression from the Classical to the Neo-Classical schools of criminology, and the impetus to separate the law from 'purely abstract formulae' (1). As Garland shows Saleilles deals with the tension between the determinism of the new criminology and the notion of free will of the individual by replacing 'a philosophical principle (all men are free and responsible) with a positive psychology (each man must be investigated, his personality assessed' (1985: 187). In this way he retains the valuable 'fiction' of individual responsibility while at the same time arguing for investigation into the psychological make-up of each individual (Saleilles 1911). This is his 'system of true responsibility – a responsibility that shall be concretely and individually applied, with due reference to the personality of the offender and the details of the case' (74-5). In effect, it is an amalgam of two opposing positions: on the one hand the concern with only the facts and circumstances surrounding the crime, and its view of the offender as incidental (a view that sees only crimes and no criminals); and the adaptation of punishment to the individual (a view that sees no crimes only criminals).

In Saleilles' analysis, the reform movement had started with humanitarianism distilled from a sense of justice but then gradually had incorporated a scientific rationale. Awareness, stimulated by knowledge that not every individual had the same chances in life, prompted a change in the conception of responsibility, thereby acceding that it may vary for different people and in different situations. Saleilles moulds this into a version of individual freedom and responsibility, which may be affected by a person's state of health, pathology or mental disorder. Hence, for example, premeditation of a crime suggests that 'the measure and degree of intent in an act corresponds to the degree of freedom in the act as realized' but it actually 'corresponds to the degree of determination that induced the act'; and the stronger the determination the more it 'constitutes the very reverse of a state of freedom' (71-2). This is an interesting epistemological point as far as probation history is concerned because if the compulsion to drink is defined as a form of diminished freedom (and therefore responsibility), then probation is conceived out of the concept of diminished responsibility. Further credence, therefore, is given to McWilliams' explanation for the succumbing of the missionaries to the scientists (Raynor and Vanstone 2002).

The assumed theoretical responsibility of the old Penal Code is, therefore, replaced by Saleilles' over-arching system of true responsibility, and the issue of what should be done with an offender becomes an inquiry into the degree of moral freedom exercised in the commission of the offence. At the same time, the offender becomes Garland's reconstituted subject in the Modern Penal System, and presents the system with a fundamental problem of clarifying the boundaries of freedom before it can decide between punishment and rehabilitation. Inevitably, then, that process of inquiry separates the offenders who are suitable candidates for reform and those who are not, those who deserve to be saved and those who do not. It is known that first, police court missionaries and later, probation officers became actively involved in assisting that process of separation. They, therefore, contributed (if only by default) to the segregation and removal from society of the incorrigible by identifying the reformable and the saveable.

To some extent, this is contingent on the eclipse of responsibility and its replacement by 'the adaptation of the punishment to the psychological character of the criminal' (Saleilles 1911: 134). But Saleilles does not abandon the concepts of responsibility and freedom as bases for punishment; instead he asserts that they do not determine its nature; and that punishment itself should only apply 'when the act is committed in a normal condition, when it is the work of one capable of freedom' (167). Therefore any deviation from the normal condition or constraint on freedom of choice created a justification for intervention, first by police court missionaries and then by probation officers. It is an intervention the success of which depends on a combination of the administrative individualisation of, for example, the Elmira Reformatory in New York State, and the humane, enthusiastic faith of dedicated missionaries;[8] and probation, therefore, became the conduit for the transfer of individualised punishment from such institutions to the community.

It is a core argument of this history that probation theory and practice are an integral part of the story of psychology's dominance in the processes of social control. The status of probation has, by and large, rested on its ability to demonstrate expertise in understanding the offender and what can be done to change offending behaviour, and psychological explanations have invariably informed that understanding. As a consequence, probation with on the one hand its commitment to humanitarian but normative values, and on the other hand its aspiration for professional status, has embraced explanations for deviant behaviour ranging from moral failing to eugenics. Moreover, it has laid claim to expert knowledge of these explanations.

In his examination of psychiatry as a political science, Rose (1996) argues that each attempt to control the behaviour of others involves a body of knowledge, and requires '[t]ruths, explanations, categorizations and taxonomies concerning human beings individually and en masse' (3). Moreover, it is the 'experts' who have a key role in moulding the problems to be dealt with and regulated, and who constitute the connection between governments and the 'sites' where behaviour is processed and responded to. Since the 19th century, psychiatry, which he describes as 'a heterogeneous complex of contested relations' between varieties of experts, has been bound up with politics and the problems of governance.

Probation, Eugenics and Mental Hygiene

According to Rose, this pivotal position has not been achieved through the application of its knowledge base to the solutions of practical problems but rather through its application to abnormality (Rose 1985). Rose maintains that between

1875 and 1925 (spanning the early history of probation) psychology developed as 'a coherent and individuated scientific discourse', and that it sought its status through its ability to deal with 'the problems posed for social apparatuses by dysfunctional conduct' (3, 5). Rose demonstrates how the theory of degeneracy brought a range of pathologies together under the heading of deviation linked to heredity,[9] and concerns that defects might be passed on to future generations. Psychology was placed ideally to throw light on these concerns.

The essence of this eugenicist analysis is exemplified by its creator, Galton (1903) who proclaims that human beings varied as much as domesticated animals, and that 'whether it be in character, disposition, energy, intellect or physical power, we each receive at our birth a definite endowment' (3). In addition, he asserts with apparent confidence that 'the brains of the nation lie in the higher classes' (10). Drawing on Booth's classification, he rates his class A, among whom he puts loafers and criminals, at about one percent of the population in London. They, and class B, the very poor who survive on casual earnings and includes those who are poor because of their idleness and drinking habits, live lives of savages and serve no useful service to the country; they ruin everything they come into contact with, and although there are exceptions they are incapable of improvement. Criminals, in particular, should be 'resolutely segregated under medical surveillance and peremptorily denied opportunities for producing offspring' (19-20). He condensed the purpose of eugenics in a paper delivered to the Sociological Society in 1904 when he avowed that '[t]he aim of eugenics was to bring as many influences as could be reasonably employed to cause the *useful classes* (my italics) in the community to contribute more than their proportion to the next generation.'[10]

Galton was also a member of the Royal Commission on the Care and Control of the Feeble-Minded (1909) that argued for 'long and continuous detention' of 'mentally defective' juveniles to change the situation that allowed 'them to become habitual delinquents of the worst type and to propagate a feeble-minded progeny which may become criminal like themselves' (13). This merging of criminality, poverty and the promiscuity of the poor into a threat to social order was not new as eugenicist themes thrived in the earlier part of the 19th century (Garland 1985: May 1991; Taylor 1998). As Taylor suggests, the perceived threat from the dangerous classes was high between 1825 and 1850, and the development of reformatory and industrial schools, and the opening of Pentonville are indications of the moral philanthropists defining young offenders and other possible future offenders as a distinct group in need of protection from the dangers of moral degeneration. This politically and morally infused welfarism remained prominent during the period police court missionaries began their work, and although encompassed in religious faith it too was concerned with the corruption and demoralising of the individual. It was, if we accept Rose's interpretation, transposed from moral intervention by voluntary societies to state intervention within an administrative framework of a whole range of sanctions such as probation, particularly for juveniles. The administration of the moral degeneracy, especially of children, needed a process of assessment and categorization through reports and psychological enquiry (Rose 1985). Moreover, it was the psychology of the individual in an alliance with the juvenile court and in relationship with probation that assumed the right to make judgements about behavioural disorders; and the missionaries and subsequently probation officers who conceptualized 'criminality on the model of the causes and spread of epidemic diseases' (167).

Experts in the field of psychology multiplied in the 20th century, and probation officers can be included as far as they profess expertise in dealing with offenders. Because the probation service nailed its colours to the mast of psychology (Brown 1934; Holmes 1912; McWilliams 1984), it can be included in this bundle of experts, and ineluctably must be viewed as part of the politics of government: its humanitarian tradition must be placed in this denser undergrowth. In particular, it is bound up with incursions into criminal justice made by psychiatry (using Rose's broad definition); and because the vocabulary of degeneracy is central to psychiatry's claim for its relevance as a science, it is an important element in any understanding of the early history of probation. That vocabulary derives its coherence from the classification of those who were a threat to the fabric of society – criminals, gamblers, drunks, paupers, imbeciles, idiots, vagrants, the mad and so on. These abnormal characteristics, so it was feared, were passed down through the generations and threatened the quality of the human stock. What Stedman Jones ((1971) terms 'the theory of hereditary urban degeneration' was not 'confined to one or two eccentric doctors' but was supported by a large section of the middle class (128). Admittedly, as Rose (1996) emphasises, the eugenicists were opposed by those committed to civil liberties and during the 1880s poverty did become a focus of attention. However, Stedman Jones argues that there was little compassion for the poor, and that instead they were portrayed as 'coarse, brutish, drunken and immoral' and 'an ominous threat to civilisation'. Therefore the impact of eugenics should not be underestimated as it promulgated the idea that pauperism was 'largely an act of will' predicated on degeneracy (285-6).

Of equal relevance in probation history is the mental hygiene movement,[11] which Rose represents as a more positive conceptualization of these problems: psychiatry, in sites such as courts and schools, assumed the purpose of reducing the social danger emanating from deviant behaviour of one kind or another. Offending had 'now entered the field of medical, educational and social activity, and in one aspect [had] become a part of the general problem of Mental Hygiene' (Le Mesurier 1935: 208). Probation officers, as social workers became caseworkers concerned with individual cases, and in practice brought together 'the home, the school, the court and the clinic, the playground and the street' (Rose 1996: 11). [12]

Rose, therefore, along with others like Garland, McWilliams and May, provides us with some clues about the relationship between the police court missionary and the early probation project and eugenics, moral degeneracy, and psychological aspiration. But what is the evidence? Admittedly, it is no greater than that of their humanitarian tradition but it is there in the statements and stories of those directly and indirectly involved. It is not the argument of this chapter that the orthodox version is inaccurate but rather that the humanitarian tradition is but one thread woven into the fabric of these other elements. The evidence of humanitarian motivation has been well rehearsed and does not need repeating here (although it will emerge in the later accounts of practice); instead an emphasis will be placed on evidence that completes the picture. It is evidence that will reveal the conflicting ideologies and motivations underlying the probation project.

The Views of 'Experts'

An interesting starting point is the writing of Hill who is widely regarded as being an influential figure in the development of the idea of probation. In the most detailed, objective account of his life available, Bartrip (1975) informs us that Hill was educated at the 'progressive' Hazlewood school established by his father, and had the narrowest of Calvinist views: 'as a nonconformist Hill was firmly in the tradition which stressed justification by hard work' (225). Undoubtedly, he was a humanitarian of his time with a concern for the moral welfare of young people who had fallen from the straight and narrow as it were, and he was keenly interested in reform. In a speech at the laying of the first stone of Birmingham prison in 1845, he accepted infliction of pain as a proper part of the punishment of imprisonment but he qualified that sentiment by proscribing vindictiveness in its application and encouraging its reformative powers (Hill 1857: 102)). He was a strong advocate of the administration of justice in mercy, and believed that mercy should be part of 'a course of treatment which will be for the ultimate welfare of the sufferer'. Prisons, to him, were 'moral hospitals' in which prisoners should be segregated, work industriously, be administered to by religious ministers and disciplined in an enlightened way (103-4).

There is evidence to suggest, however, that he could show little regard for prisoners. In a dispute with the council over the number of sessions he convened, he revealed scant concern about the fact that the limitation he imposed on the number of sessions increased remand periods for prisoners. Bartrip asks the question, '[d]id Hill favour the better treatment of prisoners only when it did not inconvenience him or when his salary was sufficiently attractive?' (203) The answer is probably no because Hill was a supporter of Maconochie's 'mark system' which rewarded good behaviour, and he advocated the idea of Discharged Prisoners' Aid Societies as an 'essential adjunct to any comprehensive reformatory system' (233). He was also a strong advocate of improved sanitation and living conditions because of what he saw as the links between disease and crime. In this sense, he can be categorized as a humanitarian and philanthropist but he was critical of other philanthropists. When writing about habitual criminals (in the context of the murder of a clergyman, Mr. Holest) – 'the idle, dissolute and unprincipled [...] this Bedouin horde' – he questioned whether the blame for their proliferation rested with 'that spurious and maudlin philanthropy which is equally ready to breathe a gentle sigh of compassion over the untimely fate of poor Mr. Holest' (160). Nor did charity escape his critical gaze: without the constraint of 'grudging parsimony', he avowed, '[t]he open hand encourages the pauper spirit – reliance on the aid of others, it weakens every motive to industry and thrift' (76).

However, his humanitarian views were circumscribed not only by the middle class perspective of his time on particular categories of offenders but also the use of the future vocabulary of eugenics. As far as 'people who make crime their calling' were concerned, in his Charge of July 1939, he argued:

> [that] something must be done towards diminishing the numbers of the class, by permanently withdrawing the criminal upon his first sentence from his career of crime; either by transportation, or by imprisonment for a long term, whenever the disciplines of our prisons shall be so far improved as to make them places where their inmates may be reformed, instead of more deeply corrupted (Hill 1857: 8).

Moreover, in the Charge of May 1840, his views on the mental and physical inferiority of criminals are clear:

> ...yet criminals, taken as a body, are far below the average of every honest class, both in natural and acquired endowments. Their inferiority is so obvious on the mere view of any considerable number of them collected together, as quickly to dispel all prejudice in favour of their powers, mental or physical (48).

Unsurprisingly he was not a supporter of egalitarianism: for example, following the Chartist demonstration of 10 April 1848 he endorsed the cultural and intellectual superiority of society's elite, and argued strongly against redistribution of their wealth to 'the inexpert, the slothful and the prodigal' (Bartrip 1975: 114). Bartrip's assessment of Hill is measured and fair; he concedes that '[i]f some of Hill's reformatory techniques appear harsh today, it must be remembered that this was a harsh age, the emotional values of which we tend to tolerate little' (246). Indeed Hill's own writings confirm Bartrip's view that radicalism and reaction permeated his character, and because his 'opinions evolved little' inevitably, he was 'left stranded by the pace of change' (381).

Edward Cox, the other prime mover in the use of recognizance, conveys a similar dichotomy of view. Unremarkably for his time, he saw the primary purpose of punishment as deterrence, and reform as 'a secondary consideration' the responsibility of which was with other agencies. He was, as is demonstrated in chapter one, a humanitarian in his attitude to deserving first offenders and his aversion to the imprisonment of juveniles. Nevertheless, he was an implacable opponent of what he described as the 'sentimentalists' who for example opposed stringent punishment such as whipping for the habitual criminal whom he doubted could ever be reformed (Cox 1877).

The Howard Association contributed significantly to the momentum which led to the Probation of Offenders Act. Timasheff (1941) refers to a paper entitled 'Juvenile Offenders' published by the Committee of the Association in the same year 'which greatly influenced the further development of Probation in England and the English colonies' (26). It was formed in Stoke Newington (Rose 1961), and its annual reports from 1873 to 1912 covered a number of criminal justice related issues, the most frequent of which were capital punishment, the supervision of discharged prisoners, children and prison, intemperance and improvidence, prison conditions, profitable prison labour, and probation. The reports convey firstly, a particular understanding of the causes of crime that is focused primarily on individual failings such as intemperance, immorality, irreligion and profligacy; and secondly, a belief that crime will not be eliminated until the Church adopts it as the work of god 'as a department of true missionary service in home lands' (Howard Association 1878: 19). Interestingly, then the work is equated with missionary work in the colonies and, therefore, with assumed racial superiority but historical accounts fail to accord any relevance to the comparison.[13]

Clearly, consideration of these reports needs to take account of the social and political context of the day, and what follows is not intended to question the humanitarian motives of those involved in the Association, of which there is clear evidence. Its pressure for prison reform, for example, focused on remunerative prison work that prepared prisoners to earn an honest living outside. The Association was concerned that the average cost of a prisoner was £34 per head and that they only earned £2 each to contribute towards their subsistence; so it argued for work that was more remunerative. However, it was perturbed about deaths through a combination of low diet and the treadmill, and while not pleading that prisoners should be 'pampered' and accepting that low diet and hard labour separately might be useful deterrents, protested about their combination (Howard Association 1867 and 1868). It also had a commitment to the reformatory benefits of long sentences, and an aversion to a succession of short sentences because 'such leniency [was] an absolute provocation to crime, and brings the law into contempt' (1868: 10). In addition, in this report, it concluded that the Poor Law had failed to relieve pauperism, and on the contrary had increased it because it had shifted individual responsibility entirely to officials.

This latter concern resurfaces in the 1873 report, which concentrates also on drunkenness and improvidence, and shows a concomitant concern about the high wages of people working in the iron and coal districts. The Association had no objection to such wages as long as they were 'accompanied by temperance and providence', and it believed that the current Poor Laws encouraged 'selfish profligacy'. It urged, '[t]he provident amongst the poor and lower middle classes in particular [to] demand of the government to protect them from the selfish and improvident' (9).

An early indication of the Association's faith in supervisory oversight as a means of preventing crimes can be seen in the 1874 report, which draws attention the 'successful reclamation of a number of drunken and disorderly persons at Birmingham by means of systematic visitation after their discharge from gaol' (6-7). The 1881 report provides a detailed account of Joseph Sturge's[14] report on his visit to the Juvenile Probation and State Agency in Massachusetts in which it is clear that one of the appeals of the system is its adherence to the idea of parental responsibility, and the fact that it is backed by 'authoritative and compulsory power' (Howard Association 1881: 4). He noted that parents or guardians were visited by state appointed officers, whose first aim was 'to secure the exercise of individual responsibility' through persuasion but that in the event of the failure of that persuasion, the child was removed from home.

The Association saw the structure in this country of reformatory and industrial schools and supervision of habitual offenders by the police as having ready-made advantages. The same report expresses continued disquiet about intemperance, and provides evidence of the Association's ideology of self-responsibility and control, and fears about social degeneration. On intemperance, it argues that the function of the law 'is to facilitate self-government and to remove obstacles and temptations from the path of self-elevation and self-control'; and on prostitution it relates the story of a young man of excellent character who had been 'utterly depraved' by three months association with prostitutes (6).

Vagrancy and pauperism are highlighted as causes of crime but what is more interesting is how the Association's proposed solutions combine social awareness, Christian values and eugenic concerns. The Association viewed unconditional charity as evil, and a more severe criminal justice response to begging as an essential part of the strategy in dealing with vagrancy (Howard Association 1882: 3-4). The idiom of eugenics is more apparent in the later discussion of juvenile offenders in the same report and that of the following year. First, this report urges that greater responsibility should be put on the parents of children whom the State has to look after because the Reformatories and Industrial schools might further poverty and thereby increase the burden on the taxpayer and spread communism (a concern repeated in the 1884 report). More explicitly and on the same subject, the following year's report lauds the 'fundamental truth' that '[e]vil communications corrupt good manners', and argues that people should not be treated as numbers but rather as individuals whose spirituality and morality should not be subverted by 'indiscriminating treatment in promiscuous masses' (Howard Association 1883: 4).

Addressing the problem of overcrowding and poor housing conditions, which the Association deemed to be a great social problem, it advocated legislation to force owners to maintain their properties. Now this is a particularly interesting example of the Association's campaigning style, and it has direct contextual relevance for its penal reform and probation campaigns. It had clear humanitarian motivation; it recognized the predicament and poor lifestyle of the lower classes but it was circumscribed by an equally clear ideological position. It proclaimed the first principle of social science to be that 'irreligion, intemperance and improvidence' are the main causes of squalor and vice, and while admitting that environment moulds people it judged that people, to a 'far greater and more general degree' were to blame for the problem. The solution to this moral problem was the further promotion of education, temperance and religion; the very essences of, among others, the police court missionaries' work (Howard Association 1884: 4).

The campaign for probation, therefore, was founded on that same ideology. In a section entitled, 'A Still Better Way – Probation', the 1896 report cites probation as an effective way of enforcing parental responsibility of pauper children boarded out and ameliorating the 'costly nuisance' of the 'INSTITUTION CRAZE'. Its definition of probation is friendly counselling backed by the threat of imprisonment in order to prevent lazy and drunken parents foisting their children 'upon the backs of the rate and tax-payers' (Howard Association: 6).

Probation remained a cause to the end of the century and into the next. The report of 1897 refers to its special advocacy of alternatives to imprisonment including probation. A report on juvenile offenders (Howard Association 1898) espouses the desirability of extending the 1887 Act to allow for the appointment of probation officers. Moreover, the 1901 report expresses its admiration for the probation system in Massachusetts, and affirms that it had repeatedly pressed for the 'same excellent principle' to be adopted in the United Kingdom (Howard Association 1897 and 1901). While it welcomed the Juvenile Offenders Act 1901 as a progressive step, it expresses the hope that supervision by probation officers would be included in the future. The reports of 1902 and 1903 refer to the campaign to introduce the Massachusetts model, and in particular Miss Hughes' recommendations (see above) (Howard Association 1902 and 1903). That of 1905 provides detail on a report by Miss Lucy Bartlett, a member of the Association's Committee, prepared following her visit to the probation systems in Boston, Chicago, New York and Philadelphia. Although she found caseloads of 150-200 in Boston and a high level of bureaucracy in New York, and warned that probation was not a panacea, she was greatly impressed particularly with Indianapolis's use of volunteers. Probation worked best, she said, when imbued with the 'human touch' (Howard Association 1905: 6). Again, the 1906 report details a meeting between Thomas Holmes and Edward Grubb (present and past secretaries of the Association) and Gladstone, the Home Secretary, in which they pressed for state appointed probation officers (Howard Association 1906). In fact, Edward Grubb supported the idea of probation and parole through correspondence with *The Times* newspaper.[15]

All this activity and attention, however, did not mean an unconditional commitment to reform and rehabilitation in the community. The outbreak of 'juvenile ruffianism' in which gangs armed with weapons such as belts, bludgeons and pistols had attacked 'unoffending citizens' sometimes with fatal results, prompted the Association to forswear its opposition to imprisonment of children in such cases. More generally, it placed biblical education of the young as a far more important means of preventing crime and pauperism than 'their cure, or ultimate treatment' (Howard Association 1898a: 7). On the same subject but in a special report, it asserts, '[n]o trifling is suitable for these. They require either whipping, or cellular imprisonment, or prolonged industrial discipline in a Reformatory. Imprisonment for considerable terms, for the worst of this class, has been found useful at MANCHESTER (sic)' (Howard Association 1898: 11). For these views William Tallack, who was secretary of the Association from 1866 to his retirement in 1901, was accused by the Humanitarian League of being against genuine reform (Rose 1961). In the same authoritarian vein a discussion on the habitual offenders of the 'Dissolute Class' ends recommending farm colonies and Magdeline institutions with enforced remunerative labour instead of prison plus care for the feeble-minded and half insane (Howard Association 1904). What is more, it was selective about who qualified for community supervision, and it is in this selectivity that the clearest connection with the general political anxieties about social degeneracy can be discerned.

At a time when Thomas Holmes was secretary, it offered general support to the idea of probation and argued that prison failed to allow prisoners the chance to develop 'moral strength' and did not reform because it sheltered people from temptation; but it made an exception of the 'dangerous classes' (Howard Association 1906). The 1906 report defines three classes of people that the State tended to release to the detriment of society, namely defectives, habitual misdemeanants and habitual criminals. The first it describes as consisting of 'demented weaklings' who have normal human needs but without self-control or moral judgement and needing a different type of incarceration. The second it categorizes as made up of women who continually flouted the law, whose one aim in life is 'to live the life of an uncontrolled animal', and who need a strategy of early leniency which if not appreciated should be replaced by life long detention. This it claims would lead to the 'purification of our streets and to a higher condition of social and national life' (24). The third it classifies as those people who lived by crime and corrupt others, and should be dealt with by an early version of three strikes and you are out. This was modelled on the New South Wales scheme whereby a third conviction meant being placed on the Habitual List and given an indeterminate sentence to be served until 'deemed honest' (25).

Support from the Howard Association was pivotal to the eventual introduction of probation into the British system, and it contributed to ideologies that were to be prominent in the fledgling organization. Two important figures in the Association and, in one case, the Police Court Mission itself, were William Tallack and Thomas Holmes. Very probably, both contributed to the opinions expressed in the annual reports referred to but their individual writings also are illuminating and confirm not only the often contradictory nature of the humanitarianism on offer in the penal reform movement but also its connection with classical criminology and some of the foundations of incipient eugenic ideology.

William Tallack was born in 1831 in St. Austell, Cornwall; his parents were Quakers. He was an ardent supporter of the separate system in prisons, and held a life-long commitment to the principle of cumulation in prison sentences, combined with productive work and supervision on discharge, despite the fact that the former tended to invalidate the latter. Rose (1961) throws doubt on his conceptual ability and contends ,'his attachment to the views of the earlier generation became a point of criticism later in the century' (25). However, he concedes that Tallack was committed to the use of statistical evidence as a basis for argument, and it was his information about the American system of probation that triggered the popularity of the idea in this country in the 1880s (141). Rose also reminds us that like other reformers of his period he was 'entirely against the 'pampering' of criminals' in what he scornfully called 'The Collegiate and Hotel Prisons of the United States' (49).

Tallack's way of reconciling his own views and the conflicts inherent in advocating reformation within a distinctly selective and punitive system was to negotiate a path between the extremes of 'morbid leniency'' and 'inconsiderate severity', and to eschew 'unwise humanitarianism' and supplant it with 'genuine humanity'. He made clear in a paper presented to a meeting of American Prison

Officers in New York (Tallack 1871) that by this he meant a reassertion of the doctrine of less eligibility and the proscribing of the 'mischievous pseudophilanthropy of Continental Socialism' (13). In promoting the idea of training in 'honest industry' as opposed to 'mere mental knowledge', he enlisted the support of the Prussian philanthropist, John Falk, who believed that teaching offenders to read and write only served to make them more dangerous.

No doubt, Tallack was pitching to his audience but his political stance is translucent and reconciles apparent contradictions. He blames the unwarranted leniency of the American system on immigrants importing the philanthropy of European socialism, and identifies poverty as the main cause of crime because it produces physical and psychological defects which are passed down through the generations. The hereditary nature of crime, therefore, is associated with 'spinal deformities, stammering, imperfect organs of speech, club-foot, cleft-palate, hare-lip, deafness, congenital blindness, paralysis, epilepsy and scrofula' (23). Moreover, while he promotes reformation as an important component of society's response, he stresses the importance (for a Christian people) of that response including a 'very considerate and discriminating application of penal discipline' (13).

In the following year, he returned to these themes in a paper that repeats some of the same phrases (Tallack 1872). His subject here is the lack of proper provision for imbecile and semi-imbecile prisoners, which he describes as a 'blot on the convict system'. Using, as evidence, a paper on 'The Hereditary Nature of Crime' by Dr. Thompson, resident surgeon of the general Convict Prison for Scotland at Perth, he reaffirms his conviction about the hereditary nature of crime. He refers also to a paper that relates the 'moral imbecility of habitual criminals' to cranial measurements, and asserts, '[t]he physical aspects of convicts have become almost proverbial. Bullet heads, low brows, projecting ears, weazel eyes, and other bodily indications of deficiency, are but too general amongst them' (101). However, while accepting the current theory he challenges its inherent determinism by arguing that they should be treated not as 'unimprovable, hateful beasts' but as morally responsible citizens and as more sinned against than sinning; and that the unfortunate classes who make up the population of the gaols, should have the opportunity to reform (including longer sentences to learn self-control). Finally, he reminds the reader that the response to crime should be supported by the 'influences of the Gospel of Christ' (141); in other words, mercy tempered by discipline.

Some twelve years later, Tallack set out his arguments for a probation system (Tallack 1884). Although he repeats his philosophy of individual responsibility, and delineates how the reformatories of Massachusetts between 1846 and 1866 had relieved 'vicious parents' of their responsibility and pauperised them, he highlights positively the authorities' creation of a State agency for juveniles and also the use of probation for adults in Boston. Then he proposes the adoption of the system in this country because of its 'moral and economical results' involving policemen or volunteers, and using the 1887 Act which along with the Summary Jurisdiction Act 1879 had reduced already the number of people being sent to prison – 'a gratifying feature of the age'. Certainly his commitment to the idea remained consistent, and in 1903 in a letter to *The Times* he drew attention to reports he had received on the Ohio probation system in order to promote its development in the United Kingdom: the experiment, he avowed, was 'well worth trying, especially in view of its wide and increasing success in America'.[16] His reformatory credentials, therefore, are well established but the more complete picture of this penal reformer reveals a complicated mixture of morally attuned attitudes towards offenders and theories that straddle classical and neo-classical criminology; what is more, they presage eugenics.

The same is true of Thomas Holmes, famous for his accounts of early police court missionary work. He succeeded Edward Grubb as secretary of the Association 1905, and, so Rose (1961) argues, his appointment marked a change in the type of secretary. Both Tallack and Grubb had been Quakers: Holmes was a member of the Church of England and the son of an artisan. According to Rose, he was 'a man of lesser ability, though equally earnest and wholehearted' who had a 'flair for writing in a popular, if rather diffuse and sentimental, style' (68). His compassion and concern for disadvantaged and troubled human beings is evident from the fact that he worked tirelessly on their behalf, even at times taking people into his home for long periods (Holmes 1908). His practice will be reviewed later but here it is his views about offenders and society's response that demand attention.

Undoubtedly, he was an advocate of reform but he was discerning about who was deserving of such treatment, and unflinching in his preparedness to exercise control and discipline over people. Accordingly he believed in a system of progressively longer sentences for those offenders who spurned opportunities for reform, and that ultimately the State should withhold 'liberty altogether from the determined habitual criminal'.[17] He was clear about where the State went wrong:

> [It] makes two mistakes, for it not only puts thousands of people in prison
> who ought not to be put in, but it ejects from prison every year many
> hundreds of criminals who ought to be permanently detained.[18]

Furthermore, he viewed drunken wives as 'criminal inebriates' whom the State should 'keep and control' in reformatories and treat them scientifically (76). Therefore, as far as most inebriate women generally are concerned, respect for the 'purity' of the streets and 'public morality and public decency' should demand that they are detained 'for the remainder of their natural lives' subject to 'kindly control and strong-handed constraint' (88-9). He judged the majority of them to be 'defective, possessed and dangerous' and needing to be 'detained and controlled'. However, he promoted the idea that the few 'genuine inebriates' should not be sent to prison but rather sent for two years to an inebriate reformatory rather than prison.[19] Other classes of offender attracted differing moral assessments and degrees of sympathy:

> The idle, loafing criminal has no attraction for me. I like him not, and have
> neither time nor effort to waste on him; but for the intelligent and industrious

> criminal I feel some degree of pity. I speak with such men, and find that they
> not only know right from wrong, but they can also weigh the consequences
> of their crime; moreover, they know perfectly well that criminality does not
> pay, and never will pay them. Further, many of them, in spite of repeated
> conviction, have earnest desires to do right (132).

Nor did he 'want criminals and offenders to have an easier time or, indeed,as easy
a path in life as the honest, sober, and industrious' or the the lives of decent people
being made harder and their difficulties increased by ill-considered efforts in
rescue work'. However, he did 'want fallen men and women to have some chance
of reform' without their demoralisation and society protected (149). Offenders, he
contended, are 'morally diseased' and therefore prisons 'should not only be the
means of protecting society against the depredations of the criminals but should
also be hospitals or asylums for the study and cure of moral disease' (150).

He was sensitive to the brutalising nature of prison, and believed that 'terrors of
the law have little effect upon brutalized men, for they feel themselves at war with
society, and, by the treatment meted out to them in prison, society has declared
itself at war with them', and that as a result they emerged from prison more
hardened and likely to offend (152). His enlightened vision of what prison should
be like is worth reflecting on in detail:

> [s]hort sentences; abolition of ticket-of-leave; interesting work and more of
> it; less time alone, and more with the schoolmaster; gradual improvements in
> conditions as a reward for industry and good behaviour; some relaxation at
> intervals, such as lectures with magic lanterns, concerts, etc [...] I would
> have good singers and first-class musicians invited occasionally to give the
> prisoners a concert. I would have also the prisons supplied plentifully with
> books, and constant additions made to the library. I would have a looking-
> glass in every cell, that prisoners might at any time take knowledge of
> themselves. I would have every warder master of a trade, or able to teach
> something useful, for work that interests must be the great factor in the
> reformation of intelligent prisoners (156).

Furthermore, it would be a system which sought to humanize and prepare prisoners
for freedom through 'gradual improvement in their conditions, approximating more
and more closely to a state of freedom' instead of 'senseless drudgery and damning
monotony' (156). His negative opinion of prisons as they existed applied also to
shelters and labour homes, which to his dismay had increased in number, and were
a boon to 'the loafing vagrant class' which he deemed very large and 'not worthy
of much consideration' (153). Nor was he concerned solely with conditions in
prisons in this country; in one campaign, he drew attention to inhumane conditions
in Moroccan prisons.[20]

It is in his thoughts about the relationship between psychology and crime that
he reveals more clearly his assessment of particular groups of offenders, and his
theories about the causes of crime (Holmes 1912). Physical degeneracy, he
declares, is closely associated with crime, '[i]n a word weakness, not wickedness,
is the one general cause of crime' (24), and he confirms this by taking the reader on

an imaginary tour of Parkhurst prison, which he describes as a 'sort of convalescent home for criminals'. In front of the reader, he warns would be: '[b]lighted bodies! Twisted bodies! And mutilated bodies! Retarded physical growth accompanied with underdeveloped minds. Bleared eyes and defective eyesight, epileptics and similar sufferers, a motley, pitiful assemblage of unfortunate humanity, and alas! Hopeless humanity' (17). The eugenist inventory includes also the 'deaf and dumb' and 'the cripple' and 'the hunchback, the maimed, the one-armed, the one-legged, the sufferers from sun-stroke, and the vast army whose lives have been spoiled through physical accidents'. Without training and control, he continues, these will become potential criminals whose 'wits become sharpened to deceive, their tempers violent, explosive and dangerous' (14-5).

He applauds the fact that in Holland (where his pamphlets on the subject had been widely distributed) the government had established a colony 'for the permanent detention and complete segregation of these helpless people' (26). Paradoxically, however, he enlisted the support of Karl Pearson (eugenist psychologist and contributor to probation meetings)[21] and Ruggles-Brise to refute the concept of a criminal type, and exposes the environmentalist in him by pronouncing that not every degenerate is a criminal, and that '[t]hey become criminals not because they possess criminal minds but because there is no place for them in our social and industrial life; because their necessities cannot be supplied in any other way', and they cannot compete with the fitter (39). He has little doubt that they are 'the direct product of defective social, economic, industrial, educational and domestic conditions' (41). With sharp insight and analysis, he concludes that the poor feature prominently among offenders because there are high levels of poverty, and it is wrong, therefore, to speak of the poor as the criminal classes. The convolution of his ideology is clearest in his conclusion about the perpetual prisoner:

> Some day we shall pity them and care for them and give them, under control, as much childlike happiness as they can appreciate – such work as they can do with simple comforts and controlling discipline: but no useless liberty, no opportunities of *perpetuating their kind* (my italics), no more of the vicious circle and no more prison (81).

In that statement, he provides one of the most illuminating examples of the competing ideological, philosophical and theoretical tensions within both the humanitarian reform movement and the probation project itself.

The views of the Howard Association, Tallack and Holmes illustrating as they do the discourse in the social and political realms within which probation materialized, are reflected also in the writings and observations of psychologists, other penal reformers, people within the probation service itself and politicians. In the debate on the second reading of his Probation of Offenders Bill, (in what can be seen, perhaps, as an early example of 'spin') Howard Vincent made it clear that he was concerned with social order. As he put it, he was not motivated by a 'spirit of sentimental philanthropy' towards habitual offenders whose crimes were the 'product of a criminal and habitually vicious mind'; rather, he regarded them as 'social pests' who should be kept in prison (Hansard 1886: 333-4).[22] In a speech to a conference on the care of the feeble-minded, Dr. W. A. Potts (1903), chairman of the Birmingham After-Care Committee, avowed that 'the feeble-minded are from their very nature feeble in all respects; they show their weakness in their moral qualities; they are therefore specially susceptible to bad influences' (89). It is for this reason, he said, that the Birmingham After-Care committee was campaigning for the use of boarding or colony accommodation.[23]

Edmund du Cane, the Prison Commissioner (1885) contributed to the idea of classes of offender which were either amenable to treatment or incurable, and so encouraged the kind of selectivity apparent in the writings of Tallack and Holmes. In his book about punishment and the prevention of crimes, he insists that the deliberate, rational offender is unredeemable and needs to be dealt with harshly. In his preface to Goring's The English Convict, his successor, Ruggles-Brise supports the notion of individual responsibility because crime is explained by the failure of people at the lower end of the scale to keep to the law because of physical and mental deficiencies. Such persons, he argues, should not be exposed 'without care or oversight to the conditions of free life, which are likely to be ruinous to himself, but dangerous to the community' (vi). Karl Pearson in his introduction to the same volume is careful to avoid the conclusion that one criminal begets another but instead states that 'all we can safely say is that the less fit elements from which criminals are drawn undoubtedly reproduce themselves'. In addition, he judges that a lack of 'social instinct' is hereditary, that it leads to crime when the opportunity occurs, and therefore, in this sense criminality is hereditary (xiii). Goring himself outlined research evidence of the link between degeneracy, physical defects, promiscuity and crime. Obviously, it is important to be circumspect about attributing a direct influence of these views on the generality of police court missionaries, probation officers and close associates. However, Thomas Holmes advocated the restriction of such breeding, as did another police court missionary with the same name (Holmes 1915).

Other philanthropic spheres associated with missionary work reflect the idea of inborn deficiencies of people defined as deviant. Miss Totman, matron of the Derby for girls and women, speaking about classification (and using a particular case for illustration) at the annual meeting of managers of homes of the fallen (my italics) said that the best guide for classification was 'the knowledge of evil unhappily acquired by the girl in question, the depth of depravity into which she [had] sunk' (Totman 1897). Similarly, W. Clarke Hall who was to have a close association with the probation service, speaking about the causes of 'Juvenile Female Vice' to the conference of the Association of Lady Visitors to Prisons (1912), reserved a final comment for 'that class...who are inherently depraved' (91); in other words those young girls 'who are naturally and inherently vicious' and who 'openly and deliberately incite boys and men to commit offences against them' (95).

Belief in depravity or moral wickedness or degeneracy (and its implications for selection as appropriate for probation) has a long pedigree in probation history.

John Augustus, the first probation officer confined his efforts to first offenders and excluded those who were 'wholly depraved' (John Augustus, quoted in White 1978). Moreover, he helped people while 'wisely discriminating between cases so as to shift the incipient sinners against the law from the hardened and incorrigible, that the more innocent should be hindered on the very verge of their criminality' (Anon 1858: 6). Clearly, the belief survived through the early years of the probation service. In a paper in the newly created probation publication, a Chesterfield probation officer (Cary 1913) defines the clientele of the service as 'victims of the moral wreckage of our twentieth century civilization' who are 'burdened with different kinds and different degrees of weakness' and 'morally sick'; and the privileged task of the probation officer as leading them towards 'ways of moral health and strength' (28-9). To him, probation officers are moral physicians who carried out their work amidst the morally diseased with the help of 'the great Physician of souls' (29).

A Stockton-on-Tees probation officer is even more explicitly eugenic in his paper on the causes of juvenile crime. They include, 'the degeneracy or degradation of development from the normal type'; 'defective physique'; 'imperfectly developed intellects through lack of moral education'; and 'degenerates and moral lepers [being] born in the atmosphere of moral and physical rottenness pervading the slums' (Helmsley 1915: 100). He argues that it is unchristian to ignore the environmental conditions of 'the degenerate class', 'these poor creatures, many of whom are victims to their circumstances, born in viciousness, immorality, mental and moral derangement' (101). For him, crime is both congenital and environmental and society's safety depends on remedies that are wholly individualistic such as instilling self-control, discipline and hard work, and if necessary corporal punishment.[24] In fact, as late as 1932 a member of the Eugenics Society was allowed space in *Probation Journal* to rehearse arguments about the biological aspects of crime (Hodson 1932).

Pervading all these accounts is evidence of Garland's conclusion that one of the major successes of the Victorian penal system was it had clustered criminality in the lowest stratum of the community, and set the people in it apart from their 'more respectable peers' (Garland 1985: 38). Moreover, that stratum was a constant source of potential contamination. All of this, Garland argues, was the outcome of an amalgamation of ideologies drawn from criminology, eugenics and religion, in addition to the gift of charity (with its baggage of duty, guilt and social superiority) and social work to ensure the moral dividend of reform of the individual. Social work within the penal system is, therefore, according to Garland a part of the political imperative to restore and maintain the social order by reforming or repressing these 'outcasts of the residuum' (115).

Christianity, Temperance and Social Work

Christianity justifies specific attention because it held a distinct position within this process. 'Let then, the crusade be proclaimed against intemperance; the missions be organized for direct aggressive effort on this special form of evil'. In this manner Canon Ellison (*Church of England Temperance Chronicle* 1873) announced the task of the CETS' missionaries; and three years later they were to extend their work to the police courts. In effect, this was the culmination of the Anglican teetotalism project begun by the Reverend Stopford. J. Rain's advertisement inviting all abstaining clergymen to make contact and the subsequent drawing room meetings organised by Samuel Bowly and Mrs. Fison of the National Temperance League (Harrison 1971: 181-3).

From its beginnings, however, it failed to escape political conflict. As Harrison reveals, many Chartists were sceptical about the extent to which the temperance movement with its exhortation to the poor to make 'moral effort' was 'promoting the interests of their class' (39); and some socialists believed that the movement sustained intemperance as an effective means of exposing the vices of the working class (403). That evangelical Christianity was bound up inextricably with the early police court missionary activity is self-evident but to what extent did it embrace the early social work venture and early probation? Bowpitt (1998) offers a reappraisal of the Christian origins of social work that throws into relief the relationship between the evolving practice of social work and the revivalism of the evangelicals underpinning Victorian philanthropy. While accepting the imprecise meaning of social work in the late 19th century, he identifies two distinct features: first, effort aimed at social improvement; and second, a conviction that social action rather than the saving of souls or action by the government best achieved this (678). Illuminatingly, he demarcates these features as the main reasons for the subsequent disconnection of social work from philanthropy, and its increasing dependency on 'the rational application of methods derived from social science and practical experience' (679). Now, this is an interesting point as far as probation history is concerned because although the tensions implicit in Bowpitt's analysis existed in the ideologies of police court missionaries, [25] a heavy emphasis on spiritual regeneration, as he puts it, is manifest in the evidence about their activities at this time. Moreover, although social science emerged triumphant in probation too, the battle lasted well into the 20th century (McWilliams 1983; 1985).

First Bowpitt traces the early connection between charity (which he describes as an evangelic form of Methodism or a kind of 'systematic outreach to unbelievers') and social work awaiting its knowledge base, and then the eventual estrangement. He puts this down to the general secularisation and decline of religious belief in the late 19th and early 20th century, and the different reactions of the churches, particularly the conceptual adjustment of the liberals in the Church of England who adopted an 'undogmatic Christianity flexibly vulnerable to scientific or historical refutation' (682).

According to his explanation, philosophical idealism (which had been brought into this country from Germany by Oxford intellectuals in the 1870s and 1880s) and its notion of the potential of the individual (the possible self) influenced social work. In essence, this was moral citizenship based on self-reliance, civic duty and fervency for social improvement, and the principal, overarching vehicle for these ideas was the Charity Organisation Society (COS). [26] The Society, in giving a credence to charity founded on 'moral and social improvement' and not on spiritual redemption, further nurtured secularization and opened the way for the 'application of social scientific knowledge to the solution of social problems' and *ipso facto* social work (683). However, social work was still a part of the effort to transform pauperism into self-reliance, and was concerned primarily with changing the individual; and the COS's objectives retained their political substance (bringing order to Victorian philanthropy; regulating the working class; domestication of women and conversely providing a professional outlet for women). Bowpitt, like other historians (Garland 1985; Young 1976), elaborates the COS's campaign against indiscriminate almsgiving but argues that the success of the campaign was ensured by its commitment to the development of the professional expertise of social work. Moreover, the fact that the Church embraced the secular base of social work within the doctrine of *Incarnation* whereby God blesses worthwhile human activity stimulated a Christian inspired value base.[27]

His analysis complements McWilliams' explanation for the victory of the social diagnosticians, and certainly, it highlights a previously neglected aspect of social work history. However, it overestimates the difference between moral improvement and spiritual redemption because in early probation history at least, the two remain interwoven. Furthermore, emphasis continued to be placed on the importance of spiritual redemption well into the 20th century. For instance, in 1937, Sir Herbert Samuel (the Under-secretary of State who introduced the 1907 Bill) in the introduction the third Clarke Hall lecture (Harris 1937) refers to social improvements and reduction in the prison population and asserts, '[f]ar more important has been the saving of souls' (9). Furthermore, in 1925, a Nottingham probation officer neatly affirmed the spiritual element of probation when he wrote that the probation officer would recognize the importance of improving factors such as education, employment and social surroundings, '[but] he will also see that along with, and perhaps above, them all goes the spiritual factor'. Probation officers, he believed, should never lose sight of 'the great evangelical principle of the regenerating and sanctifying work of the spirit of God' (Poulton 1925: 546).[28]

Their predecessors, the police court missionaries had temperance and redemption at the forefront of their minds. It was after all the main objective of the Society that they served, and as Gamon (1907) puts it '[n]o wonder then, that the police court missionary is well-intentioned but narrow minded, zealous but inclined to preach' (181).

In the early years, all police court missionaries had to be 'communicant members of the Church of England' (Le Mesurier 1935: 195). However, in 1922, following the report of the Departmental Committee the chairman of the Police Court Mission (in a deputation to the Home Secretary) reasserted their right to appoint churchmen but indicated that if the committee conceded this religious test 'they would not consider themselves bound or constrained to appoint a Churchman in every case, but would be prepared to consider each case on its merits' (quoted in Le Mesurier: 195). Despite this concession, it is clear that the predominance of the religious motive and focus on spirituality was maintained well into the century, and is confirmed by other historians of probation and the Mission. Dark (1939) paints a Hogarthian portrait of the grim state of early 20th century England and its 'ragged and hungry ...whose lives [were] divided between the gutter, the frowsy lodging and the comparatively comfortable prison cell' (10); but the probation officer's office is still, nevertheless 'a spiritual dispensary' and '[h]is work [is] Christianity in practice' (25). Hasloch Potter (1927) posits redemption at the core of missionary work; to him it is constructed 'in the overcoming power of the living Christ', and when it is transposed into probation 'the spiritual side of the work [was] preserved as clearly as ever' (10). The saving of souls was a component of the effort to respond to social degeneration, and, therefore, the political, social and religious fears outlined above are joined: reporting on the Departmental Committee of 1909 under the banner of 'Rescuing the Perishing', the Temperance Chronicle sums it up:

> It requires no very practical eye to detect the evil force which makes for moral degeneration in man, which we call sin, and which is all too evident in the police cell. There is a side of life which is absolutely beyond the imagination of most self-respecting, law-abiding citizens. With this human depravity the Mission is asked to grapple (1910).

The next chapter explores how the first practitioners thought about and acted upon that depravity.

Notes

[1] It was linked, however, to the policy of *progressive stages* (making the prisoner's sentence gradually less punitive) the philosophy of which was set out in 1842 by Lord Stanley, Secretary of state for War and the Colonies (McConville 1995).

[2] *The Times* 14 November 1856.

[3] For example, *The Times* on the 26 December reported 'a daring garotte (sic) robbery' near Sheffield, and a letter to the newspaper on 8th April about the granting of *ticket of leave* was signed 'A NERVOUS MAN'. However, not everyone concurred with this alarmism: in a letter to *The Times* a correspondent challenged the view that they were 'the authors of all crimes', and pointed out that 'not more than three out of every hundred committals are found to be license-holders' (*The Times* 1 January 1857).

[4] *The Times* 18 July 1862.

[5] See Pearson (1983: 132-142) for a detailed account of the response in *Punch*.

[6] A report in *The Times* on 13 March 1856 said that Mayhew had started the meeting by explaining that his purpose in convening the meeting was to make the public 'better acquainted than it was with the condition and aspirations of ticket of leave men'.

[7] Professor of Comparative Law in the University of Paris and in the College of Social Science.

[8] Opened in1876, it combined indeterminate sentencing and education, and exerted a worldwide influence as a model for other institutions.

[9] Also see Garland (1985).

[10] Reported in *The Times* 17 May 1904.

[11] The National Council for Mental Hygiene was established on 4 May 1905. Later in its history Lord Feversham President of the National Association of Probation Officers became its Chairman.

[12] Interestingly, the notion of treatment was part of the metaphor of salvation inherent in the work of the early police court missionaries as demonstrated by Canon Ellison, the founder of the Church of England Temperance Society in the sermon at St. Pauls in 1873 (referred to above) when he said that in encouraging temperance there is '[r]oom for the Christian physician to reconsider the practice of his noble art; to remove, if it may be so, the reproach that now rests upon it, that he must needs prescribe as medicine' (*Church of England Temperance Chronicle* 1 May 1873).

[13] The same link is made 33 years later by a H. Taylor of Gateshead in an address on the study of the nature of the child when he says that to work successfully the missionary must 'see as the natives see, hear as they hear, think as they think, and, indeed, he must be all the time 'thinking black' ' (1921) *National Association of Probation Officers,* 15, 298.

[14] An important figure in the development of the Reformatory system in Britain.

[15] On 5 October 1904 he outlined the use of probation in the Juvenile Courts of Indianapolis, and argued that the use of state appointed probation officers was 'one of the reforms most urgently needed in our criminal procedure'. A few days earlier, on the 28 September, he argued for a parole system similar to that in America administered not by the police but parole officers and volunteers. (Correspondence to *The Times*)

[16] Letter to *The Times* 21 October 1903.

[17] Letter to *The Times* 25 September 1906.

[18] Letter to *The Times* 16 June 1913.

[19] Letter to *The Times* 23 September 1907.

[20] Letter to *The Times* 12 October 1911.

[21] In a letter to *The Times* 31 May 1910 Karl Pearson asserted: 'Of a hundred first-born, a hundred second-born, a hundred third-born, and so on individuals – independent of sex – the

first two sets will have rather more, the third and other sets rather less, than the average percentages of tuberculosis, insanity, albinism and criminality'.

[22] As the publication of correspondence between himself and Hugh Childers, Secretary of State for the Home Department, demonstrates he experienced considerable difficulty in pushing the Bill through parliament: 'Lord Sudeley told Lord Belmore, I understand, on the Monday that he had not been desired to offer any opposition on the part of the Government. But when the second reading was moved 24 after he vigorously opposed it...' (*The Times*, July 26 1886).

[23] The same Dr. Potts addressed the 1928 NAPO conference on probation so had remained a figure of significance to the Service.

[24] In the same edition another officer refers to 'juvenile depravity' and the 'pernicious influence of picture shows', 'gaming on the streets' and 'the indiscriminate reading of suggestive and dangerous literature' (109-110) and suggests that the solution lies in the increased use of Reformatories and birching. Loughlin, J. (1915) 'Juvenile Crime and Some of the Causes', *National Association of Probation Officers*, 6, 109-111.

[25] See, for example, Holmes 1902: 22.

[26] Stedman Jones (1971) refers to the 'sternly individualist philosophy' of the COS, and argues that 'by systematically investigating each individual applicant, the COS was a pioneer of 'casework' ' (257).

[27] It is interesting that Stedman Jones (1971) contrasts the pessimism of people like Malthus and John Stuart Mill about the possibility of improvement in the working class with the optimism of the 'new generation' symbolized by Alfred Marshall's view that 'every man is a gentleman'; and, moreover, that he links it to 'a growing conviction among a significant sector of the intelligensia of the possibility of reconciling a modified form of Christianity with science and progress' (5).

[28] Alongside this was an article by H. Chinn on court clinics, thus juxtaposing the psychological to the religious.

Chapter 3

Early Practice: Redemption, Pledges and Terrible Warnings

American Practice

It might seem inappropriate to begin an account of probation practice in the United Kingdom with American practice but as has been suggested in the previous chapter, it is of considerable significance in the development of work with offenders in the community. It influenced the shaping of probation in America, and in turn, that system influenced what happened in this country. It, therefore, demands some attention.

Although John Augustus was not the only pioneer at least one commentator has described him as the 'undoubted pioneer of probation work in America' (Chute 1933: 228); moreover, he has left an account of his work. Glueck (1939) presents a synopsis of Augustus' approach:

> His method was to bail the offender after conviction, to utilize this favor as an entering wedge to the convict's confidence and friendship, and through such evidence of friendliness as helping the offender to obtain a job and aiding his family in various ways, to drive the wedge home (xvi).

Just like the police court missionaries, he insisted that the person took the pledge. In fact, the focus of his early interest was drunkards, and for the first year of his activities, he would secure a small fine (for men only, although he would later deal with women) on the evidence of their improved behaviour (Chute 1939: vi). Clearly, he was motivated by humanitarian considerations but he was also sure about the purpose of the law, which he argued, 'is to reform criminals, and to prevent crime and not to punish maliciously or from a spirit of revenge' (Augustus 1852: 23). As all of the histories state, he was moved to take on his role by a chance experience in court; it is worth seeing in his own words:

> In the month of August 1841, I was in court one morning when the door communicating with a lock-room was opened and an officer entered, followed by a ragged and wretched looking man who took his seat upon the bench allotted to prisoners [...] the man was charged with being a common drunkard [...] before sentenced had been passed, I conversed with him for a few moments, and found that he was not yet passed all hope of reformation, although his appearances and looks precluded a belief in the minds of others that he would ever become a man again. He told me that if he could be saved from the House of Correction, he never again would taste intoxicating liquors; there was such an (sic) earnestness in that tone, and a look

> expressive of firm resolve, that I determined to aid him; I bailed him by
> permission of the Court (4-5).

In this way the first recorded assessment and intervention in court of a person
resembling a future probation officer was made. It was a manifestation of humanity
and concern but this first probation officer, like those ahead of him, was selective.
As he wrote himself, 'I confined my efforts to those who were indicted for their
first offence, and whose hearts were not wholly depraved, but gave promise of
better things' (19). The detail of his methods is not clear from his account but a
clue lies in Glueck's synopsis above; it probably involved friendship, exhortation,
persuasion and confrontation. [1] However, it also included practical help: for
example, in 1846, a year that he describes as 'extremely arduous', he provided
temporary accommodation for forty women and employment for an unspecified
number. This is how he describes one such intervention:

> One evening in the year 1845, I was in Commercial Street, when about
> twenty emigrants who had arrived in Train's ship, entered a room for
> temporary shelter. This group and the place formed a picture of
> wretchedness, which transferred to canvass, would awaken emotions of
> sympathy and pity. There were no chairs in the room, and the miserable
> objects were seated on the floor. One girl, in particular, arrested my
> attention. She was apparently about fifteen years old, a countenance
> prepossessing, an intelligent eye, and in her general appearance, far from
> being displeasing or repulsive, as many of her companions actually were;
> she was crying, and my curiosity and interest in her welfare, led me to make
> some inquiries into her history. She had no homes or friends; her mother had
> died on passage. And she was left penniless in a land of strangers. I took her
> to my house where she remained a week or two. A lady from Roxbury took
> her into her family as a domestic, and she proved to be a very good girl [...]
> she remained with the family until the spring of 1851, when she was married
> to a very respectable man in Watertown, who had acquired a snug little
> property of about seven thousand dollars, and a happier pair could not be
> found (97-8).

Although not work with an offender, it is probably an example of an early form of
crime prevention, and in any case it is interesting for what it indicates about
Augustus' selection technique.

It is documented elsewhere that he faced opposition in court particularly from
the police whom he was depriving of money (White 1978) but it is not commonly
known that his motivation was doubted. One journalist (and Augustus to his credit
includes it in his report alongside eulogies) described him as a 'mock
philanthropist' who had been described as a Good Samaritan 'in sheer and sarcastic
derision, by those who had sufficient penetration and knowledge of human nature,
to see through his empty hypocrisy, and sufficient manliness to despise his
audacious duplicity' (78). He went on to write that he 'hangs and loafs' about the
courts, and gives himself licence to 'take uncontrolled possession of every woman
that is brought up'; and finally, that unless he desisted he would 'take it upon

ourself (sic) to teach him decency'. Just like his heirs, he too was embroiled in social and political controversy.

Practice in the United Kingdom

Categorizing the activities of the police court missionaries and the first probation officers as a distinct entity in the history of probation work is problematic. What constitutes early practice? Is it a cohesive phenomenon? When did it end and later practice begin? Truthfully, these questions do not have unequivocal answers. Rather the categorization is expedient in order to separate work undertaken in the spirit of religious evangelism from that undertaken within the context of an identifiable professional organization. McWilliams (1985) identifies the requirement that probation work should be performed by people who trained specifically for that task as instrumental in moving the probation service from 'the religious missionary ideal to the scientific, diagnostic ideal' (261). Moreover, he stipulates 1919 as being the start of demands by probation officers for training, and the late 1920s as the period in which the stage was set for the transition to a professional service. The call for training may have been a little earlier than he suggests. For instance, Leeson (himself an ex-student of the Social Studies Department of Birmingham University) in 1914 reporting on the American system stated that it was diminished 'when administered by officers lacking....education and training' (88), and even earlier, Gamon (1907) argued that the way to improve the police court missionary's status was to appoint better educated and more 'cultured' people (193). Nevertheless, his demarcation between the periods of evangelical zeal and the first stirrings of professional aspiration is a useful one. For the purposes of this chapter, therefore, early practice describes the work of police court missionaries and probation officers up to 1920, and approximately a decade before the word casework was first used by a probation officer (in *Probation Journal*) (Bochel 1976).

When Nelson and Batchelor first began their work in the Southwark, Lambeth, Bow Street and Mansion House courts, they did so within a Victorian criminal justice system. As was indicated in the previous chapter, offenders were of interest only as morally culpable individuals; the appropriate nature of charity was in dispute; society was beginning to register concerns about the impact of the morally degenerate on the 'normal' and law-abiding citizen; prison was the principal response to crime; and drunkenness was identified as a potent social problem. A few years earlier, there had been a series of moral panics about violent crimes (Pearson 1983; Rawlings 1999; Taylor 1998); and drink related offences had risen sharply between 1860 and 1876 (McWilliams 1983). [2] Stedman Jones (1971) suggests that the term moral panic might be restrictive because during this period the press was 'full of warnings' about the danger of revolution. By the time that Leeson and Chinn were practising as probation officers, what Garland (1985) describes as the Modern Complex was well established. Offenders were objects of scientific curiosity, and increasing number of sites both in and outside the community was involved in their treatment. In addition, the study of individual psychology had asserted its legitimacy as a conduit for assessment and classification of offenders; concerns about degeneracy had conflated into the science of eugenics; the Gladstone Committee 1895 had reported; and prison had receded as a punishment of first resort.

This crude taxonomy of changes in the criminal justice and penal systems masks an intricate miscellany of practice and ideologies which illustrates how broad patterns of change in systems incorporate the behaviour and thinking of individuals that simultaneously confirm and confound those patterns. Over this period, as the following examples of practice will demonstrate, religious faith, individual theories about crime, personal moral canons and knowledge of criminological and psychological theories motivated and sustained probation work. As far as they matched that of the CETS, the visions of Nelson and Batchelor were clear: they 'would rescue individual drunkards, render them susceptible to the influence of the Spirit of God and their souls would be saved' (McWilliams 1983: 134). How far they were aware of the work of George Lockyer at the Middlesex Sessions (Cox 1877: White 1978) and the first probation officer in Boston is not known but they were to have a significant role in the history of practice so are worthy exemplars.[3]

A cursory glance at the reported work of the early police court missionaries confirms the superficiality of at least some of their work.[4] Page (1992) using a report from the Rochester Diocesan Branch of the Church of England, shows that in two years (1894 and 1895) seven police court missionaries conducted 18,576 interviews with people accused of drink-related offences and made 13,171 home visits (an average of 2,654 interviews and 1,881 home visits by each missionary).

Clearly, this was the norm. Ayscough (1923) highlights the fact that in their first five years Nelson and Batchelor on top of prison meetings, mother's meetings, and juvenile meetings interviewed 16,269 prisoners and took 584 pledges (Ayscough 1923). Page provides two examples of practice: first, that of Mr. Wheatley:[5]

> he took particular care to follow up such cases by visiting them regularly, finding jobs for them and generally trying to keep them on the straight and narrow (p. 15).

The second, that of William Batchelor, the second police court missionary to be appointed, comes from his own account:

> The police and all the officials assist me in rescuing the fallen ones and preventing others. Young girls, when they are without friends in London, make application to the magistrate in the morning, and the gaolers take care of them at either court when I am not there. This is an encouraging aspect of the work. On five occasions I have been able to restore cases direct to their parents or relations (15-6).

Women missionaries rescued children who had been abandoned, and placed them in residential schools or homes; Le Mesurier (1935) posits this approach alongside finding work for men and young men, and the provision of practical help of people discharged under the Probation of First Offenders Act 1887 (190). The task of saving people was not easy, and the belief in the need for control was there under the surface of exhortation for at least one missionary, particularly with regard to females: 'I am nearly baffled to know what to do with them. I have done much to save the poor victims, but it seems to me like working against hope. I am fully persuaded in my own mind that they should be placed under medical care and enforced abstinence' (Ayscough 1923: 18). Moreover, as the following extract from the third annual report of the London Diocesan Branch of the Church of England Temperance Society (1895) exemplifies it was not only women who were recalcitrant:

> J.B. had served a long term of penal servitude. With the help of the magistrate he was supplied with a plentiful stock of goods, by which he could earn his living honestly. He had been assisted once previously. J.B. sold the goods (31).

Help was then refused, and J. B. was consigned to the category of the '"Can't" species, and therefore a failure' (31). The language of racial subdivision used is of interest here because as shown in chapter two it was a feature of a number of the accounts during this period.

The type and range of this work is confirmed by all of the main historical accounts, and as can be seen in the annual reports over a period of thirty years of the London Diocesan Branch of the CETS, survived up to and beyond the introduction of probation. Report after report shows exactly the same categorisations with varying figures. For example, in 1901 the total work included 1301 pledges; 666 people placed in employment; 562 women and girls placed in homes or restored to relatives; 900 men and boys restored to friends or sent to sea or homes, 6863 letters written; 134 employers persuaded to reinstate; 1679 women inebriates handed over to women missionaries; 4096 people supplied with clothing, blankets, food, rent, stock or tools; 7751 people materially helped; and all at a cost of £1691 17s. 01/2d (21). Four years later, the cost of the same range work of Mr. R. Marshall in Acton, Chiswick and Willesden was £214 17s 10d (1905).

Clearly, the Society had in place an information system, and it gathered qualitative as well as quantitative information. The methodology employed in individual cases is illustrated in the same report. A visit to the offender's home is described as of greater value than admonishment in court, and once there the missionary was urged to encourage abstinence, diligence and self-control but to provide practical help in relation to money and employment.

Christian influence was essential to the attempts by the missionaries and probation officers to change people (Ayscough 1923): as an early probation officer put it, they should have 'deep religious convictions' Pickersgill-Cunliffe (1913). This Christian dominated practice found its outlet in a number of sites outside of the courts. The Society set up Labour Homes and Yards in which people could do supervised work; a home for inebriate women was set up in Torquay in 1891; and in 1897 the Society purchased a Winson Green Coffee House containing a small hall and rooms where the missionaries could see people in private (Ayscough 1923). Clearly, a value base founded on respect for people, and optimism about the capacity for change existed. Ayscough cites an example of a women who was 'a notorious unfortunate' and had appeared before the courts so many times that she was in danger of being sent for trial as an 'incorrigible vagabond'. The missionary intervened on her behalf, and persuaded the magistrates to allow him to place her in a Home. They acceded to his request; she thrived and subsequently became Assistant-Matron of the Home – an early example of New Careers. (46-7).

The forswearing of alcohol and exhortations to faith were principal foci of the attempts to influence. Ayscough provides an example:

> One day a man, W.M., appeared in the dock, charged with drunkenness and assault. He had thrown a coal-shovel at his wife, and hit the child, four months old, over the eye. The Missionary went to his house to persuade him to give up the drink. He threatened to strike the Missionary with a chair. Subsequently the Missionary had the joy of seeing him, with tears in his eyes, ask his wife to forgive him. W. M. gave up the drink, after which he became a different man (44).

The lack of detail necessitates the use of some imagination about the methods involved: they appear to involve an ability to cope with aggression and threats of violence coupled with moral exhortation. No mention here of any theoretical knowledge but several of the characteristics of the later casework approach, and hints of a commitment to the importance of moral and mental hygiene.[6]

It is, however, descriptions provided by two long term Missionaries, both named Holmes, which provide a more detailed portrayal. Thomas Holmes, as he said in the preface to his second book on his work as a police court missionary (Holmes 1908), worked in that capacity for a quarter of a century; he has, therefore, an interesting story to tell, and it provides insight into his practice. However, any reading of that story should take account of the fact that he was prone to generalisation. For example, in that same preface he confidently asserts that, '[t]he poor have no ill-feeling toward the rich; they harbour no suspicions; no envy, hatred, or malice dwell in their simple minds' (viii); and that, as Rose (1961) puts it so tactfully, his writing was woolly and 'sometimes lacking in logical sequence' (68). Furthermore, it exposes the sometimes contradictory and class biased value base that pervades much of the writing about reform of offenders contemporary to his. Before the detail, though, the broad pattern of work needs elaboration.

The figures for the ninth Annual Report of the London Society were provided by Holmes and his colleague, Miss Robeson. The list follows the pattern in other parts of the report, and includes, for instance, 1123 visits made and 703 visits received; 1043 letters written; 76 pledges taken; and 195 helped with rent, clothing, tools and stock (1901: 29). Interestingly, the amount of pledges taken to material aid given is proportionately lower than the total London figures for 1905. This, might, of course, be due to the activities of his colleague because Holmes professed not to have too much faith in religious homilies as a means of rescuing people from crime. Reflecting on the misery of the people he dealt with he writes: 'I wonder how it is that folk undoubtedly think that poor humanity can be warmed, fed and comforted with tracts, or be saved with goody stories' (Holmes 1902: 22), and '[v]erily, if temperance pledges, tracts and washtubs could save humanity, we had had the millennium long ago' (20). Undoubtedly, he believed strongly in the need for practical and material help for the people he tried to save, and he conceived of poverty as a significant factor in their offending; but his theories about crime were more complicated than that.

Page (1993) agrees with Marjory Todd that police court missionaries had little contact with theories, and cites the lack of reference to theories by Holmes or Gamon or any mention of the missionaries by Goring in his work the English Convict (53);[7] and, in substance, he appears to be right. However, Holmes' writing is full of implied theory, reference to psychology and even phrenology; in fact at the beginning of his Pictures and Problems book, he refers to the fact that all the London missionaries had their heads measured by a professor of phrenology, thus suggesting at least some connection with a mainstream theory of the time. He classifies problems as psychological as well as social and legal, and his writing contains some of the language of psychology.[8] Some of his doubts about the value of pledges are evident in his expressed interest in the psychological causes of drunkardness (Holmes 1902). Moreover, he expressed the view that for men and women 'physiological and pathological causes very often lie at the root of their condition' (112). An examination of his view of prisons and the need for qualified staff illustrates this further:

> Prisons, then, should not only be the means of protecting society against the depredations of the criminals, but should also be hospitals or asylums for the study and cure of moral disease [but] to deal with human nature of the darkest and worst descriptions, it appears as though anyone will do. No special fitness is required, no training is looked for, and no knowledge of humanity is asked for; in any other department of life the thing would be absurd (150-1).

Obviously, this cannot be generalised to other missionaries but it is reasonable to assume that the flavour of his conversations with his colleagues was similar. His is certainly not the language of someone unfamiliar with the newly developing social science.

Fascinatingly, and sometimes disturbingly, his language is replete with psychological and religious allusion, and humanitarianism and authoritarianism, all drawn together into his personal philosophy about crime, its cause and treatment. It is a philosophy in which social insight and moral condemnation, humanity and punitiveness sit together uneasily. On the one hand he was fervently committed to keeping people out of prison, and on the other hand to locking inebriate women up for the rest of their lives in inebriate reformatories; moreover, he was intent on 'giving Christ' to people but he advocated scientific treatment. Drunkenness was at one and the same time the result of mental disease and wickedness, and delinquency was caused by parental neglect and indolence. Evidence of his selfless devotion to helping people flows from the pages but he asserted also that he had no time for or effort to waste on the 'idle, loafing criminal' whereas he had pity for the 'intelligent and industrious criminal'. While he did not want 'criminals and offenders to have an easier time or, indeed, as easy a path in life as the honest, sober, and industrious', he did want them 'to have some chance of reform [without] the path to rectitude and decency [being] too thorny'(149). In a very real sense his views reflect the main strands of criminological thinking of his time, and illuminatingly they reveal its contradictions and compromises; moreover, they fashion a pattern that would repeat itself throughout the rest of probation history.[9]

Although, as indicated earlier, Bochel underplays the link between the missionaries' work and later probation practice, and while Jarvis concedes the point that a simple and direct link cannot be made between the two, he does assert that they were pioneers who 'developed the concept of social workers working in the courts' and 'provided the rudiments of the techniques of individual concern and a personal relationship with offenders in the open' (9). In fact, their work was aligned closely to the more general practice by rescue workers who were urged to be patient in their dealings with young girls in moral danger (Flather 1898).

What is helpful about Holmes' work is that it provides a detailed, albeit, colourful picture about his practice and thereby, an approximation of the generality of the work of the police court missionaries. Particularly when it related to drink, as it often did, it was intensive work, as the following extract exemplifies it is best told in Holmes's words.

His acknowledgement of his fascination with the 'dipsomaniac' (whom he describes as a strange object of pity) sets the tone; it was a fascination aroused by their contradictory motivations: on the one hand, a fervent desire for help, and on the other hand a fiendish determination to continue drinking. He had witnessed it many times (Holmes 1902: 116). This particular man had written to Holmes with the words, 'I am in hell! I am in hell! Give me a hand out! You tried to save Cakebread – save me!' (116).[10] Holmes invited him to his home:

> He came, white and tremulous from his last debauch. I found him a clever man and a gentleman and most powerful in physique. He was a chartered accountant, and undoubtedly clever at his profession [...] I gave him that friendship, and he came to live with us; His intellect was in good order, his strength was magnificent, he seemed open and honest; so I felt hopeful. He told me that the drink craving would not come on him again for two months, Or perhaps three. He lied to me, for it was on him then, and at that moment he was lusting and planning for drink. But I believed him. He took up his abode with us on a Thursday, employment was found for him, and his duties were to commence on the following Monday. On the Saturday at mid-day he went to his bedroom drunk. I went up to him, and found he had more drink with him. For this we had a struggle, but he was too strong for me. So I let him drink it, hoping he would go to sleep. But he did not; he became violent, and wanted to go out. This I was determined to prevent, so I locked the room door. Then he raved and swore, and declared he would stay no longer. 'How dare you lock me in! What right have you to make me a prisoner?' he indignantly asked. I told him that he had come to me for his own pleasure, but that he was going to stay for mine, and that I was not going to lose sight of him till he went to his work on Monday. So through Saturday night I stopped with him. All day on Sunday I was out in the open air with him,

when he walked as if a fury were upon him. Every now and again I pulled
him up, and gave him a soda-and-milk, and by degrees got him fit for a
decent dinner, after which he had a dose of medicine and a cigar. When he
had finished it, he came to me and took my hand, and with tears in his eyes
said: 'By God, Mr. Holmes, but you are a man!' Yes, and next weekend (for
he continued at work during the week) I had it all to do over again. For
twelve months he stayed with us, and if ever mortal man tried to help
another, I was that man. Every bit of intelligence I possessed, every bit of
time I could spare, in fact, the whole of my being -- was pressed into his
service. He liked chess, so in the evening I played with him; he liked whist,
so we formed whist parties for him; he loved books, so we discussed
literature together; he liked church, so he went to church with us (116-8).

In this example, then, a range of methods can be discerned. It involves, first, the
development, not of what would be classified later in the history of social work as
a professional relationship but rather an intense personal relationship characterized
by personal commitment, concreteness, concern and trust; second, the use of moral
and religious persuasion and influence; and third, the use of authority and coercion.
What is of additional interest about this case is what it indicates about the
selectivity of the work. He emphasises that the client was an educated man whom
he liked, and we know that he had no time for people he classifies as idle.
Accordingly his work was selective, and in chosen cases he put in a very
considerable amount of time and energy; it was a selection informed by moral
judgement and it must have resulted in a conversely limited commitment to other
categories of offenders. This does not gainsay his humanity and humanitarianism,
simply it is in Tallack's terms 'genuine humanity' rather than 'unwise
humanitarianism'. In other words, it was constructed – socially, morally and
politically; it had its limitations.

Holmes, quite clearly, believed in the hereditary nature of crime. As he put it,
'[s]ome people are born thieves, and will steal on any and every occasion possible
anything that they can lay their hands on' (133). Nevertheless, he was interested in
the complexity of compulsive theft, and what he described as manias, as the
following description of his work with a burglar shows:

He looked at me for a moment, and then said: [...] Why do some men get
drunk? Because they must. So I was a burglar because I was compelled to be
a burglar [...] After he left me I said to myself: 'This man wants a stake in
society -- something to lose (136-8).

With this in mind, Holmes acquired an unfurnished house for him and his wife, and
stood security for a loan to buy furniture. They were ecstatic, and Holmes used this
to provide the type of challenge that would grace latter day counselling, by
suggesting he put himself in the role of victim to the burglary of his goods. For two
years he did well but his wife's drinking contributed to a further bout of offending,
and he subsequently served another prison sentence. Holmes persevered with him
and repeated his help to set him up again after his release. In spite of this, he later
committed further burglaries and received a sentence of five years. Even though he

regarded it as a failure, he retained his faith in his methods in the face of this 'strange mania'; '[p]erhaps my methods were wrong, but to me they seem right; for I hold that if a man cannot be saved by faith and hope, by friendship and respect, there is no salvation for him' (148). Thus he summarizes the principal components of his practice, and these were bolstered by very significant practical help, the use of negotiation with third parties and advocacy on behalf of the offender.

Robert Holmes (1915) provides a similar representation of early practice. At the time of writing this book, he had been a police court missionary and then a probation officer for seventeen years.[11] He believed in measures to prevent the morally degenerate from having children, and like that of Thomas Holmes his writing is permeated with (at least) the tone of eugenic language, and his generalisation from the case of a women with low parenting skills, illustrates the point:

> in truth the task was beyond my power, or the power of any person unable to be perpetually in the society of such a parent. Women of this type are left too much to themselves; too much, that is, among neighbours whose ways of going on are of the same standard. Whole colonies are formed, permeated with incredibly low notions of parental responsibility and privilege, and children suffer in consequence. Our punishment for allowing this to continue is that the children in their turn *propagate the evil* (my italics), which increases and will increase until a remedy is applied (25).

It seems likely, though, that he was inclined to believe that human failings were passed on through example rather than through the genes. In discussion about one case he says so explicitly: 'Owen's example proves the fallacy of the argument that idleness is inbred. It runs in families undoubtedly, but rather from example than breeding. Moreover, many strenuous workers are burdened with very idle sons' (Holmes 1915: 262).[12] Nevertheless, he carried with him the familiar classification of people's position in the social order, as his discussion of relationships outside of marriage vividly exemplifies:

> Judging by the results of these illicit unions it did not appear that the second choice of either party was happier than the first. Neglect, drunkenness, dirt, debt – these prevailed in both houses alike from the day that I knew them. I have noticed that where there is a legal bar to marriage, persons living together as man and wife almost invariably share a wretched home [...] It will readily be understood that a lower type man cohabits with a married than a single woman, and a lower type of woman with a married than a single man. Hence it comes about naturally that one finds wretched homes in one set of cases and fairly decent homes in another (28-29).

His practice, like that of Thomas Holmes could be quite confrontational at times, and he had clear ideas about what was right and wrong putting them forcefully to those under his supervision. In the case of Bertram, a solicitor's clerk who had been convicted of embezzlement and was not happy with Holmes' view that he should take up some unskilled manual labour, he writes:

> What you are seeking is an idle life. You want to keep on the same game that has brought you to this, and to mix with the same companions [...]. In my opinion, you are at present as idle and worthless as most I have met with. I want to help you to do better (252-4).

It seemed to work. Holmes provided him with a job into which he settled, eventually being promoted to a clerkship; he subsequently joined the Territorial Army and saw active service in the war. Such practice, direct and apparently condemnatory as it was, also contained clear manifestations of concern for people within a Christian framework.

Many of the new probation officers had been former police court missionaries, and in court, they sat alongside their former colleagues who remained missionaries. Indeed many of the accounts of probation work include missionary activity. Nevertheless, with the benefit of hindsight it can be said that the days of the saver of souls were numbered; as McWilliams puts it, the routine of assessment for probation would shift attention away from 'the soul and its potential for grace, to the mind and behaviour' (1985: 259). True though this is, and despite the slow drift towards science, the language of religious persuasion would stubbornly remain part of the lexicon of many probation officers. In fact, the literature of probation in its early years remains a curious hybrid of evangelistic fervour, scientific aspiration and what McWilliams has termed uninformed 'moral judgement': in some respects, it is a case of more of the same. Furthermore, it reveals theories about the causes of crime and of offenders still redolent of the fear of social degeneracy, and the newly established eugenics movement. The writing of the ubiquitous Thomas Holmes is a case in point. In 1912, he confidently proclaimed that he and his contemporary practitioners knew as much about the mind 'as scientists or specialists' despite their attempts to mystify the subject with the language of science (Holmes 1912: 4).

A New Voice for Probation

Practitioners, apart from those who were busy writing books, first had the opportunity to write about what they did with the publication of the journal of the newly formed National Association of Probation Officers in April 1913. In the second edition, Mrs. Cary who worked in the London courts contributed on probation work with women, which she believed to be the prerogative of female officers (Cary 1913). During the previous three years she had dealt with 108 cases: 25 for drunkenness; 18 for soliciting and related offences; 38 for theft; 2 for neglecting their children; and one for assisting the keeping of a brothel. There is no information about the remaining 24 but it is clear that in her view women were more difficult to supervise than men because they needed to be pampered more, and because it was harder to fit women out for domestic service (15). One of the ways in which she attempted to overcome these difficulties was to engage in an early form of groupwork with girls and use the concept of a social club (Cary 1915; Vanstone 2003). First, she would put them in a shelter and find them employment in service; then for two evenings a week she hired rooms at a local Church Institute in

Chelsea where girls could 'gossip', play table tennis and dance, and she could challenge their values and offer moral guidance through conversation, prayers and hymn singing, communion and confirmation, and talks from the vicar. She was not alone in recognizing the power of group situations. Miss Croker-King (1915) established a club for the 'unclubbables' at her Bethnal Green flat during the First World War.[13] What she described as a 'social reporting centre' allowed the boys to play games so that she could get to know them better. Although neither officer ran the groups with any therapeutic intent, they were aware of the value of observing and engaging with probationers in a more realistic milieu, and were therefore using groupwork of a kind.

Carr (1913) supplies a more detailed exposition of individual work; that he is familiar with at least some of the new scientific language is evidenced by his explicit appreciation of the importance of accurate diagnosis. For him, probation clients are 'burdened with different kinds and different degrees of weakness' and 'morally sick'; the probation officer's role, therefore, is to assess and 'heal their sickness':

> We surely are moral physicians, hence our first duty is to find out what the ailment is from which the person is suffering [...] the help of the great Physician of Souls [...] The intricate and tangled nature of moral disease makes it almost impossible to form a correct first impression, and for this reason we must not trust too readily to moving, melting feelings, nor to harsh and solid feelings (29).

Not only is the account distinguished by its pseudo-scientific and medical tone but also it amalgamates quite neatly, the religious and the eugenic. He continues by arguing that although each probation officer must adopt his own methods he must focus on the cause: '[w]hen the stomach or the eyes cause a headache, the physician does not treat the head, but the stomach and the eyes' (29). Furthermore, probation officers must have sympathy, so that even when they have 'to put the knife in' they should not show harshness. He adds, however, that such practice should be undertaken in conjunction with other appropriate agencies such as the NSPCC.

Several other accounts reveal a mixture of Christian homily and pseudo-science. Palin (1915) describes officers as physicians concerned with the young offender's home background and general environment but essentially undertaking God's work. Crabb (1915) warns of the dangers of officers not having qualifications as a counsellor and friend, and recommends caution about the probationer who becomes over familiar (and even more so if the situation involves a male officer and a female client.). In his opinion, the officer should be as unobtrusive as possible and a 'human friend', but at the same time should not shirk from referral back to court, or from concentrating on 'the spiritual side of the probationer's make-up': the latter done tactfully, 'will be a potent factor in securing general discipline' (99). Finally, he lists three further aspects of good practice: first, concern for the probationer's welfare; second, avoidance of constant referral to the offender's past and whether he is keeping to probation requirements; and third, visiting the home and getting to know the family.

Helmsley (1915) emphasises the moral degeneracy, low intelligence and poor self-control of offenders but at the same time highlights the significance of environment and expresses a commitment to social reconstruction. His remedies, though, remain individualistic and include: parents providing decent homes and environment; parents being punished more severely and being placed on probation; discipline and hard work; corporal punishment when the offender is 'out of hand'; parents contributing to the cost of institutionalization; and more working boys' homes (101).

The definer of casework in probation, Chinn (1916),[14] explains the elements of probation work with children. As a probation officer, he details how he visits the home in order to make inquiries into the character of the child, and pays particular attention to interviewing the father because much 'is concealed from the knowledge of fathers by easy-going mothers' (123). He regards it as unwise to question the child about the offence and to talk to the parents in his presence; and he stresses the impartiality of the report. After the order is made, he would visit the home again to bring home the responsibilities of parenthood; thereafter, he would try to work with them in a way that encouraged them to play their part. The practice elements he suggests as conducive to producing this kind of collaborative relationship are, 'kindly advice, interest in their pursuits, hobbies, and the thousand and one ways and customs of everyday life' (124). He refers to encouraging boys and girls to join Sunday school, Scouts, Boys' Brigade and clubs but emphasises the need for firmness in the face of non-cooperation and the need sometimes to give them the 'chance' of Reformatory treatment. In listing the causes of children's offending, he follows the tradition of his contemporaries, whilst adding a few of the current popular panics: cheap literature; cinemas; gaming machines; automatic sweet machines; temptation; environment; bad associations; parental neglect; vagrancy; being beyond control; and feeble-mindedness and moral imbecility. He concludes with a case example: it involves work with two boys whose other brother is in an Industrial School, and whose parents live separately:

> After a few visits I found the mother was a secret drinker and neglected the children. Father was in regular work, and by pointing out to him the conditions under which the children were living and his own responsibility he consented to give his wife another trial (125).

Chinn helped them find another home in a 'better neighbourhood'. In a final flourish, he asserts that it is the probation officer's duty 'to try and teach self-reliance and thrift', two of the classic Victorian and Edwardian motifs of the decent citizen. One commentator, however, provides a salutary reminder that because of high caseloads probation work could be very superficial with '[t]oo many cases often [meaning] a mere casual or perfunctory probation, a mere routine or careless visitation' (France 1917: 150).

A More Detached View

Other non-practitioner commentators provide confirmation of the nature of this practice. As indicated in the previous chapter the Christian framework is highlighted by Hasloch Potter (1927) in his history of the Police Court Mission. In it he relies heavily both on the work of Robert Holmes and also on the 'education in the scope and methods of the Police Court Mission' (xi) he received from his forty years as a parish priest and superintendent over police court missionaries.[15] For him the requisite element of the practice of workers like Robert and Thomas Holmes was 'the personal contact of a kindly, experienced Christian man or woman' (53).

A study undertaken by Gamon (1907) offers a more detached perspective on the work.[16] He describes his study as that of an interested observer and social reformer; and Samuel Barnett, in his introduction, adds that Gamon is a strong advocate of probation. In all, he spent twelve months visiting and observing police courts in the county and city of London; he visited Church Army homes, Salvation Army shelters and children's remand homes; what is more, he lived in the East End and familiarized himself with American probation through publications.

To him 'the friend in the police-court, par excellence, is the police-court missionary. He is the friend of all alike, and the friend simply, never the prosecutor' (161).[17] However, the eulogistic style of this description belies the trenchant nature of his critique. The missionary, he maintains, was paid a salary of £100 per annum, rising to £150; and although he was not in orders, he sometimes wore a 'semi-clerical' costume. Moreover, his wife 'like the rector's wife, affords her husband gratuitous assistance, when some special need for a woman's help arises' (162-3).

Gamon goes on to provide one of the most detailed early representations of the practice of the missionaries by someone not involved in the system. According to his account, whilst the great body of the work of the missionary was done in the court itself, he was likely to be a propagandist for the Society, giving lectures, addresses, anecdotes and 'terrible warnings'. He kept a pledge book and reported on the number of pledges taken to the courts: overall, '[h]is aim [was] to obtain a grip upon prisoners passing through the court's hand, and to influence them permanently for the good' (164). Gamon concluded that the missionary succeeded in raising the confidence and optimism of offenders, and overcoming their initial distrust by performing 'a hundred and one little services for them' (164). In addition, he was a good listener. Even so he was not just a provider; he was discerning about motivation and he was inquisitive, and, Gamon confirms, he was discriminating:

> He gets a knowledge of men, their minds, and their moods, in his work; he
> expects responses, and uses his discretion when he believes the offender to
> be merely making overtures, that his sentence may be lightened. He will not
> willingly put himself at the service of the absolutely worthless (165).

So assessment of a kind was taking place but plainly it had no scientific basis; rather, it seems, rooted in personal, moral judgements. Gamon gives the clue on which this assumption rests. Before the court sat, the missionary would visit homes; that much is already known but it is what Gamon says about the focus and purpose of the visits that is most interesting. The missionary would make surprise visits early in the morning to assess the degree to which 'his clients deserve help'; so if the client was 'seen scurrying into the backyard, leaving the missus to say "Not at home" when he should have been up and away seeking work' or if a woman was seen 'half-dressed, bearing all the marks of a slattern about her', and, therefore, 'slothfulness and despair [had] killed energy and self-respect' (166-7), the missionary would come to the conclusion that there was nothing more that he could do.

Like his American forerunner, John Augustus, he was not always welcome in the courts: although his position was officially recognized, some magistrates were reluctant to consult him, and for much of the time ignored him. His salary, education and qualifications created a lack of status, and put him in a 'wholly subordinate position' to both police and clerks (179). This depiction provides a rather different picture to that of the welcomed humanitarian of some of the orthodox histories, and offers confirmation of the more complex social, cultural and political context of probation referred to in previous chapters. The reason for what Gamon defines as the awkwardness of the missionary's relationship with some magistrates, is, he claimed, its lack of coherence, and the fact that he was a servant of the Church and not the court.[18]

Gamon's critique of the qualities, skills and practice of police court missionaries is the fullest and most scholarly in the literature of that time, and is worthy of further detailed consideration. As well as his role in court, the missionary is seen by Gamon to be a kind of probation officer in so far as he provides a 'watchful supervision and moral discipline' after the court appearance; his task is to ensure that the probationer who had been bound over knew that 'the sword of Damocles' hung over him. Also he sets down the qualities required in the missionary, suggesting that he should be in some respects like Pickwick, having a 'sunny smile and warm heart, overflowing with the milk of human kindness'. However, it is Gamon's portrait of the ideal compared to the reality that is of greater significance: it is worth repeating in full. He proposes that in addition to humanity, the missionary should have:

> breadth to sympathise with frailty, but he must also have the firmness, that alone can be of real help. He must be able to see the picture from his *patient's* (my italics) standpoint, but with other eyes; he must find hope in the gloomiest outlook. He must exhort without cant, and disarm his candour by his earnest goodwill. He must be respected no less than liked. The missionary wants all the attributes of a true friend (176).

Arguably, Gamon's aspiration for their work to be more professional is visible in the use of medical terminology and the hint of what would later be described as client-centred work but Gamon is quick to add that the missionary does not live up to this ideal. First, he argues, the term missionary is too closely associated with proselytising and the giving of sermons; second, that he runs the risk of assimilating the ideas and prejudices of the police; and third, that he lacks culture and social standing, and is 'at best, a self-educated man with no pretensions to a high rank in the social scale' (181). Of course, this may be a reflection of Gamon's social attitudes, and in any event, not everybody is in agreement with him. Page (1992) reports the view of C. H. Denyer, an experienced London police court clerk, that although the missionaries were normally of limited educational attainment they were in touch with ordinary people and influential because of, not despite, their lack of official status (51). Yet, Gamon's next point is more telling: the missionary, he asserts, although well intentioned was 'narrow-minded, zealous but inclined to preach', and gained a sense of self-importance from the condescension of magistrates and the deference of clients. The solution to these problems, he believed, was a professional system like those of America and Australia, including improved education, a hierarchy that would include a 'chief friend' with assistants, and the use of volunteers (193).

This, in itself is a limited judgement. From descriptions outlined earlier in the chapter, it is clear that the missionaries were capable of wide vision. They were also involved in sophisticated social work. Chapman (1926) tells the story of a court missionary's use of a treatment called Normyl in the case of a woman with a drink problem,[19] and affirms that his court missionaries (one for Anglicans and one for Roman Catholics) 'brought in their train the co-operation of social workers of every description' (223). Gamon's observations are useful, additionally, because they provide a counter-weight to the caricature of the social humanitarian, and the hyperbole about her or his effectiveness: Chesterton (1928), for instance, refers to the 'amazing' influence of the police court whom she portrays as 'the father of his people in all the poorer districts of London' (238); she knows of 'no better cure for physical depression or mental latitude than a morning in the missionary's room at Old Street Police Court' (239). Finally, Gamon's commentary affords confirmation of the complex social, cultural and political climate within which the missionaries practised and the roots of probation grew; and it underscores the need for professionalization. This was someway off but the limitations of the new probation officers would soon be exposed.

The reluctance to use the services of probation officers continued after the enactment of the 1907 legislation. The Report of the Departmental Committee on the Probation of Offenders Act in 1909, barely two years after the first probation officer was appointed, highlights inconsistency; of 513 probation orders made in the country, 388 of them were made in the London Sessions (3). However, the Committee's faith in probation is clear; it compared the influence of the probation officer at the time of the court appearance to the 'skilled help of a doctor to a person suffering from a disease' (2).[20]

Cecil Leeson had been a probation officer for two years when he wrote the first extensive work on the probation system (Leeson 1914); in addition, he had spent two years studying at first hand the American system. Before that, he had studied in the Social Studies Department of Birmingham University. In his description probation is a means by which 'reclaimable offenders are given an opportunity to reform'' and he has no reservations about its selectivity: '[i]t is applied to those in whom wrong-doing is not habitual, and whose youth, previous good character, or other circumstances, give reasonable hope of reformation' (3). It is an alternative to punishment, and it involves the 'friendly supervision of a skilled social worker', who studies the 'habits and surroundings' and attempts to change those 'unfavourable to good conduct'. Juveniles, he indicates, are dealt with separately away from 'the degrading associations of police court and gaol' because '[p]robation, and especially juvenile probation, could scarcely be expected to flourish in the sordid atmosphere of an ordinary police court. Merely to bring the child there, to permit him to mingle with depraved adult criminals, and to risk contamination from them, would be to defeat at the outset the chief purpose of probation' (11). He attributes juvenile crime to social, physical or mental defects of the *offender class*, and argues that they should be treated in special clinics.

He is, however, critical of practice in this country in comparison with the diagnostic clinics of America in which 'all aspects of a case are investigated' and where, '[before] the child appears in court, a comprehensive inquiry is made into his social, mental and physical condition, and upon the data so acquired a diagnosis is prepared' (25). He stresses the fact that '[t]he clinic's first object is to furnish an analysis of each case from the perspective of social, physical and mental pathology. It is concerned with the offender rather than the offence, the child being dealt with primarily as a patient, and not as a lawbreaker.' Moreover, he seems knowledgeable about and drawn to theories of degeneracy when he writes:

> [t]wo important facts are brought to light by the clinical examination of
> defective offenders. In the first place, when the offence is studied in relation
> to the defect a striking correlation is said to be revealed between physical
> and mental abnormalities and abnormal conduct; epileptics, for example,
> exhibiting a periodicity in their offences coincident with the epileptic (26).

He insists that the issue of defectives has major implications for the efficacy of probation in the United Kingdom because while attempts are made to discover 'such delinquents' the courts make no provision for them and it is, therefore, possible for 'epileptic and mentally defective offenders' to be placed on probation. In his elucidation of this argument, Leeson cites an example of a former pupil of a 'special school' going through the court procedure without his 'feeble-mindedness' being detected. The placing of 'defective offenders' on probation 'without at least making some attempt to treat their defects' is seen by Leeson as unfair to both the individual and the community (27-8).

Leeson draws attention also, to the use of volunteers working alongside with officers as part of a valuable contribution to probation practice. He identifies '[o]ne of the first, if not the first, corps of volunteer probation officers in England' as being established in Birmingham using people recruited mainly from religious organisations (31). But he is less than enthusiastic about police officers and prison officers being involved in probation work, on two grounds. First, that it is a distortion of the redemptive purpose of probation to have people who are trained to 'deter and repress their charges'; and second, that there is a moral division between those who qualify for probation and 'convicts on licence' (42-3).

Much of Leeson's description is of American practice, and is of little relevance here; he does, however, give some hints about the essential components of practice in this country. He suggests that the probation officer should assume the attitude of a 'sensible friend'; that he should be neither a 'sentimentalist' nor a 'dictator or bully', and that the 'essence of the relationship is friendship' (114). Employment, because of its 'therapeutic' effect, is emphasised as important, and he describes probation offices as being like employment bureaus; but he underlines self-help as nevertheless important. Apart from this, he contends that one of the officer's main activities is putting the probationer in touch with social and religious contacts because they will 'continue to influence the offenders' lives long after the probationary period terminates' (124). Interesting though these glimpses of the practitioner's world are, he is at his most illuminating about the theoretical base of probation in his section on selection, and he provides a checklist, which is worth reproducing in full.[21] He begins, however, by defining two reasons for selecting probation, protection of the community and reclamation of the offender, and declaring that they cannot be fulfilled by using probation for offenders 'confirmed in criminal habits'. He continues by asserting that officers are generally agreed that probation should not be used for offenders convicted of 'premeditated assaults for revenge or gain, criminal assaults on females, and crimes resulting in the corruption of children' (54).

Leeson's work represents one of the earliest appeals for a professional Service. That aspiration, which can be discerned in the writings of practitioners referred to in this chapter, was linked closely to the incipient science of psychology. Towards the end of the decade, the Home Secretary's commitment to such exhortations was made clear when he expressed the hope that probation would become 'one of the greatest units for fighting the depraved and fallen and raising the moral standard'; and described the probation officer's role as 'that of the physician, being entrusted with the diagnosis of the causes of evil and the application of the most appropriate remedies'. To him, probation was curative, 'not mere surveillance'.[22] Nonetheless, the religious base remained strong, and as shown in the next chapter the struggle between the two was to continue up to and beyond the first half of the century.

Notes

[1] A note of caution is necessary: it is apparent that both Augustus' inquiries and supervision were of a relatively superficial nature, and that 'probation periods were very short (only a few weeks from the start), and that records, plans of treatment and close supervision were not much in evidence' (Chute 1933, quoted in White: 173).

[2] This was not new. In 1764 Le Trosne's (judge at the presidial court in Orleans) said that vagabonds were more dangerous to society than wolves (quoted in Foucault 1977 p. 88), a view some 200 years later manifested in the representation of car thieves as jackals in the 1990s' crime prevention campaign on television.

[3] Lockyer's work, contrary to what historians like Jarvis, King and Timasheff have suggested, seems to have been confined to inquiry: Jarvis (1972), for instance, stated that Edward Cox, then Recorder at the Middlesex Sessions, 'appointed a special inquiry officer with the responsibility of supervising the behaviour of probationers' (p. 10). However, White describes him as being paid 20 shillings per week to use the knowledge that he had accumulated from his previous employment as a Sessions Warder to identify prisoners with previous convictions, and he reports the statement of the Committee of Accounts and General purposes, which specified his inquiry role and made no mention of supervision (p. 166). Lockyer's significance seems, therefore, to be confined to his contribution to the development of social inquiry work; as we have seen, the work of John Augustus, although of relevance to social enquiry, also embraces a kind of supervision.

[4] Jarvis (1972a) suggests that the missionaries only kept in touch with a few who signed the pledge and 'referred most of them, if they were willing, to local parish workers' (21).

[5] Probably the same Mr. Wheatley referred to in Chapter 2 who later in his career was criticized by the 1909 Departmental Committee for giving too much material assistance to those in his care.

[6] One of the earliest courses for probation officers set up by the Joint University Council for Social Studies included the subject of Moral and Social Hygiene - Macadam, E. (1925) *The Equipment of the Social Worker*. London: George Allen & Unwin Ltd.

[7] Although, during the 1920s and 1930s some missionaries encountered theories in special training courses (see Appendix 1).

[8] Later he was to write a book about psychology and crime.

[9] Evidence that Holmes reflected widely held views come from Stedman Jones (1971) who reports that in the 1880s one of the solutions to social problems in London was to move the 'casual and "loafer" class' out of the city (p.225).

[10] A notorious female 'inebriate' referred to by Holmes in the same book.

[11] He was also an associate of both the Borstal Association and the Central Association for the Aid of Discharged Convicts.

[12] In the introduction to *Them that Fall* he wrote, 'A quarter of a century's work as a police court missionary convinces me that no great proportion of "them that fall" had ever much chance of doing anything else' (1).

[13] Although there was no training in groupwork, on the Home Office training course for probation officers started in 1930 trainees were introduced to group settings through visits to prisons, Borstal institutions, Home Office schools of different types, remand homes, probation homes, probation hostels, boys' and girls' clubs, etc (Le Mesurier 1935).

[14] Bochel claims that he made the first use of the word 'casework' in *Probation Journal*.

[15] This appears to have involved a form of supervision or oversight.

[16] From Exeter College, Oxford and commissioned by the Toynbee Trust to observe the police courts and talk to missionaries, clergy and employers.

[17] Gamon refers to males only, although this does not necessarily mean that he did not observe women missionaries as well.

[18] Of course, this was not always the case; there were some very good relationships. Chapman, a magistrate in London for twenty five years writes effusively about his relationships with the missionaries in court, describing one of them, a Miss Evelyn Lance as 'a natural genius for influencing children to self-mastery' (Chapman 1926: 262-3).

[19] It is not clear what this is, but it is likely to be some kind of medication designed to reduce craving.

[20] *The Temperance Chronicle* 28 January 1910 in a comment on the report clearly saw the advent of probation as the culmination of 'an unbroken record of steady progress'.

[21] See Appendix 2. Interestingly, Leeson's list has much in common with content of social enquiry reports in Perry's (1974) survey. In fact the first attempt to change the structure and focus of reports came relatively late in probation history (Bottoms and Stelman 1988).

[22] A. Maxwell addressing NAPO conference in 1918 and 1919 - the first, *National Association of Probation Officers*, 9, 116; the second, *National Association of Probation Officers*, 10, 183-184.

Chapter 4

From Awakening the Conscience to Providing Insight

What is, perhaps, more appropriately termed the semi-professionalization of the probation service has to be viewed from an understanding of its formative historical structure.[1] Chapter 2 argued that the concept of probation developed from an intricate relationship between often-conflicting social, cultural, religious and political forces, which accentuated the heterogeneous character of the reform movement. Whilst that reform movement promoted religious morality above science (Garland 1985) probation was essentially part of a new penality based on a freshly acquired curiosity about the individual and how to change him through supervision (Saleilles 1911). It was to be expected, therefore, that probation practice would be carried by that process towards both a wider knowledge base and a burgeoning administrative and organizational structure. In other words, the professionalisation of the probation service was embroiled in the newly burgeoning mechanisms and strategies of control and was, inevitably, tied to the development of psychology and the search for *positive* knowledge about the individual (Rose 1996).

It was, Rose argues, through its ability to contribute to the resolution of social problems created by dysfunctional behaviour and the social threat posed, that psychology (and psychiatry) sought its status; and, it is argued in this book that by association probation was rendered susceptible to eugenics and concerns about social degeneracy. At the outset, it had assumed the mantle of respectability of evangelical humanitarianism but as its efforts to change human behaviour became more demanding it needed recourse to the means to achieve it. Christian exhortation in the face of complex social and personal problems was insufficient; and amidst the 'new liberalism' of the early 20th century, so was the moral status that came with Christian effort. Probation, emerging as it had from 'the moralising philanthropy of the mid-nineteenth century', which had identified 'young actual and potential criminals as a special class' (Rose 1985: 167), needed a new status. What is more, this pressure came not from managerial direction but from an unfolding practice base influenced simultaneously by the study of individual psychology (and its attendant psycho-eugenic baggage) and the growing belief that offending was a symptom not simply of moral failing (though that belief survived the century) but also of psychological defects. Hence, the process of professionalizing the practice of probation in the first half of the 20th century can be characterised as a movement from 'awakening the conscience' to providing insight into reasons for those defects.

Professional Leanings

In fact, the argument by some historians outlined in the previous chapter that the police court missionaries had little contact with theories, and by implication, psychological texts looks weaker as the 20th century begins. Ellis in the 1910 fourth edition of his work *The Criminal* makes specific reference to the probation system, and Gamon uses the term patient to describe the people with whom missionaries worked, and while this does not indicate that missionaries were familiar with theory, it does suggest that the language of the new science was filtering through to commentators. The reality is that early probation officers were much more likely to encounter psychological theories than their predecessors were.

It would not be true to say, however, that there was a specific time when practice became scientific, and in a pure sense, it never has. It has always been a varied activity depending on the particular abilities, knowledge and skills of a diverse body of people. McWilliams (1986), as indicated earlier, suggests that the slow shift from the missionary ideal to that of science and diagnosis can be traced to the methods of scientific charity, the history of the Charity Organisation Society and the use of the term 'case work'. Rightly, he highlights the role of Mary Richmond in pioneering the scientific basis of social work in her 1917 book *Social Diagnosis*; moreover, he exposes what he sees as a flaw in her diagnostic model:

> Treatment does not arise directly from the facts; rather diagnosis is an interaction between social facts and moral evaluations, and treatment is a moral prescription of what ought to be done in the light of the moral evaluations to be made. Further, as facts are not the theory-free entities envisaged in empiricist epistemology, and as the selection of facts in diagnostic practice is influenced not only by theory, but also by values it must be concluded that this methodology of social diagnosis is gravely flawed (246).

Certainly, probation officer interest in the application of psychological theory to practice occurred earlier than Bochel (1976) suggests. For example, in 1912 Holmes had written his quirky critique of psychology and crime; in 1914 Leeson had provided a blueprint for a professional service in a checklist for inquiry that has all the hallmarks of professional diagnosis; and three years later the annual conference of NAPO was addressed on the subject of phrenology and the association of 'moral depravity' with an 'ill-balanced brain' (Hubert 1917: 152-3). Leeson is particularly interesting on this issue. On the one hand, his writing reveals clarity about the shortcomings of practice that relied completely on personality but on the other, it indicates a belief that personality was the single most important element in probation work. However, his enthusiasm for the American system of setting tests akin to entrance examinations for would be probation officers, his consistent reference to cases, and his emphasis on statistics confirm his preference for a professional Service. Unsurprisingly, therefore, he warns, 'the system loses greatly when administered by officers lacking [such] education and training' (p. 88).

Official recognition of this viewpoint is manifest in the Report of the Departmental Committee on the Training, Appointment and Payment of Probation Officers (Home Office 1922). Even though the Committee placed a heavy emphasis on the personality of the officer and did not think the job would attract university graduates, it did stress the need for recruitment 'of men and women of higher qualifications' (p. 14). It did not specify, however, what type of training. Two years later in an address to the Howard League, Carey (1924) asserted that the probation service needed 'men and women of high culture and of broad education and profound knowledge of human nature if the work is to be done as it should be done' (109-10).

McWilliams (1986) is probably right in his judgement that it was not until the 1960s that 'psycho-social diagnosis' had 'swept aside many (though not all) of the earlier understandings' (255). Yet, a perusal of probation writing from the beginning of the 1920s reveals that the language of social science *was* cropping up amidst the idiom of commonsense and religious morality. For instance, Ayscough (1929) in a discussion of young offenders exemplifies how probation at this time was tentative about its psychological credentials. He placed them in three categories: harmless (or trivial offenders) who might warrant probation; abnormal who need expert treatment; and victims of a problematic home situation in need of removal from home or intervention of a new influence. Conversely, he suggests that even when psychological treatment was required probation might have a part to play, and supports this by reference to Burt's 'excellent book' *The Young Delinquent* and its definition of probation as not 'mere surveillance' but 'an intimate and active relation, which deals with all factors of the child's life' (Ayscough 1929: 23-24; Burt 1925: 193). A paper about probation from the point of view of a female officer furnishes another example of the tendency to venture into the realm of expertise (Hemsley 1920). Her solution for young people with parents who had no concern for moral decency, was removal from home – the need, 'physical and moral well-being', the remedy, moral education in a home. In nine and a half years, this particular probation officer placed 386 females in homes, and her concern for the moral health of the young extended to the 'evil of the ice-cream saloon' because its cubicle system allowed 'undesirable social influence' (222).

In confident style, Chinn (1920) extols the fact that in Birmingham officers had recommended successfully the appointment of a medical officer to examine offenders who were supposed to be 'physically, mentally or morally defective'. In the case of a fifteen-year-old boy on probation for larceny, it had been effective in exposing tonsillitis and its effect of making him dull and stupid as a cause of his offending. According to Chinn, following examination by the medical officer, surgery and three weeks of convalescence he was found a job, and became 'a useful member of society'. Chinn refers also to a case in which the medical officer diagnosed tuberculosis as 'a direct cause of delinquency' (248-249). No doubt convinced by the efficacy of a more informed approach to the work, he finishes by arguing for greater coherence in the reforming efforts of the Service with officers working in a more systematic way, and suggesting that the route to this was through the appointment of properly trained and adequately paid officers.

Another officer while accepting the eugenic standpoint on inherited wickedness accepts that causality includes social circumstances (Rankin 1921). As an *expert*, he espouses the value of experience over theory, and then asserts that he and his colleagues find that the young people they have to deal with 'prove that the downward twist in human nature has not changed – they run the same course that their fathers ran' (321). Although he elaborates a theory in the guise of common sense the paper is interesting and valuable in terms of insight into the practice and theory of probation in more than this sense because he reports on his own research involving gathering problem cases with suggested solutions from officers around the country. He does not describe it as research or confirm the numbers involved but it is informative all the same. Six problems with their solutions are presented; and because they are real cases, they merit detailed attention.

The first difficult case involves a child charged with theft and wilful damage who truants from school and who has parents of 'dissolute habits' and weakness of character. The parents want him removed from home until he is capable of earning a wage. As a solution, it is proposed that the probation officer finds out why the child is behaving the way he is and why he is out of control, and that if it is proved that the parents encouraged the offence they be bound over under section 99 of the Children Act to improve the home.

The second case is a sixteen-year old boy charged with attempted burglary who is the eldest in a family which the father has deserted, and in which the mother is 'bordering on imbecility': he is unemployed and the family are very poor. In this case, the dilemma facing the officer hinges on recourse to the workhouse or the duty 'to befriend and otherwise assist'. The proposed solution is the availability of a relief fund to every probation officer, and the actual solution was temporary financial relief, the provision of food and clothes, the finding of employment, and the utilization of the local Board of Guardians to find the father and procure his contribution to the family.

The third case, a homeless, destitute and unemployed man, aged thirty who is bound over to keep the peace, is described as 'not being to fond of work', not very able and not as 'deserving as many others'. It is suggested that he is placed in a work home in which he would have supervised work and care until he could be reconciled to his wife.

The fourth case is one of his own; a twelve-year-old boy who was a ringleader in offending and had little controlling influences at home. He had been placed on probation for shopbreaking. Supervision involved an innovative but idiosyncratic approach:

> I began by emphasising my desire for his friendship, and my desire to help him. I found him mentally wrong; he had been examined by a doctor, but he refused to certify him; still I felt he was so and do now. In a few weeks he was again in Court on a similar charge; the parents made an agonising appeal to me. This was my opportunity for dealing with them, and gained a pledge if I succeeded in getting Probation Order (sic) again they would follow my instructions and control him and co-operate in my methods. I obtained a new Probation Order. Knowing the lad had some regard and

affection I appealed to latter virtues and feigned illness, got him concerned, and then told him he was the cause of a big pain under my heart; thus he became interested in my welfare. I ventured to suggest that he could help me to get well, and he could give me the right medicine by letter. The idea took and I helped him to prescribe my remedies. If conduct good he sent me a bottle on paper labelled 'This will do you good'; if conduct not so good bottle labelled 'A little nasty,' and on my visits I was either better or worse. He became interested, and remained at home away from the company he kept owing to parents becoming more anxious to help. After some time I asked him for a tonic to buck me up, as the medicine he had sent me was doing me good. Then I was convalescent – this meant I visited less frequently. Later I changed from medicine and tonic to a few pills, pointing out the advertisement about Williams' Pink Pills, and so he finished probation satisfactorily to the wonder of Police, who were sure he never would go straight; but he has done to this day (322).

Case number five involves a youth who had been placed on probation for 'wandering abroad'. The author found him lodgings and a job in a local colliery. He lost both, and subsequently fell ill with pneumonia and pleurisy, at which point the officer took him to the workhouse infirmary. After absconding on several occasions, he arrived at the officer's home but refused to enter, and the only way that the officer could appeal to him was '*by threatening to thrash him with a stick*' (my italics). Finally, he took him to a Poor Law home, informed the police that he was there and that 'he was ripe for certifying mental defective' (322).

The final case, a young married man who with his 19-year-old wife had been charged with neglect of their child who had died. Both were deemed 'border line' cases, were semi-starved and poorly clothed. The suggested solution by the officer, who supplied the problem, was work, which was found thereby improving the situation.

Rankin then provides some general advise if probation is to be a viable alternative to the reformatory. It involves having an efficient method; studying the case; formulating a plan; listing available agencies which might contribute to the success of the plan; using members of the community on the offender's behalf, and acting as the offender's advocate.

These case examples provide a remarkable insight into the eclectic nature of probation practice and its infusion with yet to be theorized methodology set alongside lay approaches. They contain reference to the importance of investigation alongside the language of both moral and degenerative classification; an early form of behaviour modification; and role reversal alongside coercion and threats of physical violence. Moreover, they incorporate a strategic approach that juxtaposes the use of other agencies and recognition of the importance of material aid in the alleviation of environmental problems (a form of systemic intervention) to a belief in moral frailty as a cause of crime.

They coexist alongside descriptions of work that owe nothing to science and everything to a kind of layperson's guide to successful relationships. For example, a young girl on probation for disorderly conduct and from an 'immoral home' is given special attention:

She is rather difficult to win [...] something special must be thought of for her and her friends. A little party or club will be the thing. A cosy room, a fire and a kettle boiling. Flowers or plants on the table, tray cloth, with cups and saucers. Different kinds of fancy work and a merry book, such as 'harum scarums' read aloud. The girl becomes confidential. A blouse with some of the new stitches learned worked on it takes the place of the old dirty dress, and the close of the winter sees a merry, sharp-witted, self-respecting girl who is not likely to be arrested for disorderly conduct again (Kenyon 1921: 318).

Is this a panacea for crime, or a simple solution to a minor problem? Whatever, an explicit combination of the scientific and theological approach to practice came two years later but this time premised on the concept of manhood. Membury (1922), in flamboyant language, defines the probation task as building men who fit with the 'Master Builder', the starting point being bringing the probationer in contact with 'One great Sympathetic Superman'. Juxtaposed to this task are diagnosis and enquiry into both the psychological and genetic background. In addition, he is inquisitive about motivation, the offender's perception of the offence, and his strengths. In explaining the latter interest, this officer reveals it as his method of establishing friendship through the expression of belief in the individual, a method that then involves the sharing of personal experiences of life's dangers. The methods used, he argues, should be underpinned by absolute conviction to facilitate confidence and courage, and backed up by material and practical help, if required. There is nothing groundbreaking here but what he says about the constraints on help, and what appears to be a prototype client-centred approach is very interesting: 'Do not press your services if he prefers to act alone in finding work. He may be doing it to avoid being "labelled" '; and if at school 'enter into his view of school life' (346). If the probationer is unhappy at school, he urges officers to seek school transfers, and to visit the school and work with his teacher. Leisure time is highlighted as particularly important, and officers are advised to refer the probationer to 'Educational Classes, Sports Clubs, Scouts, Brigades' and other recreational activities such as gardening and woodcarving; to encourage reading; to introduce him to friends; but more importantly, to link him with a religious organization. The intent though is not to narrow down the probationer's mind; instead, he advises, encouraging 'largeness of mind', and extolling 'the duty of the individual to the race, the duty of the parent to the child, the choice of partner in life, always allowing scope for the liberal expression of his own mind'. Finally, he insists that officers must take into account the 'complexity and diversity of human nature'(346).

At this point in probation history, probation officers were grappling with the difficulty of trying to respond in a considered way to people's offending and related problems in a changing political and social climate. For instance, in the face of the declining influence of Temperance Societies, Smith (1922) presents the case for the use of probation with first offenders convicted of drunkenness. Another former police court missionary who ran a hostel for young females (Stead 1922)[2] refers to the mixed response of her former colleagues to the changes brought in by the Probation Act. She argues that the changes required both magistrates and officers to study more closely social conditions and the causes of crime 'both hereditary and environmental' – that 'queer jumble, physical, mental, spiritual, which makes up humanity in the abstract and in the individual' (373).

Both the incipient nature of probation practice and a continuing concern about deterioration in social and moral standards offer a reason for the Service's problem. Society demanded solutions, and the probation service was the object of expectations from without and within. What is more, because of the increasing secularization of society, the Service was experiencing a crisis of identity, and some within it held on to the certainties of theology. A paper read to the Worcestershire NAPO branch laments the indifference to God, public worship and the Sabbath, and expresses anxiety about the slump in moral standards across the whole class spectrum (Musgrove 1923). In promoting the solution of Christian friendship and influence to these problems she highlights the opportunity provided by access to people's homes, and delineates what is required from officers: 'a large, steadfast, strong, loving spirit; self-sacrifice', and 'the wisdom and experience of doctors, lawyers, nurses and many others' (435). She warns that the 'very low standards prevailing in the homes' to be visited will shock officers but counsels them against judging the lives of probationers by their own standards.

Her paper provides a glimpse of not only the desire for the characteristics of a profession but also a subsequently well documented and institutionalized value base. However, some saw the system of dual control, whereby officers appointed by justices remained representatives of various societies, impeding this progress – a progress contingent on a unified service, allegiance to one authority and professionalism (Barrow 1923). On the other hand, the commitment to theology in the only probation publication remained doggedly strong (Poulton 1925). Appeals to spirituality as a component of probation coexisted alongside reports on experiments in progressive social work such as the East End Boy's Hostel and Club based on principles of community integration, mutual help and self government (National Association of Probation Officers 1925); and accounts of pioneering work with young offenders in America (Pratt 1925). In turn, these coexisted with progressive moves to deal with the practical problems faced by probationers; for instance, London had an Employment Officer (Page 1992). Undoubtedly, the latter is an example of helpful innovation but despite this, the language associated with concerns about degeneracy laces some of the descriptions of him and his function:

> The manager, Mr. A. J. Pilgrim, has a most comprehensive knowledge of human nature, the secret places of the criminal heart are open to him; he recognizes all the hidden vices, calling upon them each by name. Nothing perturbs, nothing upsets him, he remains eternally interested, unflaggingly eager, competent to cope with any convulsion of unregenerate man or woman.
>
> Of late a fresh type of borderline case has appeared. Among the new poor who since the War have found themselves reduced from quiet comfort to a wearing condition of uncertainty, there are a number of women who in early middle age have to earn their living without any trained means of

doing so. They retain that reticence as to their difficulties, which is the hall-
mark of their class (Chesterton 1928: 250).

It is fair to say that such language masks evidence that in the second half of the
1920s probation was moving into a new era. In a paper given to a NAPO
conference in Leicester, Walter Stanton, who had worked in the police court
mission and then the probation service for forty years, places the role of the
probation officer in a new liberal era of criminal justice (Stanton 1925). Probation
work is in his view focused both on children and on young people at a critical
juncture in their lives, and faces difficult problems that require intelligent
responses. While the paper acknowledges the value of a good education, the
qualification of experience in the 'university of the world' is deemed paramount
(501). In the same edition, however, a magistrate challenges that view with an
explicit demand for professionalism (Trought 1925). Encouraged by his knowledge
of developments in America, he argues for probation to be placed on a par with
teaching in terms of conditions of service and status; for scientific treatment rather
than punishment to be the ideal in Juvenile Courts with all the 'stigma of
criminality' being removed; for a recognition that there are 'no criminal children,
only unfortunate ones'; for the utilization of 'medical and mental clinics' in the
search for causes of crime; and the abolition of fines and birching (510).

These arguments attracted support from officers such as Chinn (1926) who (in
an address on the problem of adolescent sexuality to NAPO conference) provides
one of the earliest examples of a practitioner's public discussion of psychological
theory in relation to criminality.[3] The connection with criminality is tenuous, and
Chinn justifies the focus of his paper with the fact that a large proportion of those
appearing before the courts are aged between 12 and 18. He concurs with Stanley
Hall's assertion that the causes of most offending careers can be related back to
adolescence, and acknowledges the constraint imposed on probation officers by
their lack of knowledge of a 'profound' and complex subject. Then he extrapolates
a theoretical explanation of the process of adolescent emotional and physical
growth, which draws on what he has read. He reports that 'McDougal in his
"Social Psychology"' points to the increase in frequency and strength of excitation
of two great self-regarding impulses – self-display and self-abasement – due to the
enrichment of the consciousness of self and of the self in relation to others'. Next,
he defines the ideal relationship as not based on equality but 'respect, admiration
and consideration for woman' (601). His attention is then drawn to the response to
these 'newly awakened ideals and emotions', of the 'town children' with whom
probation officers have most contact. He asserts authoritatively that such children
are introduced inappropriately to sex because of the overcrowding and squalor, and
denied access to the opportunity that country children have to deal with the 'vague
inexpressible feelings of adolescence' by 'long solitary and extremely valuable
rambles'. The results, he argues, are aimless parades on the street, truancy, running
away from home, succumbing to the 'lure of the cinema', the warping of 'the deep
religious aspirations of adolescence', the suppression of individuality, and the
'extinction of sentiments of modesty' (602). He ends by offering some guidelines
for probation officers: first, referral to group situations such as scouts, brigades and

clubs; and second, the provision of sex education. Chinn is very detailed on the latter. Probation officers should recognize the complex components of the problem, such as fear of abnormality, curiosity that might lead to anti-social behaviour, and the loss of self-esteem through self-abuse. Chinn asserts that the loss of self esteem is temporary, and that, therefore, probation officers should point out 'that in reality very little permanent harm is done if the practice is not indulged in excessively' but also emphasize 'the evil in the habit' and the fact that it is not just an insult to self but also to God (602). This concluding advice to his colleagues is full of the terminology of psychology, such as 'neurosis and unhealthy states' and 'excessive morbidity'.

As will be shown, the influence of psychology increased in the second half of the 1920s, and reached new heights in the 1930s. Appropriately, therefore, this section ends with an examination of a paper given to the 1928 conference by Dr. W. A. Potts of Birmingham. He is a significant figure in the probation history of this period, and clearly an influential one.[4] He begins by warning about the risk of probation being viewed as a punishment, and asserting that assessment of suitability is of paramount concern. As far as physical weakness or mental disability is concerned, he stresses the importance of probation officers having sufficient time to put things right by indeterminate terms of probation. In his view, all cases that came before the court are underdeveloped physically, morally and spiritually, and it is the probation task to give them the 'vitamins that they [lack]' (672). He acknowledges the great difficulty that probation officers have with 'mentally defective' cases, and offers the study of the psychological side of problems as a potential aid. In his view, 'psychological and mental defects' figure largely in cases that come before the courts, and it is important to investigate factors from the very beginning of the child's life. He refers to the conclusions of 'a very eminent Swedish psychologist' that the minds of criminals have 'never developed in individuality, in the capacity for shaping their own life or for fitting in to social life' (672). In addition, he outlines the important stages in the development of a child's life, and stresses particularly the importance of the period between ten and 14 years when the child has 'to learn to fit into social life', and the period between 14 and 21 when the adolescent has to develop responsibility (672). Finally, he endorses the importance of scouts and guides in the process of teaching teamwork, and the importance of learning self-control. This is a further example of the increased exposure of groups of probation officers to the perceptions and teaching of psychology, and expert confirmation of both the efficacy of aspects of their practice and the validity of some of their beliefs. As the 1930s dawned, it was a tendency set to increase very significantly.

As has been suggested in chapter two, the probation service would eventually commit itself to the strictures of psychological theory but the growing influence of psychology has to examined in context. Firstly, the religious base of the Service was still strong, and available evidence of discourses within the Service during the 1930s suggests a tension between the intellectual and moral demands of both religion and psychology. (Moreover, as has been argued previously, the psychological complex itself was made up of competing influences.) Second, the language of degeneracy was crucial to the claim of psychiatrists for the importance of their sciences. As Rose (1996: 8) makes clear, the degenerate class 'appeared as different forms of expression of an underlying pathology of constitution' acquired by amoral behaviour and passed down by the highly promiscuous. Influential though this perspective was, it represented only one (albeit very important) *political rationality*, and the eugenicists were opposed by civil libertarians and the Mental Hygiene movement which itself had carved its own niche in the treatment of offenders.

The Age of the Expert and the Launch of Probation Journal

At this point, evidence of the training of probation officers and police court missionaries also becomes noticeable. In the 1920s and early 1930s some police court missionaries were attending, or undertaking correspondence courses in social science that included economic history, problems of poverty, social psychology and the psychology of crime; and in 1930 prospective probation officers began attending the Home Office National Training Scheme (Le Mesurier: 66).[5] The introduction of the scheme was not without controversy, and the debate preceding its introduction reveals the ambivalence towards training felt by those in and close to the Service, and the sense of threat to its traditional foundations. William Clarke Hall (NAPO 1929) at an official conference of probation officers convened by the Home Office, warned that training alone would not make a good officer:

> If we forget we are running a tremendous risk of killing the soul of probation, and without the soul it would be a dead machine, useless for carrying out the great work it has undertaken (7).

He went on to argue that the essential qualities of an officer were the quality of personality; indefinable religious spirit; a broad view of human life; the highest ethical standards, and an understanding of those who fall below those standards. He said that while he had known good officers not tied to one particular religious creed, he had never come across an officer without a religious spirit. In the same debate, Sydney Edridge cited the influence of personality as paramount; a Mr. Watson warned that training might erode the 'certain heart sense' that was the foundation of the work; and the Reverend Harry Pearson argued for training but stated that the officer needed to remain a kind of 'Father Confessor'.[6]

Symbolically, the publication of the journal *Probation* is of critical importance because it inaugurated the professional voice of the Service, and the first paper in the journal on the method of probation illustrates perfectly the status of probation practice at the end of the 1920s (Warner 1929). It lays down the aspirations of the Service with confidence and clarity. Probation, the author proclaims, had passed the 'creeping and crawling stage', and arrived at a time for critical reflection on its progress to date and its future direction. Her recent experience in America had convinced her that the Service should become scientific but not as seemed to be in America to the exclusion of common sense and instinct; rather, she argues, what is required is an amalgamation of sympathy, understanding, common sense and science. She compares officers to doctors, and then sets out a charter for professionalism that includes diagnosis to help assess suitability; expounding theories; record-keeping; an 'individualised' plan worked out with the probationer and designed to help him help himself; reviews of the plan; links with other agencies; home visiting; and office interviews. Those interviews, she avows, should not be 'perfunctory', and 'should be long enough for the probationer not to feel that the probation officer [is] impatient to get on with the next probationer' (11).

She was not the only probation officer to have visited America that year. Chinn (1929) in his report on his trip there states that officers are given psychiatric training, and that the 'emphasis on individual treatment is largely due to the work of the Child Guidance Clinics' (27). Here, then, was the professional approach urged by Leeson some fifteen years earlier, being actively encouraged by some practitioners: it was not a new imperative but it was opportune. Waiting in the wings were the experts who would provide the knowledge base on which such an approach needed to be built.

In that inaugural volume of the journal, Creighton-Miller's paper to the NAPO conference (1929) provides an early example of the promulgation of the technical language of psychology. Speaking about the motivations of the 'juvenile delinquent' he employs terms such as 'mal-adjusted', 'the regressive', 'cases of inferiority', and 'cases of resentment'. With transparent confidence he refers to the example of a red headed boy convicted of travelling on a train without a ticket whose 'unconscious motive' is attributable to teasing about the colour of his hair; and he alludes to the 'mechanisms whereby the delinquencies of the juvenile are produced' (14). A trend is established.

The following year the influence of Cyril Burt is visible in a contribution by a Dr. Burns (1930) on the psychology of the individual.[7] Burns begins by referring to Goring's refutation of the existence of the criminal type, and Burt's assertion that crime is not inherited. However, he then re-iterates Burt's version of the hereditary principle, that what is passed down through the generations is 'inferior material in some but not all criminals; either physical weakness and underdevelopment, or temperamental instability: with low powers of resistance to moral infection' (39). Burt had indeed been the main opponent of the link between inherited idiocy and feeble-mindedness with offending. However, in Rose's view he had taken this position because of his desire to claim offending and general problem behaviour as the intellectual property of the psychological not the medical field, and to allow psychology to be located within the realm of reformation and treatment. From that standpoint, the problem was not inborn or physical and, therefore, demanded psychological solutions targeted at the 'inner mental life of the delinquent.' A 'set of biological instincts' or tendencies were inborn and were subject to the influence of the environment (Rose 1985: 194). This kind of compromised eugenic position stimulated by the Mental Hygiene movement is clear in Dr. Burns' paper. Therefore, the criminal is produced by the 'interplay of environment, and the raw material which is to be moulded by it', and the loss of the 'social sense' caused by 'defective early training' (Burns: 39-40). Much of the input from the field of psychology that followed affirms this theoretical and ideological position.

Possibly the same Dr. Burns (1930) who was physician to the children's department of the Tavistock Clinic for Nervous disorders, seems less reticent about his eugenic credentials in a paper published later in the year.[8] In this, he advocates the use of the probation officer's personality 'to free probationers from problems that have twisted essential goodness' (52), and offers guidance on causation and the direction of inquiry the probation officer should undertake. First, he links offending to 'mental defect or some *racial poison* (my italics) in the family' (52). Then, he provides a checklist of inquiry which covers the nature of the potential person; the extent to which 'the dice are loaded against him'; evidence in the personal history of mental defect, lack of intelligence, need for supervision and control, disease or neurosis; the degree to which he is 'an inferior type physically'; the psychological environment; the material and moral state of the home; mental deficiency or disorder in the background; and poor peer influences. With apparent reticence, he concedes that poverty and overcrowding are worthy of consideration but suggests that their importance is relative to their combination with other factors.

Dr. Suttie (1930), also of the Tavistock, concentrates more on intervention. For him the 'normal' delinquent is the product of 'self-indulgence and recklessness, indiscipline, thoughtlessness, conceit', and the probation officer's task is to help the process of growing up. This is achieved by providing personal support and encouragement for the individual as they move through the 'shock of exposure and the strain of disgrace' (69). Advocating what appears to be an early form of *Restorative Justice,* Suttie hypothesises that disgrace creates a kind of excommunication that stimulates changes in attitudes and values, and the discontinuation of taboos. Probation officers, therefore, must bear this in mind along with the potency of anti-social incentives, and the need to foster an 'affective dependency in the probationer'. The objective of treatment is to lead the 'patient to experience good fellowship and tutelage', and he advocates a kind of crisis-intervention at the time of the court appearance –'the psychological moment for the probation officer' (69).[9]

As Suttie suggests, a typography of offenders is woven into the textual analysis of these psychological offerings, and there are judgements about the jurisdiction of probation's effectiveness. In a typology of causes, Creighton-Miller (1931) lists suggestibility as amenable to education, rebellion as worth spending time on, deprivation as requiring personal help but mental defect as providing very little scope for probation. His is, however, a broadly inclusive approach: probation is the opportunity to show the probationer ('primarily a herd animal') that he is an 'object of love' and not a 'pariah' (99).

The transcript of an address made to the Midland branch of NAPO conference by a contributor from Nottingham University (Sprott 1931) affords a much more detailed exposition of the application of psychology to crime. It is of significance particularly because of its direct reference to the use of psychoanalytical theory in probation practice. From a neo-classical position of concern with the individual, and with echoes of Saleilles, Sprott asserts confidently the psychological position:

> For psychology there is no such thing as an act of stealing, an act of rape, or an act of truancy; each of these performances requires interpretation, we have to find out how it fits with the personality of the person who has performed it; we must discover if we can what were the motives, conscious and unconscious that led to its performance (123).

He reminds his audience that this way of viewing crime is familiar to them, and refers to the work of the American psychologist Healy, and in the United Kingdom that of Burt and Le Mesurier (in her book 'Boys in Trouble' 1931). Children, according to Sprott, are born with inherited tendencies requiring the constraint of moral education in order to teach delayed gratification. He sets out a critique of four methods of treatment for those cases where that education has been either faulty or not absorbed. The first *pain*, he dismisses as negative and counter-productive. The second *exploitation*, he explains, involves demonstrating to the individual that the undesirable behaviour stands in the way of satisfaction from other tendencies that are more important to him. The third, *social methods*, he describes as being used in the Borstal system, and in particular at Lowdham Grange where it involves placing the individual in a 'pungent social atmosphere' that he will gradually absorb because of the advantages that this kind of society will offer him. However, it is the fourth, *transference*, which he credits as being the most important. As he puts it, 'the child 'identifies' himself with one or other of its parents or with parts of both', and 'the emotional attitude of the child to its parents is transferred onto someone else, perhaps onto a series of people, in later life' (124). Then, he outlines a method to be 'used consciously and scientifically' that was to survive in probation practice certainly until the early 1970s.[10] Sprott provides a succinct description of the practice method:

> The probation officer must woo the delinquent into this relationship, must stand to him or her in the position of father or mother or both, and use the emotional attitude which has been established as a basis for influence (124).

With a final flourish, he tells his audience that use of the personality on its own is not enough but that transference must be used with 'an enormous amount of skill'. Interestingly, in the discussion that ensues, officers are reported as indicating that much use was being made of the third of his treatment responses, the social method.

Increasingly during this period, as Le Mesurier (1935) was to emphasize a few years later, the subject of delinquency was entering the arena of 'medical, educational and social activity', and in her view, was therefore becoming 'a part of the general problem of Mental Hygiene' (208). It is interesting therefore, that Rose (1996) identifies the Mental Hygiene movement as the creator of more fertile ground for the application of psychological theories and techniques than the Eugenics movement. The reason for this, he suggests, was that it created optimism about the potential for changing behaviour because explanations of delinquent and deviant behaviour shifted from inherited defects to poor mental hygiene in the various sites of influence in a child's life. In this sense, it is unsurprising perhaps that this influence that was more pervasive in probation discourse at this time; for example, Dr. Feldman of the National Council for Mental Hygiene contributed to an early volume of *Probation* on the problems of the normal adolescent (1931). This is not unexpected because the weight of medical opinion was against a 'full-scale project of eugenics', and towards the improvement of the race through the enhancement of mental hygiene (134). That said, the Mental Hygiene movement, embracing as it did the application of a range of 'dynamic psychologies and therapies' (Rose 1996: 10) did not entirely eschew the concept of hereditary defect. What is more, the editor of *Pobation* was willing to give a voice to a prominent figure in the Eugenics Society (Hodson 1932).

Mrs. C. B. S. Hodson had been General Secretary of the Eugenics Society from 1920 to 1931, and was appointed a Life Fellow in 1937. She was a pre-war supporter of the National Socialists in Germany, and issued statements such as 'the protagonists of the new eugenic era in Germany appear to hold a middle course'. Of the German exhibit of 1934, she pronounced, 'there is comparatively little about the Jews, and the point stressed is that alien races are all right in themselves and provided they keep to themselves but that they must not be allowed to 'poison good German blood'. In addition, she indicated that the exhibit also covered 'the problem of the 600 black bastards on the Rhine'. Subsequently, in a letter to Wing Commander James, she wrote, 'I fear some of us will have to stoop to a good deal that is vulgar if we are really to get Eugenics home to the masses, but very possibly they do not matter'.[11] In the *Probation* article, Hodson expresses confidence about the growing awareness that 'a great deal of law-breaking rests ultimately on the inborn make-up of the individual concerned' (151), and characterizes the habitual offender as not only being unable to distinguish between right and wrong because of 'a moral blindness' but also as uneducable. However, she is more optimistic about the average offender and the probation officer's ability through 'personal friendship, environmental aids and the like' to ameliorate the problems caused by 'faulty heredity' (151-2).

In apparent contrast, Dr. J. R. Rees, the deputy director of the Institute of Medical Psychology, in an address to NAPO conference reproduced in the journal, classifies early delinquency as normal; '[i]f only', he speculates, 'we could get all magistrates in this country to realise that they themselves have been delinquents' (Rees 1932: 183). But then in grappling with the problem of 'Sin v. Illness', Rees drifts into what Garland defines as the 'compromise formulation' (Garland 1985: 100) in which freedom and determination are both part of the individual's make-up. So while promulgating freedom of choice via an early version of 'growing out of crime' (Rutherford 1986), he claims that the majority of offenders 'have not been able to make that clear choice, for nine tenths of the things that happen to bring them into our hands result from illness, disorder of the mind or personality. They are people who are mentally sick' (Rees: 183). Finally, in an analysis which typical of its time seems to be a hybrid of eugenics and mental hygiene, Rees places biological causes in offenders who are 'constitutionally lacking' alongside environmental causes such as lack of parental care and lack of 'education in moral and social standards' (184).

In the NAPO conference of the following year Dr. J. A. Hadfield, lecturer in psychopathology and mental hygiene at London University picked up the same theme (Hadfield 1933). The transcript explains that crime is sometimes a disease and sometimes not, and uses the example of a 13-year-old girl who has committed theft: the cause could be, physical disorder such as underdevelopment of the brain; menstruation; exhaustion; bad home environment; anti-social tendencies; or psycho-neurotic compulsions. In it, he stresses the importance of training probation officers in the identification of behaviour disorders.[12]

This 'two-sided' study of the individual is, according to Clement-Brown, what is meant by the scientific study and treatment of delinquency (1934). In the report of his address to the Midlands NAPO branch, he claims that social workers fall into either the hereditary or the environmental camp, and that they are suspicious of science. In a call for a more scientific approach, he extols the work of Burt, Healy and Cabot, and explains how science is a way of making sense of the 'generalisations of our experience' (298). In what must be one of the earliest references to the idea of risk assessment with a probation audience, he illuminates the possibility (through detailed investigation) of discovering 'what type of individual and home would make a 'poor risk' on probation, and in what type of case there would be a high probability of success' (299). The caveat, he adds, is the dependence of the idea on social workers accepting scientific discipline and recognizing the importance of their link with researchers. Although he does not say so in the context of his analysis it is reasonable to assume that the issue of heredity versus environment would be a crucial one in determining risk.

Despite the fact that throughout the 1930s conference addresses and journal articles provided probation officers with alternative versions of crime causation, the compromise Mental Hygiene position prevailed. de B. Hubert (1935) told conference that the idea of inherited moral imbecility with its implied need for eugenic measures was 'far too pessimistic'. However, the written report shows that like Burt and others, he did not leave it far behind. In addition it illustrates his commitment to the position that the 'hereditary factor is merely a tendency towards crime which needs specific influences to develop it' but when it is developed through faulty relationships with parents, it 'may be regarded as illness in the same way as one regards ordinary symptoms of nervous disease' (363-364). Significantly, it advocates the use of psychotherapy but in the discussion about 'high grade defectives' and 'psychopathic personalities, it asserts that the 'most promising approach' seems to be analysis of 'their hereditary relationships and attempt (sic) to control their propagation' (366).

Barton Hall, honorary physician to the Liverpool Psychiatric Clinic, explained personality to the Lancashire and Cheshire probation officer conference (Barton Hall 1934). Understanding of the delinquent's mind, he informed them, needed to be predicated on an understanding of four aspects of personality, intelligence; temperament; instinctive force (namely, 'vital urges which compel the individual to express himself'); and character development. Furthermore, such understanding had to take account of both inborn and acquired characteristics (329-30).

Brown (1934), Wilde Reader in Mental Philosophy, Oxford University, exhorted the Midland branch conference to greater co-operation with psychologists so that they could heighten understanding of the causes of crime. In this paper, he locates crime closely to mental and physical illness but identifies a number of contributory factors that includes: lack of self-control; sexual abuse; love of excitement; problems with self-assertion; physical illnesses such as encephalitis and lethargia which can lead to kleptomania and moral deterioration; hereditary factors such as alcoholism and epilepsy; and environmental aspects such as parental violence and moral lapses. Unlike most of his colleagues who appear in the pages of *Probation*, he gives some attention to the practice of probation officers in the face of these causal factors. Having first argued that the core focus of that practice should be fulfilling 'the individual's need of love and understanding', he lists its desired elements. They are intuition; influence; encouraging the probationer's commitment to the ideal; the provision of 'emotional, ethical and intellectual' re-education; putting the probationer in touch with the spiritual world and using prayer as 'a stepping-stone to faith'. For him psychotherapy must be not only mental but also 'spiritual reclamation', thus helping the probationer to a 'spiritual awakening' (276).

An almost unfathomable array of definitions of abnormality and disease permeates psychological discourse at this time, and some practitioners and outside experts attempted to steer a path through the resultant maze. For example, one contributor presented a technical elaboration of court responses and the distinction between mental deficiency and abnormality (Norris 1934); and Hamblin Smith, the Medical Officer of Birmingham prison confidently proclaimed '[t]hat there is always some abnormality in a criminal offender' and that '[c]rime is a symptom of disease' (1931: 81). Yet in another paper Suttie (1933) dispels the idea that mental abnormality has physical causes, because of emerging knowledge that 'subtle factors' in upbringing produce 'morbid effects' on behaviour (230). For him, therefore, investigation and interpretation of life histories are crucial. Moreover, quite exceptionally Kydd (1936), a tutor at the London School of Economics, in an address to the Sussex Branch Summer School, urged officers to see the individual against the economic background of unemployment, slum clearance, Hire-Purchase debt and the cost of living.

As Brown demonstrates (see above), religion was not forced entirely from the stage; it infiltrated psychological discourse while the theologians tried to reconcile increasing scientific knowledge with Christian belief. Although there were worries about the waning influence of religion,[13] it was not all pessimism: some gave credence to the new science (Talbot 1934). The Right Reverend Neville Talbot defines the probation officer's influence as a reflection of his Christian faith and ideals but then acknowledges the role of psychology in work with offenders; moreover, he emphasizes the need to explore the link between faith and science.[14] From his perspective, the fact that psychological knowledge emanates from God eliminates any possible discordance. In an address to the Weekend School of the Lancashire and Cheshire branch at the end of the decade the Reverend Leycester King (1939) confirmed further this rationalisation of the link between religion and psychology. The report of his address in *Probation* declares that probation work is 'straightening twisted, distorted creatures', and 'is necessarily connected with the religious sphere. Both from the objective and the subjective side the work is or should be supernatural' (99). While psychology is of some help, it continues, it is because the delinquent comes to the probation officer disorganized spiritually that the supernatural is most important. He was not alone. Scientists also rationalized the relationship between faith and science. While firmly wedded to the ideal of psychotherapy, Hopkins (1934), a lecturer in Psychology at London University, still acceded to the importance of spirituality. He portrays probation practice as the development of friendship with the offender that acts as an 'escape valve for his emotional tension' and helps 'wean him out of his egoism and get him to submit to a discipline of his impulses'. Nonetheless, its ultimate goal is to lift the offender 'to the happiness of complete and lasting spiritual marriage with the ideals of society as a whole' (64).

Despite these protestations and the continuing significance of religious conviction in the life of probation, psychology had assumed by the end of the 1930s a dominant position in the ideology (at least) of the experts gathered on the sidelines of the Service. Of course, that is not to suggest that the existence of the rhetoric of these various experts is in itself evidence of influence. It is clear from the content of the journal that a range of probation officers through conferences, summer schools, training and reading the journal itself during the 1920s and 1930s, were exposed increasingly to psychological theories underpinned themselves by discourses such as those of psychoanalysis, eugenics and mental hygiene. Moreover, the fact that during the 1920s probation officers and police court missionaries experienced training in the social sciences is well documented. Ayscough (1929), an early advocate of the use of psychological treatment to deal with what he terms 'the complex', refers to the National Police Court Mission of CETS Diploma Course established at the University of London. Rimmer (1995) reports that these Diploma courses had been available since the beginning of the century, and that those who undertook the courses at the London School of Economics 'were being taught by such authorities as Beveridge, Tawney, Hobhouse, Laski and Dalton' (177).[15] It is probable, then, that exposure to these teachers rendered some probation officers susceptible to their influence.

Besides, the theory and practice of probation in America had been a potential influence because probation officers from the time of Leeson had been paying professional visits there; and it seems likely that psychological discourse had become entrenched in the American Service well before the United Kingdom. Contributions to a book of essays in honour of Herbert Parsons provide evidence of this (Glueck 1933). Yet as in this country there was still some way to go. Glueck (1933a) in his introductory chapter suggests that although probation 'substitutes intelligence and humanity for ignorance and brutality in the treatment of offenders' its technique needed to be enhanced by psychology, mental hygiene, social casework and adult education (14). In the same volume, Ferris (1933), the Director of the Domestic Relations Division of the Recorder's Court in Detroit, classifies the 'art and science' of probation as being in its infancy. However, next he describes an advanced form of investigation designed 'to produce a clear picture of the offender, his traits, habits, abilities and tendencies' and to discover causal factors such as 'social, economic, moral, mental, hereditary etc'; and the use of case histories and treatment plans (140). Weiss (1933), a former probation officer of the Boston Juvenile Court, argues that probation work is social casework along the lines of Mary Richmond's model, and provides a practice example:

> John M had been in court four times, once for larceny, twice for drunkenness and the fourth time on two complaints of larceny in two different courts at about the same time. The larceny case in the first court involved approximately $250 while the one in the second consisted of a number of thefts totaling nearly $1,000 (190).

Detailed information about the family 'was collected by the probation officer from John himself, from his parents, from his wife and her father, from two previous employers and from three social agencies to which the family was known.'

> The probation officer had several long interviews with John, and went over the whole situation with him. His childhood and youth were discussed, and so were his marital life and his professional career.
>
> At this point, the probation officer did her most intensive thinking. Had he the stuff in him to make good, or was his attitude of remorse merely a temporary mood? Was he essentially weak or did he have qualities in him on which one could build? Was it possible that these years of unhappiness could so completely cover up those qualities, or did they not exist in him at all? If they did exist, what were they? His children were fond of him; he had been a good worker at one time; he had tried to please his wife; he had been a good son to his parents. But this had been years ago; could these qualities revive under wise guidance? The probation officer remembered having seen in the back yard of John's house a skillfully constructed aquarium with a miniature amusement park around it; the oldest boy pointed at it with pride and said: 'Daddy done this for me.' The work of art was of fairly recent date. The probation officer weighed all this against the crushing mass of unfavorable facts. She decided to take the risk though she was fully aware of the grave responsibility involved. She claimed later that, very probably, the aquarium had given her the courage to try it.
>
> From the moment she had made this decision, the probation officer changed her course. The process of finding out became of secondary importance; the main point in the diagnosis had become clear, and the attention was now focussed on treatment. The final decision would still depend on John's response to the first steps of treatment (190-1).

What then follows is a model of practice redolent of later cognitive work, and contains elements of task-centred and systems approaches:

> She began by trying to build up his courage. Then, she spoke of the children, how they needed their father and how much he had to make up toward them. His relationship with his wife was not touched upon at this point, but John was asked to work out a plan of how he could repay the money that he had taken. During the next two interviews, concrete plans were discussed so that John could see his way out, and when he began to take the attitude that all he

needed was courage and a 'chance' from the judge, probation was recommended after the continuance of two weeks had elapsed. The court agreed with this plan.

The work of reconstruction had to be attacked step by step. The social agency agreed to give John a small loan (not as much as it would have cost the community if John had been sent to jail) to set up a small business as a plumber. The wife who had been ill was sent to a convalescent home for two months, and the children were placed with John's parents. After six months, John had paid up most of his restitution, whereupon his father paid the rest. A year later, John moved the family into a suburban bungalow, bought a secondhand truck for his business and had some savings in the bank. The probation officer's most difficult job, after John had regained his self-confidence concerning his work, was to win the cooperation of his wife. The worst crisis was reached when she bought an expensive set of furniture on the installment plan without consulting her husband. The probation officer succeeded in persuading the company to take the set back without any loss to John. The result was the last great scene by Mrs. M. From that point on, she began to make progress also. After three years of probation, the situation was sufficiently stable for supervision to be discontinued' (190-2).

This impresses as a very methodical, collaborative approach based on an open, practical strategy, and rather different to the psychoanalytical method, and combination of psychiatry and social service advocated by Bernard Glueck (1933); and suggests, perhaps, that practice on the ground may have been rather different to the theory of the classroom.

This may well be true of probation in this country at that time too. Clarke Hall (1933) who contributed to this collection of essays, endorses the view that the success of probation depended on a number of factors. First, he argues, probation officers should have a distinctive personality; a good general education; a very careful training in the best courts and under the most efficient probation officers; and special study in sociology and economics and some knowledge of psychology and of criminal law and practice. Second, that there needs to be a careful selection of cases for probation based on full inquiries into character and circumstances, either on bail or in custody; realistic recommendations: appropriate involvement of medical opinion; treatment plans; and long periods of bail so that the person can be tested out (291-2). Finally, because 'there are many offenses committed owing to physical and psychological causes which are curable by the right method of treatment' that there is a need for 'a medico-psychological examination of offenders showing symptoms of abnormality' (293). In support of this, he refers to the fact that 'two of the London juvenile courts have in regular attendance at their sittings, doctors belonging to the Tavistock Clinic, the Child Guidance Clinic and the Jewish Free Clinic. Clarke Hall acknowledges also that 'England owes much to the United States, not only in giving the lead in study, investigation and example, but in direct financial assistance from two of its leading citizens' (294).

What is difficult to deduce from a distance of well over half a century is whether these various influences had impact, and permeated practice. The best clue lies in what some of the practitioners of the time wrote and said; however, several caveats are important to any examination of these accounts. First, at this point in the history of probation, policy is likely to have had little impact on practice, and therefore practice was idiosyncratic; second, the accounts are written by people who are not necessarily representative of the average officer; and third, it is clear that the amount of time that officers spent in contact with their probationers was limited. On the latter point, Rimmer (1995) refers to one probation officer working in Essex in 1939, who had a caseload of 70 plus 148 matrimonial cases in one year: and de Constabadie (1930) suggests that in view of the fact that officers see their probationers for approximately an hour a fortnight 'it is not surprising that the desired effect is not always achieved even in cases of normal mentality' (43).

In his many contributions to the journal, Chinn provides a detailed template for practice, which reflects the influence of the psychologists and American casework (Chinn 1930, 1931, 1931a, 1932). Following one visit, he argued that the home visit should entail in-depth study of the family and neighbourhood (including its spiritual dimension), particularly when the offence is caused by 'maladjustment' in the home. Moreover, it should be facilitated by systematic, surprise visiting in which sympathy is conveyed through a balanced approach as an official and a friend. He recommends a slow, objective approach in which notes are not taken and care is taken to avoid looking around the room. Treatment, he continues, should be planned, and the work should aim to teach people to do things for themselves 'and lead them to a realization of their responsibility as citizens as well as members of a family group' (1931: 84). Chinn, therefore, provides an interesting insight not just into the ideal of probation practice but also the fusion of the ideologies of support through treatment and individual responsibility. Another probation officer, underlines the importance of probationers facing up to the 'facts and responsibilities of life' (Francis 1932: 168) but also introduces the idea of adaptability through modifiable treatment plans aimed higher than just reducing offending. He sees confident, better citizens as the ultimate goal.

Clarke Hall (1931) reiterated the scientific approach in a contribution to a debate at NAPO conference on a resolution that investigations should (in principle) be undertaken on all people under 21 before the court sentences and that it is desirable to investigate physical and mental conditions of the individual:

> Probation should only be used after taking into account the personal and environmental history of the offender, his relation to society and his suitability for reformative treatment (132).

In the same debate, Chinn (1931a) put the case for pre-trial investigation for the sake of the individual and the community, and emphasized suitability as a critical aspect of the potential success of 'reformative treatment'. What is more, the written report of his contribution exhibits his psychological and social degeneracy credentials in a reference to a case that was unsuitable because the young lad was 'undoubtedly a high grade defective displaying that element of cunning common to the type' (131). The rest of his input is pervaded by contemporary psychological explanations for the offending of young people; so, for instance, in late adolescence 'habits have not become fixed' and 'anti-social behaviour is, more often than not conditioned by circumstances that have proved too strong for his immature nature' (132).

In the same report, Dr. Burns (1931) of the Tavistock Clinic supports the resolution because while not all 'delinquents are perverts or neurotics', the causation of criminality is subtle and complex, and rests on three forms of deprivation: 'physical, mental and environmental'. In delineating these forms, Burns re-emphasizes the eugenics/mental hygiene compromise. In his terms 'physical deformities warp the mind'; 'deep-seated organic effects, such as of the endocrine glands' effect behaviour; 'intellectual retardation and emotional or temperamental instability with lack of control' are defects found in approximately a third of delinquents; and a lack of intelligence causes inferiority, resentment, jealousy, and inability to conceptualize social order and the social contract (133-4). Two other practitioners bring a less technical slant to the debate in their support. A Miss E. C. Paine (1931), an officer at the London juvenile Court advocates investigation because of both the danger of judging by experiences, and also the need to discern between cases that need 'medical or psychological help', those that need 'a friend and a helping hand', and those who 'call for the blind eye and common-sense' (135). Finally, Mr. C. E. Clift (1931), a probation officer in Wolverhampton, makes the point that probation officers are better equipped to investigate 'the physical, moral and religious training of the prospective probationer' than the police (135).

Contributors to *Probation* at this time convey not only the influence of psychology and social awareness but also the resilience of moral judgement, Christian mores and class perspectives. Hence offending is 'the product of nine or ten subversive circumstances' (Mayling 1933: 219); failings of individual economy and instability of mind (Goldstone 1932); and 'the relaxation of the standards of an ordered life' encouraged by psychologists (Way 1932: 187).

Some Memoirs and the Handbook of Probation

Commentators like Mary Ellison (1934) who worked for six years as a probation officer, avow that the technical nature of reformatory effort was in the minds of those who framed the 1907 Act: '[t]his curative form of supervision is best understood by those who are properly trained and experienced in such methods' (xii). She writes about environmental difficulties, motivation and the 'equipoise' required between the needs of the community and the offender. She places emphasis on the effects of poverty and unemployment on people's behaviour but she also reveals her leanings towards more individualistic explanations for people's offending. Middle-aged shoplifters 'are no ordinary offenders! The root cause of this delinquency is physical. Such women need medical care and skilled supervision' (96); and on theft, '[p]sychologists say that theft is often a love substitute. This was obviously demonstrated by two girls in different walks of life, whom I knew well' (97). She is less liberal though in her attitudes to some women subject to domestic violence:

[t]hey are neither mentally nor morally deficient within the meaning of the Act, yet they have no backbone nor sense of responsibility. They produce endless children in whom they take no interest, who are brought up at the ratepayers' expense. Their jolly, care-free ways and splendid physique attract them to men of much the same calibre, who keep them for a time while the fancy lasts [...] These are girls for cave-man methods; the hiding and the black-eye answer where reasoning would be futile (65).

Furthermore, she believes in hereditary, biological and environmental causes of crime. Therefore, 'gangsters are both born and made'; the growth in gangs is due to increasing unemployment; in large cities young offenders are drawn from 'boys and girls of more than average intelligence' and 'feeble excitable adolescents of low grade mentality' (78); and 'delinquency is often due to a deficiency of sugar in the diet' (99). She admits that her beliefs can be confounded sometimes; for example, the fact that parents of low intelligence can produce intelligent attractive children surprises her. While she argues for adequate training, at the same time she believes in the supernatural, recounting an instance of a colleague feeling intuitively that she was needed at a prison, turning up, and finding that the woman she asked for 'was longing to see her' (145).

Ellison conveys not only a combination of professional and lay perspectives but also a blend of sympathetic interest with gendered, class-laden antipathy. In her discussion of alcoholic women, she bows to the authority of Dr. Hall Morton, the Governor of Holloway prison who had stressed in an article in the *Howard Journal* that institutional treatment using probation and conditions of residence was essential for those in the advanced stages of the disease, and urges psychological help for such women. However, she has little regard for what she describes as 'border-line mental cases' who drink: '[t]hey are disagreeable, slovenly, immoral, unpleasant people and of such poor material that there is little to appeal in them' (179). In her view, prostitution is seldom the result of poverty but rather that of 'laziness, mental or moral defect, broken hearts', and the connection between 'laziness and mental or moral defect' is evident across class boundaries (200). In contrast, she exudes sympathy for the addicted daughters of respectively a veterinary surgeon and a doctor.

Helpfully, Ellison provides an insight into her approach through an example of her work with a girl of 'low mentality and poor spirit' (206). Following the court appearance (for an unspecified offence) she took her to a Lock hospital because she was in need of special treatment. Some time later the matron alerted her to the fact that the girl was intent on running away, and Ellison dismissing the idea of convincing her that she would be a public danger, instead showed the girl pictures of 'infected girls' (presumably with venereal disease) with the result that she did not run away (208). She then encouraged the girl to tell her life-story as a 'process of self-revelation' to 'shake off the past' (223); and gradually built up a friendship based on mutual understanding. Ellison describes the process:

Gradually, Sally began to feel more secure and settled. I, on my side, began to ask more of her than at first – that she should make an effort to stay where she was placed in work, that she should make allowances for the moods of

others, remember how difficult she was herself. I encouraged her to look to
the future rather than the past (223).

Finally, she made her a loan to start a boarding house. In some ways this
illustration reveals a planned strategy of the development of a trusting, influential
relationship interwoven with the use of a methodology embracing 'shock
probation', life history work of a confessional kind followed by future planning,
progressive challenging, encouraging empathy, and solid practical help. In essence
then, an apposite example of humanistic social work draped in a professional coat.

Harris (1937) recollections span a longer period. He was appointed to
Lowestoft as a police court missionary, and in 1907 became a probation officer so
his work reflects early as well as later practice. An anonymous review of his book
in *Probation*[16] is critical and asserts that Harris ignores the principles of modern
casework, and reveals a naiveté that 'makes him forgive very freely the devilry that
may be found [in every human heart]'. Certainly, the book is idealistic in its
portrayal of probation work but the criticism is not wholly justified as his account
of the methodology of the probation officer shows.

In his view, the probation officer is a sympathetic, understanding friend who in
his efforts to 'help the offender back on to the right track', listens to the
individual's side of the story, deals with each case according to individual need and
then decides on 'remedial measures' (22). Harris sketches his own approach: he
always interviews in his study and begins by saying, '[n]ow we are going to have
one good talk about the whole thing, and then we will put it behind us for ever and
start afresh' (23). He divides his work into three parts. The first interview, which is
a 'very solemn half-hour', contains part one – '[t]he surgical or heart-searching'
section when the individual tells the story of the offence – and part two, the
'advisory section' when he gives advice about rules and the way of life to follow.
The final interview involves a 'heart to heart' talk, and a ritual burning of the
recognizance paper to symbolise the expunging of the offence. This, he explains is
'the new method of curing the offender, or rather helping himself in his own
environment amongst his own people' (24-5): it is about '[g]etting close to the
offender's mind, and understanding his point of view', sympathizing and removing
obstacles 'across the path of his moral recovery' (32). It may not be classical
casework but it contains some of its elements, such as the notion of diagnosis and
treatment, empathy, listening to the probationer's viewpoint, and structuring the
work. Harris reflects also his contemporaries' affinity for psychology; he
anticipates positively the time when a psychologist is attached to every probation
area to help detect 'minds at mischief', and when 'kinks in character will be treated
as diseases rather than faults' (46).

This particular era of probation and its openness to theoretical representations
of causation and treatment of crime reached its symbolic apogee with the
publication of the Handbook of Probation (Le Mesurier 1935). Therein is
encapsulated the collective aspiration to professional status. The nearest the
Service had come to this was Leeson's book of 1914 but that work because it was
based so heavily on the American system had served merely to highlight the
incipient nature of practice and policy in the this country. The book (originally the

idea of Clarke Hall) constitutes the first attempt to draw together the diversity of practices and theories into a coherent set of guidelines for probation officers. In so doing, it attempts to create a professional identity for a vocation set within both an historical, legal and theoretical framework. Accordingly, it delineates the duties and functions of officers, models for investigation and report writing and advice down to the detail of, for instance, the frowned upon practice of 'almsgiving' (580). It highlights the importance of 'the humanitarian aspect of the relationship between probation officer and offender'; establishes the priority of responsibility to the public who '[pay] for, and [have] a right to expect protection'; endorses the 'religious spirit' as an essential component of successful work; emphasizes the need for training; and posits psychology at the heart of probation thought and practice. Emphasis is placed on the maxim that probation officers have to understand 'that there are unconscious motives as well as conscious ones, and that these affect their own conduct as well as that of those they are trying to help' (61-62).

However, Le Mesurier herself is realistic about the diverse quality of probation practice, and this problem was no doubt part of the rationale for the handbook. Four years earlier, she had said as much in her work on adolescent crime (Le Mesurier 1931):

> Now in practice there is every sort and kind, every degree and grade of probation work, from the positive and inspiring to the negative and colourless, from the most efficient to the least competent (185).

Moreover, McWilliams (1985) has exposed the dilemma of the authors of the handbook who in seeing the way forward 'was through the pursuit of the "psychological method" recognised that most officers lacked the skills to implement it' (269).

Any analysis of the nature of practice needs to take account of the glossing effect of the written representation of what people do in their work, and it should be cognisant of the practical realities of the ordinary working situation. Two final accounts from the 1930s illustrate the unsophisticated, theoretically vacuous and routine practice of some officers, and reinforce McWilliams' point. The first describes a series of home visits involving friendly, interested conversations and inquiries mixed with practical suggestions and private judgmental inferences; and then sums up the 'detailed work' being undertaken:

> the visits, the reprimands mingled with encouragement, the mental strain of trying to see things from other points of view, the sorting out of the genuine and the 'sponger', the hopes frustrated, to say nothing of the diplomacy and tact needed to harness one's devotion to Acts of Parliament (Tyrer 1936: 58).

The second by George Threlfall, a probation officer in Wigan in 1937, illustrates vividly the effects of caseloads above sixty coupled with matrimonial caseloads of near 200:

> The pressure of work was such that one could not talk to each of the men

separately, and what we did was to have three card tables in our small reporting room, which was outside the court, and on each was placed a little pile of forms. The probationer was expected to fill in the form giving his name and address, the name and address of his employer, and his earnings. He then gave the form to one of the POs who shook him warmly by the hand and said 'How are things going?' On being assured that all was well, he was then told 'Come and see me in a week (or fortnight's) time. We had a semi-official issue of cigarettes which we handed to the men – and that was the end of reporting (Rimmer 1995: 180-1).

There is scant evidence of casework or treatment here, nor psychologically informed interventions into people's lives. Nevertheless, they have as much claim on the accurate representation of practice as any other accounts, and they serve as a reminder that practice within professional human science organizations is likely to be as heterogeneous as the problems and lives of the subjects of that practice. Nevertheless, a model of sorts was emerging, and increasingly the professional discourse of probation was characterised by reference to rationales and methods that can be loosely gathered together under the broad heading of casework and its companion treatment. The entrenchment of that model as the professional motif of the Service was not too distant.

Notes

[1] I suggest that the failure of the Service during the 20th century to commit itself fully to evidenced-based practice puts it into the category of a semi-profession.

[2] It was not only probation officers. Of the police court missionary, Chesterton (1928) claims that 'the secrets of psychology are open to him, nothing surprises, nothing appalls. Like a surgeon on a battlefield he is ready to tackle every kind of hurt, minister to the most curious and most baffling spiritual disease' (241).

[3] In addition, this paper is distinguished by a list of references.

[4] Like McDougal (who was a member of the Eugenics Society and a member of its Consultative Council in 1937), Potts was a contributor to the journal *Eugenic*: for example, W. A. Potts 'Racial Dangers of Mental defect' Eugenics Association, 11 Lincoln's Inn Fields, London which is referred to in Trought's 'Probation in Europe' published in 1927.

[5] According to Macadam (in *The Social Servant in the* Making. London: George Allen & Unwin Ltd 1945) the Home Secretary approved a scheme of training and recruitment under the auspices of the Probation Training Board in 1937. For the outline included in Le Mesurier see Appendix 3. However, a report in *The Times* 8 August 1930 states that the Home Office training scheme was planned for the autumn of that year when seven candidates were to be selected as assistant probation officers on an annual salary of £150.

[6] These views of the essence of probation are given emphasis by Gertrude Tuckwell JP , chair of the National Association of Probation officers in a letter to *The Times* 15 September 1933 in which she writes: 'We must never lose sight of the fact that real probation is first of all a question of human contacts-of friendships, which generally begin long before the Court decrees, and continue, often enough, long after the period of probation officially finishes.'

[7] Burt, whom Rose (1985) describes as the 'architect of psycho-eugenics', was a member of the Eugenics Society and sat on its Consultative Council in 1937 and 1957, and was recognised as a figure of influence in the Handbook of Probation (Le Mesurier 1935). Information obtained from the list of members on AFRICA 2000 website.

[8] Although it is likely that it is the same person, initials are not provided in the first paper by Burns so the papers are presented in the list of references as if they are by different people.

[9] In that year, lectures at the Tavistock were advertized, and in 1931 a discussion group for probation officers held at the Tavistock was advertized as poorly attended. The impact of psychological inputs, therefore, was not always evident.

[10] I remember clearly, transference being discussed by colleagues in the 1970s.

[11] Source International Federation of Eugenic Organisations, A Survey of the Zurich Conference (Hodson as quoted in the Eugenic Watch internet site http://www.africa 2000.com).

[12] Interestingly, the Departmental Committee on Persistent offenders 1932 disavowed the theory that crime was a disease but accepted that some crime was due to 'abnormal mental factors' (Report of the Departmental Committee on Persistent Offenders 1932 p. 46).

[13] In an address to the 1932 July NAPO conference the Lord Bishop of Chichester warned of the dangers of the weakening influence of religion in relation to crime in the face of the growing impact of psychology (Source - *Probation*, 1, 12, 1932).

[14] Russell (1923) made an earlier attempt to do this when he traced the definition of psychology to classical mythology: ' Psyche is a beautiful maiden, emblematic of the soul. Then you have ology, knowledge: in other words knowledge of the soul' (p. 410). Russell, R. (1923) 'An Introduction to the Study of Psychology', *National Association of Probation Officers*, 19, 409-410.

[15] Beveridge, who was Director of the LSE from 1919 to 1937, was a member of the Eugenics Society, sat on its Council in 1928 and was a consultant to the Council in 1937 and 1957 (source AFRICA 2000), and Laski, according to Searle (1976) was 'a zealous eugenist in the years before 1914', and although it was a phase in his career it was not 'a transient adolescent hobby' (13-14).

[16] Review of book by Jo Harris 1937, *Probation*, 2, 11, p. 170.

Chapter 5

Folk Theories, Practice and the Heyday of Treatment

Although it has been argued that the foundations of modern casework can be discerned in the work of the Family Casework Agency set up by the Charity Organisation Society (Paskell 1952; Stedman Jones 1971), in retrospect, the 1930s can be seen as the decade in which those foundations were consolidated in the probation service.[1] This occurred mainly through the contributions of outside experts and the medical model, which as can be seen from the last chapter was a kaleidoscope of psychological colours. As McWilliams (1985,1986) suggests, the medical model and casework are different: the former is characterized by a definition of crime as a disease, where the latter is essentially the process through which practice is organized and given a rationale.) The medical model influenced heavily the particular form that probation casework would take but it was not until after the Second World War that it is discernible as a professional construct; this became apparent when more writers on casework came from within the Service itself.

The Growth of Professional Confidence

Probation, understandably, contains far fewer papers in the 1940s but the beginning of a growth in the confidence of the profession is evidenced by an increase in papers from within the Service. The war years inevitably slowed down professional progress but they stimulated some interesting concerns about causes of crime that included the dominance of the mother in the home (Kennedy 1941); the increased influence of female teachers (Gwym 1941); and free expression in education (Percival 1941). While she agrees with her colleagues' analyses, Ralli (1941) proffers solutions, some of which suggest a very different attitude to compulsion. These are, first, parents keeping in touch with their children who have been evacuated; second, special foster mothers for difficult children; third, more hostels; and finally, no enforced leisure but play centres and voluntary Youth Service squads for the 'no-collar boy' (230).

Although psychological theory unadorned by technical language rises to the surface of these explanations, the guerrilla campaign of the religiously minded continued into this decade. An address to the 1943 NAPO conference hones in on the anti-psychology theme (Alban Atkins 1943). The Right Reverend attacks 'weird philosophies' such as fatalism and determinism that explain away moral responsibility, and argues that these 'false' views mixed with 'pseudo-psychology' and peddled by 'muddle-headed theorists and sentimentalists and cranks', confuse the issues and the work. The ingredients for an explanation of crime are mixed together and seasoned (paradoxically) with a touch of determinism, the inheritance of predispositions and the doctrine of original sin; they include parents with lack of religion and the correct moral philosophy juxtaposed to hunger, evacuation, poor housing, each of which 'make for degeneracy of the mind and body' (66).

Reflection on these kinds of theories needs to take account of what was happening as far as crime is concerned during the war. Pearson (1983) provides insight into what might have been stimulating debates about causation and remedies. There was considerable racketeering as well as worries about violence from large numbers of deserters, hooliganism, looting and vandalism by children and youth (241). At least one contributor to *Probation* urges caution (Cottam 1943); he uses statistics to expose the exaggeration of the rise in juvenile delinquency and argue that probation officers should refuse to be panicked. At the same time he repeats the standard list of causes, and adds some of his own, namely too much emphasis on examinations and lack of sex education. The theory that delinquency is 'a symptom of an underlying disorder' informs his solution; so Play Centres are needed as an 'outlet for bottled up instincts, and relief for emotional tendencies in a legitimate way instead of in anti-social conduct' (73). Other analyses are less sophisticated. For example, Vigor (1945) uses his own idiosyncratic classification system of delinquents and the required response. Broadly, he argues, they fall into three groups: the purely mischievous, the untrained and the products of bad homes. For the first he proposes a 'good old fashioned smacking'; for the second, the training of parents or improved moral education in schools, and clubs; and for the third, boarding out to a fit person (113).

Such a conglomeration of pseudo-scientific, religious and common sense theorizing, highlights the need for a benchmark denoting the standard of practice required in an organization with professional aspirations. Expectation was high, and the demand was for skilled and trained professionals. In this respect, Rose (1947) provides an interesting wish list of skills and qualities. It includes, a professional outlook; high efficiency; the human motive of friendship; inner warmth and sincerity; sympathy; optimism about human nature; a capacity to see the probationer's point of view; a preparedness to establish the right to be critical; knowledge of poverty and deprivation; knowledge of the probationer's neighbourhood; the skills of guidance not compulsion; being moralistic; good physical and mental health; intelligence; a thought out philosophy; fluency in both verbal and written expression; streetwise attitudes; maturity; leadership qualities; flexibility and prescience; industriousness and decision-making skills; reliability; and a commitment to increasing self-confidence and self-reliance in the probationer. However, juxtaposed to a practical list are the less tangible ingredients of personality and spiritual resources. Accordingly, he asserts, '[e]ach officer should be free to translate his principles and aims through the medium of his own personality' (167). Thereby, in integrating autonomy into a professional taxonomy Rose renders explicit a tension within the professional aspirations of the Service that would flavour its discourses throughout the rest of the century.

Significantly, it was at this point that early attempts to develop groupwork as a probation method were made (Vanstone 2003). In 1947 probation officers attached to the East London Juvenile Court took advantage of Basil Henriques'[2] offer of the use of a camp site at Highdown, and after one unsuccessful attempt (which seemed merely to encourage delinquent behaviour) established a programme of activities. The combination of small groups with an experienced leader and activities such as sport, fishing, boating and daily prayers ensured a more constructive experience (Pearce 1950: 15). Two years later, Merfyn Turner[3] established the Barge Boys' Club using a sailing barge called the Normanhurst berthed at Wapping (Page 1992). As Page indicates, groupwork was beginning to gain acceptance as a new technique worth supporting. Certainly, experimentation was taking place but support from managers was not universal (Vanstone 2003). One of the respondents to a survey by Rimmer (1995) described experimentation with groups of young girls similar to that of Cary and Croker-King but added that her Principal Probation Officer and a Home Office inspector had reprimanded her for deviating from her normal duties.

By 1948, trainee probation officers were being taught social psychology, and a component of the course at the University of London's Diploma course was 'Recent Advances in the Study of Groups'. This involved life in groups; the influence of groups on individuals; group therapy and training; leadership dominance; and the leaderless group (Vanstone 2003) Furthermore, in 1953 and 1954 they were involved in the Arethusa Camp set up on the sports ground of the training ship Arethusa at Upton, Rochester, Kent (Pratt and Ratcliffe 1954). In addition to these experiences, placements in the Tavistock Clinic, the Henderson Hospital, Borstals and prisons, meant that some officers were beginning to be influenced by the group psychotherapy developed by psychiatrists during the Second World War (Barr 1966; Landers 1957).[4] According to Landers, Wormwood Scrubs,[5] seems to have been at the forefront of experimentation in group therapy, and the principal influence in this respect was the work of Doctor Moreno in New York.[6] Landers describes the use of methods based on Jungian therapy deemed appropriate because they resonated with social attitudes and religious experiences of a significant number of prisoners who attended the groups.

Following the pioneering work of Dr. J. C. Mackwood in British prisons Maxwell Jones[7] adopted Moreno's therapeutic community ideas in Belmont,[8] and it was here that probation officers had direct experience of group therapy, the growth of which is evidenced by one of the first attempts to deal with the ideological and practical problems of, and reservations about, officers' involvement in this new method (Hawkins 1952). In her view, groups provide a more natural situation in which reaction and behaviour can be observed, confidence built up, and bad influence countered provided the individual remains in focus. Interestingly, she proposes that officers should allow the group to develop its own code of ethics in order to be able to identify what attitudes and behaviour need to be challenged.

Enhanced Training

Many of the skills and qualities described above by Rose (1947) were required in work with groups as well as with individuals; so, how then were officers being prepared to attempt to aspire to the ideal set by Rose? Macrae (1958) provides an account of the official history in which two developments have considerable significance. First, the Probation Training Board was set up on the recommendation of the 1936 Departmental Committee on the Social Services in Courts of Summary Jurisdiction; and second, in 1946 the Home Office invited the National Institute of Industrial Psychology to construct an analysis of the probation task and to devise an improved selection process. The selection procedure, which was still in operation at the end of the 1950s, involved the use of rating sheets by inspectors to assess applications; enquiries to referees; an intelligence test; interview by selection committee; an observed group discussion; an individual interview; and for those recommended for training, a medical examination (in some cases where there were concerns about temperament, by a psychiatrist).

A former officer [9] describes the experience of going through this process in 1951, having previously been turned down, he suspects, because he had been a conscientious objector during the war:

> I was accepted by a board sitting in the four corners of an interviewing room, with about a dozen applicants, asked to discuss some subject like 'capital punishment'. There was also a written – I think an intelligence test!

Training varied depending on age and experience. Those under 30 were expected to have a Social Science diploma (or undertake one) before a period of specialized training; and those over 30 undertook the specialized training only. The training at Rainer House lasted for nine to twelve months, and it involved a residential component in which lectures were given on casework, law, social administration, criminology and specialist areas of probation work. The same officer explains that he spent three months at Rainer House 'receiving talks about various people in law, psychology etc'. Macrae also specifies lectures on human growth and development by psychiatrists, seminars relating theory to practice and tutorials by the probation inspectors on the application of casework principles (211). The practical component varied depending on experience but all students underwent a six-month placement with an experienced officer. This new training formula had come about, according to Macrae, first because of 'a much closer integration of theory with practice, due to a growing confidence that theoretical principles are demonstrable in practice', and second, because the tutor 'knows that he is rather a teacher of the specific skills common to sound social casework practice' (212). This represents a view of the Service as a coherent and integrated professional organization, which as will be seen later, not all interested commentators shared.

Macrae's account reveals that there were also in-service courses including group meetings run by psychiatrists; ten-day courses on casework supervision (of officers); advanced matrimonial casework training; and training for the trainers. What is more, the Service was involved in an experimental use of four-year courses in applied social studies at the LSE, Birmingham and Southampton universities. Overall, Macrae believed, 'it [was] now a reasonable assumption that a probation officer on first appointment has some knowledge of the principles underlying human behaviour and has tested them out in practice' (213).

Some acquired knowledge through a process bordering on psychoanalysis. An officer signing herself or himself as Oedipus describes the experience of being in a 'study group' run by 'the Doctor' and a psychiatric social worker! The nine officers met once a week for a period of eighteen months in a group, which they were told, had no leader. It became clear to the officers that the object of the Doctor's and the PSW's interpretations was the 'unconscious' motivation behind their behaviour; and the writer gives a clue to their approach by describing the two leaders as parents. For instance, the Doctor and the PSW always arrived together, sat next to each other and left together, never taking part in post group discussions. Furthermore, they were the object of considerable anger and suspicion. Despite this, the writer reports that they learned about the 'dynamic relationship between probation officer and probationer'; how to interpret the 'client's psychological defences'; how 'the client's initial attitude to the probation officer was often largely conditioned' by early experiences; the true meaning of hostility; the 'element of sadism' in plans for rehabilitation because of the unrealistic demands made of the probationer; and how the officer sometimes internalized the ideas of the Doctor. In addition, their religious beliefs in free will were challenged. There was also much practical discussion and the writer points out that the Doctor never used psychoanalytical jargon (even transference) or mentioned Freud; and overall, the group are said to have learned considerably from the group (OEDIPUS 1956: 10-12). Not all officers, however, valued such an approach. In a letter in the following issue of the journal, an officer describes this 'toying with self-analysis' as superficial and a 'retreat from the reality of dealing with people'.[10]

That view is itself seen as a misinterpretation of the meaning of casework by an anonymous student reporting on the experience of undertaking the Carnegie generic applied social studies course (Anonymous 1956). The student confirms the broad content outlined by others below but provides a valuable insight into the training through some detailed comment about learning outcomes. Students learned to understand 'the underlying disturbances which compelled their clients to behave as they did' (50); how to promote 'normal development' of the moral conscience; an increased knowledge of psychodynamic principles in understanding human behaviour; and the full implications of client self-determination. This extension of their knowledge of people itself led to greater self-awareness. However, the course was not just theoretical, and the writer elaborates on the skills of interviewing. They learned 'to become more observant, more sensitive in interviewing, to record selectively and to adapt [themselves] to different types of administrative procedure' (51). The range of forms of treatment to which they were introduced covered practical help and the 'giving of insight', while they were also introduced to the theory of groupwork, their function in relation to the community and other agencies, and their responsibility for social policy. This account, as will be seen, confirms the recollections of former officers who provided their recollections for the study on which this book is based.

The Experience of Training

One former officer who undertook the Home Office Training course in 1946 provides an interesting account. [11] His first placement was in the Cotswold Approved School, Ashton Keynes in Wiltshire run by the London Police Court Mission (later renamed The Rainer Foundation). Having completed what seems largely to have been an observation placement, he moved to a placement in Liverpool:

> I spent two months with the Liverpool Personnel Services Society, a voluntary organisation, whose activities embraced the provision of help to all sorts and conditions of people in need. Homelessness, paternity claims, neighbours' quarrels, matrimonial difficulties, hire purchase arrears and other debts, tenancy questions – indeed, the wide range of problems that confront a probation officer in his task of dealing with offenders in the milieu of their families.

The placement included basic training in casework principles, prioritizing and recording, and was followed by a move to a naval base on the Isle of Sheppey where he shadowed the local probation officer.

> I was advised that I should be his shadow and watch his every move except where circumstances were such that the presence of another person – even though in training – would be likely to preclude a relationship between officer and client. I learned a tremendous amount from this doggedly persistent, infinitely patient officer.

He continued with the theoretical part of the course at the Home Office Training Centre in Cromwell Road, Kensington with some lectures given at the Institute for the Study and Treatment of Delinquency:

> The lecture subjects were headed 'Criminal Law', 'The Causation of Crime and Juvenile Delinquency', 'Medical Aspects', 'Recording', 'Remand Enquiries', 'the Nature of Personal Influence', 'Approved Probation Hostels', 'Homes and Lodgings' and 'Matrimonial and Family Case Work'.

The lecturers included probation staff, Dr. Denis Carrol (a prominent psychiatrist) [12] and Dr. Kenneth Soddy, Director of the Osnaburgh Street Psychiatric Clinic in London. He stresses that realism, objectivity and humility were urged upon them and that 'the syllabus represented an endeavour to give the students the basic tools to cope with the human behaviour problems in corrective work.'

> Perhaps the only time difficulties were experienced was in relation to a 'practical visit of observation' recommended – to attend the all-night opening of one of the Lyons Corner House restaurants at Charing Cross, Leicester Square, etc., to watch the prostitutes who came in with clients throughout the night and went out with further clients when they met there.

However, too many of us could not go at the same time for obvious reasons, and it became quite difficult to endure such a long night without sleep and remain fresh enough to benefit from the lectures the following day.

Thereafter he completed the course through a placement with another experienced officer, which provided opportunities to apply theory to practice. After he qualified he took an external Diploma in Social Science at London University comprising four years of weekly lectures that included Social Structure, Social Psychology and Social Philosophy and Criminology taught by Dr. Herman Mannheim.[13] Cyril Burt examined Social Psychology, and Eysenk taught part of it and the officer concerned recalls the idea of hereditary factors being prominent alongside Freudian theory. However, as can be seen from appendix four the content of the course was broad, and provided comprehensive cover of the prominent theories of the day. In his view, the Service placed a heavy emphasis on post-qualifying training because 'the Home Office required their personnel to keep abreast of current thinking and development in order to try and ensure any tendency towards complacency and mediocrity was minimised and that they were equipped to give efficient service to which the public is entitled.'

Another former officer who undertook the London School of Economics Social Science Certificate from October 1946 to June 1948 and the Home Office course at Rainer House provides the following insight into both the selection procedure and the content of the course: [14]

> [The] process of entry followed application to the Home Office. Subsequently I was called for interview. This was by the Home Office Inspector. Another interview followed. I have no idea who those people were except that I knew one. He was Mr. Morely Jools, Secretary of the London Police Court Mission.
>
> A letter followed, telling me that I had been accepted for training at L.S.E. again, subject to interview. The interview at L.S.E. followed shortly and I was accepted.

The Certificate Course in Social Science included the study of Social Philosophy and Psychology, Social and Industrial History, Social Economics (including Economic Theory), and Social Administration. He undertook placements at the Dr. Fitch. School for Maladjusted Children, Newton in Bowland for four weeks; the Family Welfare Association in Brighton for eight weeks; and the Probation Service in South Shields for six weeks. Visits during the course included the East London Settlement, Courts, Workhouses, a Personnel Department (factory), and Anna Freud's Child Clinic in Hampstead. Following training, he took up his first post in Birmingham and began with a caseload of ninety.

An officer who undertook the Rainer House course in 1951 recalled that all the teachers were practitioners. A R. L. Morrison, Clerk to the Justices of one of the London courts introduced students to the court procedures for probation officers and the law pertaining to probation work. The Tavistock still had a prominent part in training through Dr. Henry Dicks who lectured on marital work and marital interaction. This officer recollected that it was strongly psychoanalytical, and shocked some trainees. A psychologist taught casework, and Dr. Pamela Mason, who worked in a Borstal, lectured on women and gender issues. Home Office inspectors were involved teaching the practical aspects of probation work in courts. Trainees, according to this informant, went out to lectures at the ISTD (Institute for the Study and Treatment of Delinquency). In addition, they were taught a very basic form of criminology but nothing about what was effective in reducing offending; rather, they were 'taught to become good quality professionals using intelligence and discretion'. As far as theories about causation are concerned, students were encouraged in the view that there were no simple causes, and that it was the function of the probation officer to examine histories because the causes of delinquent behaviour were rooted in school and family problems and developed over a lifetime.

With minor modifications, the core element of training appears to have remained constant through the 1950s and 1960s. Another former officer who trained in the mid 1950s described the kind of Service he entered, and the nature of the training. He recalled that members of the Service were:

> still very much in a traditional set with various ingredients, while some were quite clearly representative of a working class trade union orientation. They were at the same time Methodist – Salvation Army backgroundish, so the whole set up was quite congenial to them. On the other side it was very much master, servant, Church of England, Cathedral based kind of orientation. I remember one saying to me – a highly placed person in committee and all the rest of it – 'The only thing that interests me in selecting officers is, are they or are they not a communicant member of the Church of England'. I always remember those were the very words.

Religion, therefore, remained prominent but a new religion influenced training, and by implication, practice. At Rainer House, the 'tutors so on were psychiatrists [...] it was perfectly the normal thing to hear people talking about transference, working through transference and that kind of stuff'.

But for this officer, the nature of the raw material entering the training process was vital. Entry was confined to people to people who were at least 28 and had 'quite a bit of experience of life'. His personal history and experience provides an interesting example:

> Well like most people my age, I have had 5 years in the services in the War. I have worked in South Africa, Rhodesia, Portuguese East Africa in business [....] My interests were philosophy [....] and I was interested in psychotherapy and that sort of thing [...] what makes people tick. I wasn't necessarily wanting to be in a particular direction. I simply had a very powerful curiosity. I wouldn't say necessarily I was all frightfully touchy feeling and wanting to help everybody and love everybody necessarily.

It emphasizes the importance of learning through reading, and gives a flavour of the content and expectations of training, and an interesting insight into the continuing influence of the Police Court Mission:

I think Father Biestek was appearing on the scene. I think one of the things that always disappointed me slightly about probation service was how rarely people went to prime sources. The latest penguin devoid of a footnote was the thing and although it's fair to say in London if you were interested they would finance you to the membership of things like Lewis' Medical Library [...] Rainer House itself was administered by the London Police Commission that presented, as far as the probation service went, a sort of residual remaining influence and power [...] they still retained the actual ownership operation of Rainer House and they always played a small part in the actual training programme in the shape of, I think his name was Lawrence, the Reverend Lawrence who appeared I think [...] I had him for a couple of sessions or something like that when they were talking about the moral aspects of their work [...] also there was a powerful input of relevant law. When I say a powerful input anything you needed to know about the law and this was based on the 1933 Children Young Person Act (subsequently amended over the years) and the 1948 Criminal Justice Act and you were expected to really know anything in the Acts that were relevant to our job, breaches and all the rest of it [...] and that would make up something in the order of a quarter of the total input I would have thought. There was another slot and almost similar size called Criminology and part of that was, well, criminology problems, but flavoured with a bit of sociology that wasn't specified as such but was clearly recognisable as predominantly from Mannheim [...] So there was that part of it. The practical machinery part of it [...] As far as the guts of the thing went, case work it was undoubtedly primarily concerned with people really as individuals although they are OK embedded in a family, there weren't very much thought of as embedded in a society of particular characteristics or particular consequences.

The account then expands on this particular point and provides a rationalization for the dominance of individualization:

Having said that people weren't so daft as to imagine (of course) that the environmental factors weren't powerful. It was recognised, however, I think that [...] if you are seeing somebody for 20 minutes once a week, you are not going to restructure society very much in their favour in the course of 2 years and that's still true perhaps [...] It was very much a question of the probation officer being quite clearly as it were an agent of society for court and whatever he did in the way of being social worker as it were was performed within that framework of expectation on him by society and through society.

According to his account, the main theoretical tenets of the course were Freudian 'possibly sprinkled with a bit of the other psychologists you had for Morals [and] Offending', and this fits with the theoretical drift of much of the writing referred to in this chapter. However, he suggested that the notion of individual responsibility was not lost altogether because '[m]ixed with that still was the assumption that somebody was responsible for their own actions anyway'. Moreover, the concept of family seemed pre-eminent, and the influence of Bowlby and Attachment Theory seems to underlie what he recalled:

> There was a recognition about the importance of the family although I think it's true to say this meant the mother; fathers were rarely referred to very much or seen as much of a formative agency in the family except in the negative sense. Fathers were private, fathers were drunkard, fathers were sectioned and you didn't get a terribly good reception if you raised the issue of the father in casework discussions or on training courses.

Dennis Carrol and Dr. Tourquet of Harley Street, he recalled, taught casework at an intensively theoretical level. Officers were it seems themselves the subjects of casework:

> So these were the people [the trainers] that handled that and you had to be very careful about by disagreeing with them or betraying any feelings for whatever reason they chose to cast as evidence of your own formative shortcomings in infancy and so on.

Writing some fifteen years later Hunt (1964) confirmed the resilience of the broad ideological position evident in this account when he classified an offence as a symptom of 'illness [...] consciously designed to bring authority into the picture' and identified its cause as 'a failure of the socialisation process'; casual delinquency, therefore, was 'poorly sublimated aggression' (239-241).

According to another former officer, Dr Dicks was still teaching matrimonial work in the second half of the 1950s, and he 'was willing to go deeper into the psycho-analytic stuff with those of the students who wished for this'. This officer undertook his training in two parts: the first, a two year Social Science Certificate at University; and the second at Rainer House with placements on the Wirral. This written account is interesting because it reminds us that trainees were not mere malleable, compliant learners. Previous life experience provided a filter system as he explained:

> Causation of crime [...] teaching about? Well, from my Air Force and industry/commerce (i.e. upper middle class) personal experiences, I took what we were told with a pinch of salt. All of it *was* valid: but in relation to a narrower spectrum of the clients than I felt was being assumed. *Criminal* clients I mean: as distinct from the *wider* variety of clients who actually came voluntarily to US social work agencies of the kind familiar to the US authors of the textbooks on which we were being trained. Having said which, I was probably more conscious of this than some of the other students being half-American myself as well as having more awareness of British upper middle class offences [....] Lots of people with every social-maladjustment did not commit it: and lots with little reason did.

This analysis resonates with Hardiker's (1977) argument that probation officers used 'a relatively commonsense rather than positivist model in their daily work' (149) and 'held a treatment orientation towards some of [their] cases and not to others' (152). She carried out her research nearly twenty years after this officer undertook training, and it demonstrates that older, Home Office trained officers tended, in a general sense, to be more treatment-orientated than younger graduates. However, it is of relevance here because it touches on the residual effect of an approach to training in the Home Office that remained relatively constant over at least a twenty-year period.

Some officers were direct entrants who had not undergone qualifying training. However, even those officers underwent university-based in-service training like the following ex-officer. She depicts a vivid illustration of the impact of such training on a personal ideology honed in a working-class upbringing:

> I had a diploma in sociology but at that time they were taking direct entrance so I became a direct entrant [...] I suppose having been brought up in the [a working-class area] I had all sorts of notions about people getting into trouble because of the pressures from their background. I don't actually believe that now as a cause but I think that's what I brought in with me. Really, the sort of nature of the pressures within families and things to do with poverty and poor housing. Really I suppose the sort of sociological perspective and that was enhanced by the diploma in sociology but I very quickly changed to what's now called the psychodynamic approach because that's one that the Home Office within training; and that sort of stuck with one and obviously I still hang on to sociological approaches but I think pressures are predominantly internal ... there are some external.
>
> I think I came in with the notion that things came from outside into people and the [...] course I think sort of made me think about what came from the outside into people but what people made of [problems] inside themselves and how they then reacted to the outside world because you know what always puzzled me and always still puzzles me really is how come some people survive without becoming delinquent or going mad and other people don't. [...] there must be something going on inside them that makes the difference. So I think the [...] course gave me a sort of way of thinking about things and about the internal world and external world. I think I had been more sort of routed in the external world prior to that [...] I can't remember a lot of the other people and we had a very nice Home Office inspector who subsequently went to Bradford University and I think I can't remember his name now but the Home Office had some sort of input into it.[15]

Her account confirms the Freudian basis of the training informed as it was by the 'input from analytically oriented people'. Psychoanalytical casework and the psychotherapeutic model within which it was contained, survived in training certainly up to the end of the 1960s. For instance, I analysed every client contact during my final placement using the device of process recording and supervision that bordered on analysis, and two other retired officers who attended the Rainer House course in the mid 1960s recalled psychoanalytical casework as the prime method. One remembered particularly being taught law by a Clerk to the Justices, criminology by Alan Little and marital work by Dr. Dicks. Whilst providing confirmation of the general approach, the other recalls the pragmatic dimension to the training:

> Only a few were graduates and I suppose the level of teaching had to be scaled to accommodate those who had been out of school a little longer. But again I think it served to reinforce the message that effectiveness was not just about head knowledge and smart techniques [...] So the course gave people sufficient information about the system in which they were going to operate but was not long enough or challenging enough to develop professional skills or explore the role we were to play [...] I guess we were a pretty conventional and conforming group and with Home Office Inspectors close at hand were disinclined to express views or behave in a way which might lead our card to be marked [...]Seminars on social casework with experienced practitioners – something I found myself involved in a few years later – were valued because they were seen as equipping us for the task in hand but I think it was all fairly basic stuff and did not really reflect the kind of therapy which the more recent manuals described. Biestek 'The Casework Relationship' I recall as being an exciting book which opened up a new world but I reckon that the kind of approach it presented had not really penetrated the probation culture. The future seemed to lie in a more refined and psychoanalytical application of casework method on a one to one basis with psychiatry as the professional discipline of greatest influence. Friedlander's Psycho-Analytic approach to Juvenile Delinquency was a book we rushed to buy [...] The Tavistock Clinic was something of a Temple. I reckon that we were conditioned to think more in terms of curing rather than managing offending behaviour and there was little emphasis on collaboration with other agencies.

Misplaced Confidence?

It *was* an era of confidence. The papers presented to a European Seminar on probation in 1952 represent a confidence best seen as part of the period of renewal after the Second World War. Despite the fact that there was no research evidence that probation or the psychodynamic model on which probation practice was purportedly based reduced offending, these commentaries ooze a sense of certainty. For example, Younghusband (1952) uses the USA National Commission on Law Observance and Enforcement Report No. 9, to confirm her assessment of probation practice as scientific. Fry (1952) promotes the art and science of probation, blending as it does diagnosis and treatment with the personality of the officer, and then proclaims '[i]ts rapid spread is itself evidence that its basic philosophy is in harmony with the trend of thought in the last fifty years' (66). Finally, Paskell (1952) trumpets probation as the civilizing element of criminal justice.

One of the key contributors to Home Office training is less sanguine, believing that there was 'a real difficulty in training officers in the scientific and critical habit of mind necessary for such a thorough diagnosis of causes and systematic planning of treatment' (Carroll 1952: 108).[16] Nevertheless, he gives a clear insight into the nature of his contribution to the effort to do so. He lays out an account of what he calls 'the nature and use of the personal relationship involved in the diagnostic and therapeutic work of the probation officer' (107), dividing the process of probation into the five stages of examination, the establishment of the treatment situation, treatment, closure of treatment, and the period after probation. The therapeutic approach is not confined to the officer whose use of techniques is deemed likely to stimulate either a 'therapeutic attitude' or 'an anti-therapeutic attitude' in the probationer. The language of psychotherapy permeates his account but it is the psychoanalytical concepts of both positive and negative transference that lie at the heart of the probation officer's use of the relationship with the client. So '[s]uccessful personal treatment of the offender is only possible if he develops a friendly feeling towards the therapist [and on] the emotional side the officer begins by deliberately exploiting the capacity of the offender to form a positive transference – a wholly subjective factor in the rapport' (112-13). Finally, as if to acknowledge the tensions that the Service is experiencing in the shift from science to religion, Carroll highlights some of the problems with a religious approach but admits that in some circumstances religion can be 'a most potent agent of reform' (114).

William Minn (1950) who had led probation training in the Home Office during its formative years (1931 to 1941), while promoting casework, provides a less scientific view of the probation officer's approach, and stresses that the first duty of the officer is to ensure that the probationer does not commit further offences. For him casework is more about helping probationers to help themselves and overcome their 'inadequate sense of reality' (134). In similar vein, Newton, an Assistant Chief Probation Officer and contributor to the LSE course, in his description of training in the mid 1950s introduces a note of realism, and thereby shows that some probation officers received an insider perspective on the work in their training. In somewhat ironic tone, he announces that after the diminution of the influence of religion '[t]he age of scientific interest dawned and the magic of the I.Q. shone all around' (Newton 1956: 123). He maintains that up until 1954, when the Applied Social Studies course at the LSE was inaugurated, little attempt had been made to link theory and practice with the result that students emerged from training imbued with knowledge of psychoanalytical psychology but with 'little idea of how to help their first probationer respond to themselves' (124). He describes a situation in which some students attempted to help through personal insight and interpretations but lacking the necessary skills soon gave up; some fell back on their own life experiences in relationships in order to develop their own techniques; whereas others saw probation being more than practical help and helping people adjust their behaviour as being very important. He presents what is probably a realistic assessment of the state of practice based largely on trial and error. Moreover, he places it on a continuum from 'highly skilled therapy with a strong psychiatric flavour and focused on the probationer's unconscious, to 'rescue' work with a strong emphasis on manipulation of circumstances and environment, without much consideration of either the probationer's conscious or unconscious wishes' (125). The majority of officers, he insists, were providing practical help and at the same time using 'persuasive argument, encouragement, straight talking, exhortation and suggestion, attempts to change the direction of the probationer's behaviour towards an honest and industrious life, and finally, to enforce a measure of control and a checking-up authority in order to prevent unlawful behaviour' (126). Casework was, to be sure, the province of the gifted few.

In truth, NAPO recognised the need for mechanisms to ensure the effective application of casework techniques as early as 1956. In a statement accepted at the annual conference of that year and reproduced in *Probation* (NAPO 1956), the Association accepts that supervision and casework are 'deeply interwoven' (97), and that there is a need for special training in the techniques of supervision. The statement sets out the basic principle of supervision that the supervisor is often better placed to clarify the 'meaning of what is taking place as treatment proceeds', and that as a result the officer can be helped to use the relationship with the client (note, not probationer) 'therapeutically rather than react blindly to the case or situation' (99). Correspondence in the following issues of the journal shows that this view was not universally accepted, and suggests that a debate was taking place in the Service.

Newton's is, of course, a personal view from a management perspective but it is likely that he was far closer to practice than the *managerialist* of the 1990s. In any event, it is difficult to judge practice devoid of an empirically formulated knowledge base. For a major part of the modern history of probation the assumption of a knowledge base has been enough; whether interventions actually helped people to choose a non-offending way of life seems to have been another matter. Newton's analysis stands out in its self-critical style but he too is of his time and seems to have assumed that the linking of theory to practice is enough without evidence of its effectiveness. He declares that 'new probation' is about responding to emotional needs at the right stage to assist maturation, and that this recognition that unmet emotional as well as economic needs are a cause of crime has added a further dimension to probation officer skills. This new methodology teaches the probationer 'the subjective meaning of his day to day life experiences', and in using it the officer aims 'to enlarge the probationer's area of positive action' and 'to diminish the force of his negative feelings by helping him to discharge them with' and to reach 'healthy maturity'. Moreover, it adds a new-found sensitivity to 'the meaning of the probationer's own story', and Newton illustrates his point with an actual recording from a case in which a father had requested help in controlling his adolescent daughter. The extract describes work following a breakdown in the relationship between the father and the first officer:

> [...]Father switched on the light took a long look at me. He seemed alert and very tense, ready for battle, so opened the interview by saying I supposed he was wondering who I was and why I had come; he nodded, and I told him that I was a Probation Officer, that had heard about his recent troubles and I was sure he must be very worried and unhappy. Perhaps also he was a bit confused by all that had happened, and I was wondering if I could be of any help to him. He flushed and began an angry tirade against the dishonesty of Probation Officers. Telling me he was considering proceedings for slander, he pointed to a pad of note-paper and a pencil and warned me he would make notes of our conversation for his legal advisers.

I accepted this as natural in the circumstances, also telling him I had not come to criticize or to order him about, as perhaps he suspected, but only to see if there was anything we could do to make things, easier and happier for him and his family, as I suspected they were all unhappy about recent events. In a quieter voice he told me about his feelings at the way things had been taken out of his hands he had felt 'cut off.' He said that not only had his opinions not been asked, but he had been criticized and 'put in the wrong' from the start. He showed fear at what else might be done to break up his family and protested that such action was contrary to what the public expected of court officials.

I recognized his feelings of fear and anger, saying also that he must have been hurt by all that had happened and that I thought anyone would feel like this, if they saw things the way he did. I could see he must have felt confused and perhaps cut off, when no one seemed interested in him, or his point of view-that was why I had come, and I was hoping I might be allowed to help him find his way through all these difficulties. He flushed and looked very near to tears. When he spoke again, he told me in great detail how the opinions the magistrate had expressed about him were wrong –but that he could understand how people could be mistaken due to his nervous manner [...] With tears now swimming in his eyes he told me he was a reasonable man and could talk sensibly if given the right opportunity but he got angry when people accused him and did not give him a chance [...] I thought this a natural reaction but said it was a pity he had felt like that about the court, as it was only trying to discover what was best to do and this was not easy if it was denied his help [...] He gave a history of his family and described the kind of relationships he had with each of his children and then showed more fear for the future of his family [...] I said we were as interested as he was to see that she got the best help so that what he feared did not happen. I knew he was angry now and that he might have good reason to be, but beneath his anger I thought he was worried for his daughter and wanted to help if he could. Weeping openly he said deep in his heart, beneath his hurt and anger at what she had done, he still loved the child (128-30).

After two interviews in which the importance of active listening is evident, the father was co-operating actively and his final comment to the officer at the end of the second interview showed his gratitude for the help – ' You have given me back my self respect.'

While illustrating what is possible, by and large Newton challenges the lack of application of theory to practice. However, then he contributes his own version of the pseudo-scientific approach by accepting that maturation theory is relevant to offending. Although his analysis provides a salutary note of caution, it still stands alongside other expressions of confidence in probation as a technique that survives the decade. Raeburn (1958) extols the virtues of probation as the 'second chance', and in what appears a kind of universal assumption Dawtry (1958) attests that '[p]robation, once used for the simple or youthful offence, is now regarded as a form of treatment for serious social problems where the work of well trained caseworkers is required' (183). Still, Dawtry does acknowledge doubts about the efficacy and direction of training, and while claiming that supervised casework has been welcomed warns of the re-adjustments required of older officers.

Here the concerns are merely about refinement of technique and application of theory to practice, and yet at the same time Wilkins (1958) published his findings about the effect of probation in one of the earliest 'nothing works' message. In an analysis of 97 male offenders and a matched sample he found 'no significant differences in the outcome of treatments in terms of further convictions': in short, probation was doing no better (nor worse) than custodial sentences (207). Even though Wilkins used the results to argue that more people could be placed on probation instead of Borstal or prison, and the results were based on a small sample, it remained true that efficacy of 'casework' was decidedly limited. Perhaps unsurprisingly, this did not deter officers from pursuing the professionalism that the expertise of casework endowed, and as Bochel (1976) argues, general confidence in professional aspirations was linked to casework (183). It was to experience further blows but for the moment the written rhetoric of probation remained impervious to doubt and instead was dominated by the debate about the definition of casework.

The Resilience of Casework

In truth the centrality of casework to at least the rhetoric of probation practice is evidenced by the fact that there was no reference to casework in the 1935 Handbook, whereas King's 1958[17] equivalent apportions a quarter of its content to social casework (Bochel 1976). Casework, King (1969) announces, is a response to the needs of those people unable to resolve their problems on their own. To her, the caseworker is distinguished from the generality of workers in the social services by the fact that 'the help he gives is specially adapted to the needs of each individual and is given through the medium of a personal relationship developed for that purpose' (52). She follows this broad definition of casework with a set of basic principles and methods as applied in a probation setting, and in so doing gives explicit recognition to the influence of the Freudian school of psychology. In particular, she emphasises the importance of the influence of early parental relationships (initially with the mother) on later maturity and its impact on socialization and future behaviour. She continues by arguing that poor parenting and the imparting of inappropriate moral standards by the parents are likely to lead to an inability to lead 'a socially acceptable life' whilst on the other hand, if the standards of the parents are rejected, 'an underlying sense of guilt and a conscience so strict that he [the offender] either seeks punishment to assuage his guilt or is too inhibited to face responsibility at all'. Moreover, in her view these feelings are 'largely beyond conscious control' (54-5). King maintains that these insights have become available at an opportune time when, because increased material prosperity and the Welfare state have diminished external pressures on people, there is a need to concentrate 'on internal conflicts and problems' (56). However, she does draw a distinction between psychotherapy and casework by suggesting that casework is concerned also with the individual's social environment and 'the individual's difficulties with social relationships'; and that it is not about delving into the unconscious but rather providing 'the client strength to meet his difficulties' (57).

In the definitive guidelines on probation casework that follow, King includes the classic ingredients of the social casework approach. These are the worker's use of her or his feelings and personality in the process of helping; the response to transference; creative listening; starting where the client is and dealing with their feelings; going beyond the presenting problem; giving insight; and (although the need is less) 'manipulation of the environment' (64). These ingredients are then framed within a menu of social diagnosis, treatment plan, interviews conducted at home or in the office, and case-recording and assessment. She pays attention to some of the special problems of probation casework, such as having to accept the offender but not their offence or confidentiality in a criminal justice setting. Offending is presented very much as a 'social breakdown' much like ill-health, and the approach is deemed not normally suitable for those who for a variety of reasons 'have no desire for change and feel that society is entirely to blame for the predicament in which they find themselves' (84). Casework is, therefore, entwined with the processes of selection and exclusion characteristic of probation history.

That blueprint was re-enforced in 1961 by the publication of Biestek's *The Casework Relationship*[18] (1961) which described casework as 'a way of helping people who have psycho-social problems' (134) gives one of the most vivid descriptions of the essence of the approach, and in so doing combines the rhetoric of religion and science:

> The relationship is the soul of casework. It is a spirit which vivifies the interviews and the processes of study, diagnosis, and treatment, making them a constructive, warmly human experience (134-5).

In an attempt to confound the impression that casework is a 'pseudomystical experience', he breaks down its elements into a matrix of three directions and seven principles. The directions are the needs of the client, the response of the caseworker and the awareness of the client; the principles, individualization, purposeful expression of feelings, controlled emotional involvement, acceptance, nonjudgmental attitude, client self-determination and confidentiality (17).

The influence of theories promoted by the likes of King and Biestek is confirmed by contributions to *Probation* during this period. Golding (1959) not only provides a clear account of a caseworker's thinking and practice but also stimulates a written debate. His paper is motivated by his concern about the ineffectiveness of probation work, and his attempt to deal with this problem is to unravel the components of effective psychotherapy. The psychotherapist's task is to give the client insight in the hope that the client will take on board the insight and adjust accordingly at both conscious and 'pre-conscious' levels. The influence of psychoanalytical theory is clear in his admission that he has to remind himself frequently that in many cases 'the consciously expressed difficulties are projections of difficulties which the probationer cannot or will not admit, or of whose existence he is unaware' (47). He describes his methodology with particular clarity: at the pre-sentence stage, this involves the formulation of a 'full social history' based on information from other people in the probationer's life and only a brief interview with the probationer (who presumably is unaware of his problems). Subsequently psychotherapy in depth is undertaken but only with 12 to 15 people in a caseload of 70. The process involves six weekly, 45 minute interviews to assess the need for either continuation or 'outpatient treatment' of one interview every three or four weeks. Interviews are based on several principles, namely gaining understanding; preventing the probationer from fitting the officer into a 'reference frame' that permits 'unthinking, pre-conditioned behaviour' towards the officer; assuming a balance between authoritarian and friendly extremes to allow 'the possibility of transference arising in a way which is less rigidly motivated or initially determined'; and remaining 'colourless' so that the probationer can see reflection or transference 'in [him] undisguised, unaided and unenhanced by [his] own personality' (48). Discussion of the offence is proscribed 'for at least two months', and emphasis is placed on conveying expertise and interest, and being non-judgmental. Golding finishes by arguing for the use of technique and knowledge, and disavowing (without intended irony) the need to elaborate on his philosophy and motivations 'always supposing the unlikely event of [his] knowing' (49).

Not everyone shared Golding's ideas. One correspondent to the journal argues that probation is not psychotherapy but a process of education aimed at changing attitudes; another while acknowledging the overlap between casework and psychotherapy and the need to use the mind, asserts that officers should use their 'hearts and feel'. Focusing on a different issue, two officers are critical of Golding for treating the client in isolation from the changing 'milieu' of relationships (Probation Forum 1960: 68-70). However, other critics do not wander far from the path trodden by Golding. For example, Thornborough (1960) while stressing that probation officers are not psychotherapists, criticising Golding's inflexibility and locating casework at the heart of the process of keeping people out of trouble, nevertheless promulgates the use of insight giving into unrecognized feelings, the parent-child analogy, transference and the security that comes from strong, firm but trusting and warm relationships (89-90). Farrimond (1960) attempts to introduce clarity into the meaning of casework in probation because it lead to vagueness, uncertain theoretical foundations and a dearth of critical verbal and written debate but fails to provide a definition and reiterates the centrality of casework theory to probation practice (Farrimond 1960).

Most contributions, however, follow Golding's line. Holden (1960) proclaims that effective supervision is 'geared to the client's unconscious reaction to the caseworker', and the theory of psychoanalysis has 'illuminated' understanding of the problems officers deal with (119). Another officer attempts to demystify casework by contending that psychotherapy is a form of casework if the caseworker does it, and that casework is not the domain of a small elite (Forder 1960). Garrett (1961) sees a distinction between newly trained caseworkers and older officers who need to be brought up to date. Sanders (1961) urges the extension of theoretical knowledge to underpin casework that 'is now made on the understanding of human relationships and the modification of personality and attitudes' (142). That theoretical knowledge, however, gives way to the mystique of personality for another officer (Aylwin 1961); to him the officer's 'personality is the paramount factor in achieving success; self knowledge, "deeply ingested" is the key'. In this officer's view, practical help reduces mutual respect, is 'a handicap to treatment' and should be given a low priority (179).[19]

Although a reading of these contributions reveals how diverse definitions of casework were, the Morison Committee Report (Home Office 1962), which had been briefed to enquire into the probation service, showed no inhibitions in endorsing it as an approach to working with offenders. Casework embedded in the behavioural sciences according to the committee was the emblem of the Service's professional status; and probation officers were professional caseworkers like other social workers. The Joint Under Secretary of State to the Home Office pledged the government to the training of probation officers to fulfill this professional work (Fletcher-Cooke 1962). To the Chairman of NAPO the early chapters were an inspiration to read but the report itself 'was never intended to be more than a dawning image of the birth of a profession' leaving the Service itself 'to sketch the plan and perhaps begin to lay the first foundations' (Sanders 1962: 22). If it was needed, therefore, the Morison Committee gave official approval to the core methodology of the Service, and in retrospect the 1960s can be seen as the zenith of the casework method (and by implication the treatment model).

During this period probation rhetoric as represented by the writings of probation officers and as illustrated by some of the informants in this book, is generally about the 'what' of casework and not the 'why'. Even critical analysis was conducted within the framework of casework, although at first sight there is a suggestion of an assault on the treatment model that predates the *Non-Treatment Paradigm* of Bottoms and McWilliams by fifteen years. Focusing on the relative ineffectiveness of probation to reduce offending Keidan (1963) speculates whether the fault could be 'in the emphasis [officers] place on the clinical approach, that [they] expect too much from the relationship between the caseworker and the individual in the probation setting and accept too facilely that early childhood experiences, especially relationships within the family, are decisive factors' (71). Influenced by theories of sub-culture and peer influence, Keiden eschews psychotherapy but nonetheless promotes diagnosis of the emotionally and mentally damaged, the educationally sub-normal and psychopaths, referral to other agencies and the use of group therapy.

An attempt to codify a set of principles of probation, within which casework methods could be placed, became a kind of preface for numerous contributions on the subject throughout the 1960s (Leeves 1963). As Leeves describes them, they are that probation is a part of the criminal justice system, balanced between help and the use of authority with the purpose of stopping people from offending. Accordingly, both officer and probationer have obligations and rights and responsibilities constrained by this over arching purpose. In addition, the work of probation officers is based on a belief in the worth of the individual, respect for the person, justice, self-determination, and confidentiality. Finally, officers themselves should be committed to the pursuance of statutory duties and the aims of the Service, individual professional development, and an irreproachable personal life (68-70).

Folk Theories

Parkinson (1965; 1966) who was to develop his own distinct and controversial brand of casework challenged the passivity of some casework approaches, and what he appears to define as collusion between officer and client. In his view, the techniques of probation 'encourage ingratiation processes' (59). To counter this tendency, he devised a theoretical paradigm drawn from the psychoanalytical model. It is a kind of potpourri ontology within which, for instance, the docility of clients is the 'expression of a more fundamental dividing off of angry childhood responses to frustration from the rest of the personality, making it possible for the offender to show mild responses to everything that does not directly conflict with his primitive needs' (59). Furthermore, the child is coerced 'to relinquish a sense of its own omnipotence and attempts to achieve omnipotence through its parents'. According to Parkinson therein lie the 'roots of social development and education' but with delinquents this 'takes a disturbed form and in combination with a splitting process produces psychological systems in which the client finds himself totally committed to extreme attitudes – passivity or aggression, dominance or submission, delinquency or "obsessional (sic) honesty", intensive sexuality or impotent indifference' (61). Moreover, 'enuresis is certainly in part an enjoyment of passive feminine feelings of pleasure and of a yearning for a return to the imagined irresponsibility of babyhood' (62).

What is interesting about this officer (despite the fact that he was a controversial figure and maybe not typical), is that he presents probation historians with a very clear example of the influence of psychoanalytical theory and the idiosyncratic development of ad hoc personal theory in practice situations. It is based on his direct experience with probationers, includes challenging of conventional wisdom and uses of psychological methods outside of the psychoanalytical model (cognitive-behavioural work for instance); it is what might be termed folk theory and practice.

Scmideburg[20] (1965) in an address to the Third International Conference for Psychotherapy, called for psychotherapists to learn from probation officers because they are more in tune with the fact that crime is 'a moral phenomenon caused by lack of social and moral feelings' and they try to give the probationer a 'social philosophy' (5-6). He praised Parkinson for presenting technique in concrete terms (Schmideberg 1965a), and attacked the 'indiscriminate permissiveness and non-judgementalness' (sic) of some casework as 'unwieldy, phoney, weak, inflexibly stereotyped, thoughtless, geared neither to the individual nor to the situation, therefore ineffective, or worse' (66).

Another paper picks this theme up and interprets Schmideberg's argument as a plea for a psychological approach underpinned not by psychoanalysis but a social perspective (Lickorish 1965). In this argument, moral neutrality is eschewed and supplanted by social learning theory. Accordingly, '[c]riminal offenders are deficient in social learning and no medical means can correct this deficiency' (68); and what is needed is re-learning and re-education via the use of a relationship which is based on common-sense, genuineness and warmth but which is down to earth and intolerant of the probationer's 'symptoms'.

In a paper published the same year the creator of the principles of probation, Leeves (1965) criticises Monger's recently published book on casework because he only gives one interpretation of everything, and fails to present 'casework as a developing (as yet only partly understood) science of human relations and communication, capable of modification' (66). Farrimond (1965) laments the lack of any body of casework knowledge (presumably he had not read Monger), and rehearses familiar principles drawn from a work by Heywood.[21] Currently, he argues, caseworkers are inclined to ascribe the label casework to actions that are merely those 'of a reasonably educated person who has been brought up by sensible and kindly parents' (10).

Work in groups provides further evidence of officers' attempts to move beyond that definition of a caseworker (Vanstone 2003). Parker and Bilston's (1959) work in the Social Rehabilitation Unit at Belmont Hospital engaged them in a therapeutic community in which approximately thirty percent of patients were probation clients some of whom were under treatment via section 4 Criminal Justice Act 1948. Typically, it involved daily meetings chaired by a patient, open discussion groups facilitated by a doctor, and its own internal discipline system; in effect, it was treatment premised on an early form of empowerment.

Other descriptions of probation officers' work in groups is couched in the social scientific language of therapeutic intervention, and is, therefore, very much part of the history of the treatment model (Bilston 1961: 150). In this way groupwork with teenage boys is justified as (amongst other things) the provision of mutual support; the dilution of transference; insight development; and the formation of new diagnoses. Justifying his approach with reference to the work of Maxwell Jones on community therapy, and Foulkes and Anthony[22] on group psychotherapy, he sets his aim as achieving changes in social attitudes more than fundamental changes in personality: acceptance and equality are encouraged, role play is used, and the group members are described as participating in their own treatment. Influenced by the therapeutic community model, the approach can be seen to prefigure one element of the later *Non-Treatment Paradigm* (Bottoms and McWilliams 1979).

Another officer (Bagshaw)[23] asserts that his work with boys aged 15 to 18 and his study of Slavson,[24] had led him to the conclusion that treatment in groups was appropriate for 'character-disordered clients'. Some accounts, however, suggest less ambitious aspirations, and perhaps more accurately reflect the reality of practice. Ashley (1962) professes the simple aim of encouraging a small group of adolescents (convicted of theft, burglary, taking and driving and in one case buggery and gross indecency who share the same problems) in *meaningful* discussion on any topics that they care to raise in order to find common ground. As leader, he collates viewpoints and verbalises their feelings as they discuss topics such as the cinema, girlfriends, sex and Lady Chatterley. Although he professes little knowledge of groupwork techniques, he shows some insight into scapegoating, leadership and the roles people play in groups; and he does discuss the dangers of contamination. However, there is no apparent focus on offending.

A later account of his work provides an insight into his leadership style and theoretical influences such as Bion and psychiatric work with neurotic patients

(Ashley 1965):

> My role was, as before, rather like that of a catalyst in a chemical process, in that I believe I enabled the reactions to go on between the group members without becoming directly involved in them, though I cannot press this analogy too far since a catalyst, at the end of the reaction, remains unchanged, and this was certainly not so in any case. I did, from time to time, attempt to bring together their viewpoints and verbalise their feelings when these seemed to be becoming obscure (7).

Interestingly it is in descriptions of groupwork in the journal that work with females finds most (albeit still limited) expression. McCullough (1962) states specifically that her approach to groupwork with girls in a hostel setting is the application of casework theory to groupwork. Her description of closure, for example, reveals her knowledge about group dynamics and group process:

> The meetings last from an hour to an hour and a half and I begin to close them after an hour. This piece of 'structure' I have introduced deliberately – in the delinquent authority situation people tend to want to prolong a meeting you are trying to close whereas faced with an indefinite period of time they seem more likely to resist with silence (36).

In this and another description of a leader-centred approach which exploits tension within the group, she encourages the development of self-understanding through interactions with others, and focuses on anti-authority feelings and non-verbal communication, she provides an illustration of a technical approach to working with groups that seems close to a psychotherapeutic model (McCullough 1963). This is true also of work with five young female shoplifters in which another officer maintains a passive leadership role despite anxiety in order to fulfil the group's aim of 'internalization of authority' (Freeguard 1964: 18).

So during this period debates about casework whether within groups or with individuals tended to be about its detail and occur within an acceptance of the basic validity of the model. One former officer, however, casts some doubt on the universal acceptance of at least some of its aspects. Diagnosis and its implication that the probationer was 'a diseased person who is going to have something administered to him', he recalled, 'didn't carry much weight amongst the courts and most officers were wise not to pedal it too much in courts', and that officers were 'as persons of vocation and not of profession'. Nevertheless, he confirms the dominance of casework in officers' thinking while also putting it into a realistic practice perspective:

> As far as the guts of the thing went – case work – it was undoubtedly primarily concerned with people really as individuals [...] Having said that people weren't so daft as to imagine of course that the environmental factors weren't powerful. It was recognised however, I think, that if you are seeing somebody for 20 minutes once a week, you are not going to restructure society very much in their favour in the course of 2 years [...] It was very

much a question of the probation officer being quite clearly, as it were, an agent of society for court.

Another in his recollection of conversations confirms this practical slant on the nature of casework in practice with a probationer:

> I would want to talk about the here and now. What are you doing with yourself? How are you spending your time now? Why did you? How did you go to? How did you get to being? What are you doing now? What about other friends? I would want to talk about what they were doing in the sense of work, leisure, school. I would want to talk about how are your relationships? What are you feeling at home? What are you feeling about your wife, your children, your father and your teachers and your employers? How are you handling, how are you managing these things?

The dominance of the psychodynamic model features in the recollection of the direct entrant quoted above:

> It was a predominant model. It was the way of thinking but you used to get the odd ex-army officer sort of [...] coming and I can remember one of them – I won't name him – who sort of thought he was still in the army rather than in the probation service. But mostly it was, yes, a psychodynamic agency. In the 70s, there would have been floods of priests you know and the Pope said they couldn't marry so they all joined the probation office!

Moreover, her account provides a clue about how she sustained influence and a clear insight into how she worked:

> We mainly talked with each other. There was lots of, I suppose, airing and sharing with each other really, and also in the 60s when we became [...] we broke away from [...] and then was a professional association rather than the union. So you would meet them and talk over professional issues and have professional conferences to which we invited sort of other professional colleagues and sometimes the magistrates and so there was an awful lot of talking with each other. I think friendships were mainly within the service.
>
> You would always start off seeing them weekly. That's why I had three report evenings a week and we would see people weekly for ages and ages and we mainly went for 3 year probation orders. People would turn up and we would see them one after the other. Usually there would be something that we had been talking about, you know the client had been talking about the theme in their life and they would just sort of bring it and continue talking about it. I can remember a little boy who had offended that I was seeing every week and his mother was in the psychiatric hospital and he wasn't very good at talking and so I gave money for him to have a fish tank which he built in my office; and each week he built part of the fish tank and whilst he was building it he would talk about things that were going on for him and I think we used to call it talking over a third object in those days. And I had a toy table that the children would play at and draw at and they used to talk whilst they were doing those sorts of things and in a way,

thinking about it now, although we weren't sort of aware of it that's what child psychotherapists do. They have materials for the children to play with and draw with and communicate through that medium and we were doing that without having the sophisticated knowledge that that's what should be done. I can remember with the older women one of the things a lot of them used to discuss was sort of endless children and sort of poverty and I can remember one woman who desperately wanted a hysterectomy and her husband didn't want her to have it because he reckoned it would ruin his sex life.

Her description of her theorising shows the influence of psychoanalysis:

I can remember doing home visits and discussing this […] I think what was in my mind that informed my discussions with people was something to do with them if you want the notion that early separation and early deprivation affected the way people felt about themselves and their ability to make relationships so it's probably always attachment theory and you know some of the sort of Freud's thinking about early formation that informed the way I thought about and addressed what people were talking about […] and the sort of notion that people generally wanted something different and better for themselves that they weren't actually happy offending.

The recollections of another direct entrant illuminate his understanding of what casework entailed:

I would start off with a very careful, detailed social history with everybody. So you would want to know a lot about where they came from – and for me that was never about 'were you breast fed?' – but I really wanted to learn what their life experience was from birth really. I can remember saying to mothers 'How was childbirth? How was this thieving little fourteen year old? How were the other kids? How were the parents with each other. So you start off with a detailed knowledge of a person and what had brought him to be this child who wouldn't go to school, who thieved or whatever and try – what's the word – diagnose – and formulate a plan for working which could include schools, youth club, the parents. Through talking you explore these things and see if you could encourage him into not thieving but more importantly his being a happier guy.

For him the personal theory that underpinned this approach was that the client's experiences 'made him what he is', and that those experiences included 'our mothering, fathering and schooling'. Moreover, the 'anti-social behaviour, the fighting and the thieving will be to do with that and may be to do with anger and depression, unhappiness' and 'displaced problems' and 'peer group pressure'.

From outside the Service, there were some indications of the doubt about the model implied by these last two reminisces. In a paper published in the same year that the Service assumed responsibility for After-care, Morris (1966) suggests that rehabilitation is a 'hazy concept' and that offending is as much about environmental factors as emotional maladjustment. She advocates neighbourhood work, and the collection of data to begin the process of testing for effectiveness. For the time being, however, confidence in the model persisted, and it remained a central part of probation training (Home Office 1966). Instead of engaging in critical debate, some writers concentrated on various related issues such as the need for more skilled supervision of the caseworker (Haines 1967; Frayne 1968); its infiltration into prison work (Parris 1968); reconciling casework and compulsion (Felton 1967); the opportunity of intensifying casework through Day Treatment Centres (Leeves (1972); and widening the response to diagnosis through a whole range of provisions (Wood and Shember 1973).

Although the Seebohm Committee Report (1968) stimulated a debate about whether probation should become a correctional treatment service or remain a court social work service (Murch 1969; Addison 1969; Fishwick 1969), there was an acceptance that casework remained central to officers' methodology. As Braithwaite (1969) puts it, '[a]ny system which might divorce diagnosis from treatment should be avoided, since, as caseworkers know well, the two processes are indivisible' (59). It was a methodology with tenuous links with a uniform, professional knowledge base. A study of the reading of a random sample of 200 officers concluded that officers drew more heavily on their own personality and experience than reading but of the literature read, that on psychology was most strongly correlated to literature on social work practice. Sociology and social work research on the other hand were strongly rejected as being in anyway useful (Brown and Wallace 1969). Therefore, whilst the descriptions of casework in this chapter exude confidence it may be that they reveal its basic weakness – a weakness that was about to be exposed.

Notes

[1]There is evidence that probation had a valued place in the Criminal Justice System at this time. In 1930 the Home Secretary addressed the annual meeting of the Manchester and Salford Hundred prisoners' Aid Society on the welcomed reduction of the prison population, the main reason for which 'was the use of the Probation Act' (*The Times* 10 March 1930).

[2] Basil Henriques was a London magistrate, member of the London Probation Committee (from 1937) and a prominent supporter of the probation service.

[3] Merfyn Turner was the founder in 1951 of Norman House in London, a hostel concerned with the rehabilitation of prisoners. He subsequently founded other homes, was a prison visitor and a writer and broadcaster on the problems of prisoners. According to Page (1992) he was appointed warden of the Normanhurst (a converted sailing barge and home of the Barge Boys' Club referred to above) prior to being 'a youth club leader with practical experience of the East End and of Cardiff's Tiger Bay' (214). He is the author of *Safe Lodging. The road to Norman House* published in 1961 and *A pretty sort of prison* published in 1964.

[4] Sohn (1952) identifies the 'first conscious and directed use of the principles of group psychotherapy' in the work of Dr. J. H. Pratt with tuberculous patients. As he puts it, 'A group meeting in Boston, under Dr. J. H. Pratt, were given instructions in personal hygiene and their records were checked. They enjoyed the social stimulus of such meetings and felt encouraged: so Pratt extended the method to include patients with other chronic diseases' (20).

[5] Landers quotes the claim of Dr. Macwood that 'Wormwood Scrubs was the first prison anywhere to use a social group of prisoners specifically for treatment' (328).

[6] Jacob Moreno, a psychodramatist and group psychotherapist was born in Bucharest. Between 1921 and 1925 he founded *Das Stegreiftheater* (the Spontaneity Theatre), and in 1936 (in America) he founded the first theatre for psychodrama (Therapeutic Theatre). In addition to being the originator of psychodrama he was, according to Landers, an innovator in ideas about how dynamic, interpersonal influences impinge on the individual.

[7] A leading figure in the development of the therapeutic community in hospitals and educated in Edinburgh, he worked at Maudsley Hospital before becoming medical director of the Social rehabilitation Unit at Belmont where he pioneered the treatment of psychopaths within a therapeutic community. In the notes on the author in his book *Maturation of the Therapeutic* Community published in 1976, it states that he rebelled against orthodox psychiatric treatment and instead developed 'social organisations which promote social learning and growth in their members.' This included prisons. His influence on the development of groupwork in probation was, perhaps, more implicit than explicit. Although the therapeutic community model was not adopted in its pure form in probation, some of the concepts featured in therapeutic communities, such as collaborative work with patients, daily ward meeting and the staff review meeting, can be found in Bottoms and McWilliams' *Non-Treatment Paradigm* and the values inherent in Priestley and Mcguire's *Social Skills and Problem-Solving and Offending Behaviour* models. Moreover, they permeated early practice in day centres, and in fact the first programme of the Sheffield Day Training Centre was based on the model. It was, however, quickly abandoned in the face of the reality of testing such an approach in a statutory setting.

[8] The Social Rehabilitation Unit, Belmont was later renamed the Henderson Hospital.

[9] An informant to the original PhD research.

[10] Letter to *Probation Journal*, 8, 2 (1956: 29).

[11] Taken from an unpublished memoir.

[12] A Dr. Denis Carrol is recorded as a member of the Eugenics Society in 1948. Source Africa 2000 website.

[13] See Appendix 4.

[14] Letter to the author.

[15] It is likely that this is Robert Foren who went on to co-author *Authority in Casework*.

[16] It seems that his name is spelt both as Carrol and Carroll. I have used whatever spelling is in the particular source.

[17] This refers to the first edition but the text used in this study is the 1969 third edition.

[18] A future standard textbook on training courses, referred to as a basic text as late as the 1970s.

[19] For a further assault on the worker as 'technician' see Goslin, J. (1964) 'The Great Deception', *Probation*, 10, 11, 168-170.

[20] At the time, a prominent exponent of psychoanalytical theory and practice.

[21] An Introduction to Teaching Casework Skills.

[22] Their book, *Group Psychotherapy, the Psycho-analytic Approach* published by Penguin Books in 1957 is referred to as the most frequently read by the respondents to Barr's survey. Their approach was Freudian but was also influenced by Gestalt psychology - 'The therapist's attention is focused primarily upon the interpersonal or 'transpersonal' relationships between the members of the group and not exclusively upon the internal psychodynamics of individual patients' (McCullough and Ely 1968).

[23] Letter to Probation Journal, 9, 11, 168.

[24] American expert on group psychotherapy. Sohn (see above) cites S. R. Slavson's group therapy classes with problem children during the 1930s in New York as of significant influence in the development of group therapy. According to McCullough and Ely (1968) his theoretical model was drawn from Freudian ego-psychology as used in individual psychology. So, for instance, concepts such as transference, ego-strengthening and reality testing were an essential part of the dynamics operating in groups. He applied his model in a number of different agencies, including a neighbourhood centre.

Chapter 6

The Emergence of Doubt: the *Non-Treatment Paradigm* and Alternative Therapy

The treatment model and casework were about to experience an assault from several directions (Raynor and Vanstone 2002). As will be argued in this chapter, the result was fragmentation rather than disintegration of the treatment model. Nor was it the end of casework, the written and spoken emblem of probation practice. Instead they both endured albeit within an approach based more on collaboration with the probationer. Indeed as the examples of practice described later in this chapter show, psychology prevailed and the individual remained the target of change.

There is evidence of a relatively early concern to initiate collaborative relationships with clients: for instance in 1978 Fielding (no date) undertook a survey of training in one Service and found a significant number of officers committed to Task-Centred Casework and placing an emphasis on client self-change. However, this was sometime after the first critical assaults on the treatment model. One of the first came from Wootton (1959). She used the evidence of the dominant position of psychiatry in the 1919 National Conference of Social Work in the United States to support her argument that social workers had sought their professional status through an uncritical use of psychoanalysis, claimed mystical powers and created an illusion of effectiveness.

At the beginning of the 1970s, Reid and Epstein (1972) were no less disparaging when they concluded that, 'practitioners of interpersonal treatment today are guided by theories that are no better supported by empirical data than was Dr. Rush's theory of depletion' (40).[1] Indeed, one of the former officers interviewed who was involved in regional training during the 1970s recalled the lack of influence of research findings and 'a low level of concern about effectiveness'. In his critique of rehabilitation, Bean (1976) throws into sharp relief the explicit use of medical terms, and questions the link between the growth of humanitarianism and the rehabilitative ideal. He argues that while it had influence it is more likely that there was a general trend away from inhumanity and that the 'reformist position arose at the same time as this general trend' (8-9). He aligns himself with the radical non-interventionist position that therapy or treatment is premised upon an 'institutional definition of reality [that] requires a body of knowledge that includes a theory of deviance, a diagnostic apparatus, and a conceptual system of curing souls' (13). Furthermore, it requires experts, and he includes probation officers in that group who obscure a hidden moral agenda by diagnosing, treating and manipulating 'offenders' psycho-social worlds' (42). According to Bean, there are two flaws in the social pathology model: first, it ignores the wider social context; and second, its target, social disease, is not tangible like physical disease.

He confirms that the expertise of probation officers derives from psychoanalysis, which he describes as a generic term covering 'a host of theories based on unconscious mechanisms' (46). According to his critique, it provided a ready-made theoretical framework for diagnosis and treatment, it satisfied the demand to understand the 'inner man', and it did not have to be restricted to medical experts. As he reminds the reader, all of the probation officers involved in the probation research project in 1966 gave casework as their principle theory and their foci as personality, emotional adjustment and family. However, in Bean's view, the model's failure lay in the inadequacy of its theoretical base and the unrestrained power of its pseudo-expertise.[2]

The reality of the practice situation was a little more complex than Bean implies but Folkard and his colleagues (1966) confirmed both the degree of discretion and the emphasis on attempts to change the individual's personal and social world through direct personal influence and support. In their study the most frequently used form of supervision involved low support and low control, whereas the least frequently used were situational control (high home visiting, low support and high control) and situational support and control (high home visiting, high support and high control). High control was associated with low success, and the main determinant of type of treatment was the officer providing it.

Practical help may have been more prominent than is suggested by this treatment model (Willis 1983), and as has been argued elsewhere officers' belief in the efficacy of rehabilitation was sustained through the early assault on the model and indeed the pessimistic research findings of the 1970s (Cooper 1987; May 1991a; Vanstone 1993). Nevertheless, the fault lines were already there. Radzinowicz (1958) had already exposed probation's failure with what are now known as high risk offenders, and even optimism generated by success with first offenders was dimmed by the findings of 1970s research (Folkard et al. 1976; Lipton et al. 1975). Indeed, in a survey of the efficacy of sentencing, on probation Brody (1976) concluded:

> Probationers on the whole do no better than if they were sent to prison, and that rehabilitative programmes – whether involving psychiatric treatment, counselling, casework or intensive contact and special attention, in custodial or non-custodial settings – have no predictably beneficial effects (37).

This challenge was always equivocal. For instance, the IMPACT experiment (Folkard et al. 1974; Folkard et al. 1976) while adding to the doubts about the efficacy of treatment, did suggest that it depended on the matching of treatment to particular categories of offender.[3] Although not statistically significant, its finding that offenders with low criminal tendencies and high levels of problems responded more positively to supervision trailed a kind of early *What Works* premise. What is more, as Raynor and Vanstone (2002) have explained, the psychological theories on which the treatment model was based, while widely used in training, were never empirically tested in Britain. Instead its popularity may have been due to the fact that 'the underlying theoretical assumptions about causation of delinquency provide[d] a way of reconciling a controlling function with a strategy for treatment' (Waterhouse 1983: 64). These elements of external control and expert treatment had significant advocates (Foren and Bailey 1968; Hunt 1964; Hunt 1966).[4] Ultimately however they led, Raynor and Vanstone (2002) have argued, to a number of more collaborative and inclusive models: namely primary and secondary contracts between worker and client (Bryant et al. 1978);[5] two separate services (Harris 1980); social work based on systems theory (Pincus and Minahan 1973);[6] socialist probation (Walker and Beaumont 1981); radical social work (Hugman 1980); and the *Non-Treatment Paradigm* itself (Bottoms and McWilliams 1979).[7]

In spite of these developments, a cursory perusal of the post-paradigm period reveals that the break with the treatment model has not been a clean one. There are numerous examples of different types of work that demonstrate this point but it is beyond the scope of this book to describe in detail every theoretical model used in probation. The following have been selected for several reasons. First because they are promising methods of influence that demonstrate clearly an attempt to link a specific theory to practice; second because they are based to some extent on a reformulated treatment model predicated on increased collaboration and the use of contracts with clients (see Corden 1980); and third because they were identified in an interview with a former Regional Training Officer as a significant part of the curricula of three of the four Regional Staff Development Units established by the Home Office in the early 1970s. Confirmation of the impact of this training comes from Ainley (1979) who in a small-scale survey showed that although the methods were sometimes dissipated the skills were transferred to other areas of work. They are presented descriptively, with a deliberately limited commentary and followed at the end of the chapter by a discussion that generalizes some conclusions from the individual examples.

Intermediate Treatment

The camps with young probationers might be seen as an early form of Intermediate Treatment (IT) but its arrival on the social work scene was stimulated by the work of Thorpe and his colleagues at Lancaster University in response to the high number of juveniles being placed in Care for welfare reasons (Thorpe et al. 1980), and its status as a method was confirmed by the 1969 Children and Young Persons Act (Lacey 1984). Positioned between supervision in the community and residential experience it was a reaction to the confusion about welfare and justice thinking that accelerated children up the sentencing tariff. Lacey (1984) constructed a theoretical and practice paradigm premised on prevention work through high and medium level intervention in low intensity groups. However, probation accounts cover outdoor activities coupled with problem-solving activities, and included diverse approaches such as sea voyages (Durbin 1982); structured groupwork programmes (Hankinson and Stephens 1984); canal trips combined with an intensive programme focused on self-control and decision-making (Harding 1971); activity groups (Bunning (1975; Carpenter and Gibbens 1973); and therapeutic centres (Voelcker 1969). No doubt, to some extent IT achieved its aim of countering the pathologizing impact of the treatment model but 'often in probation practice the treatment model was transported literally from the office to the field' (Vanstone 2004a).

Family Therapy

Family therapy which first found prominence in IMPACT experiment is relatively unique in probation practice in as far as it was based on systemic intervention in families (Thornborough 1974; Vanstone 2004). Practitioners who used the approach focused among other things on co-working; family dysfunctions; engagement with family interaction; and therapeutic intervention in the family as a system (Thornborough 1974; Ireland and Dawes 1975; Thompson and Clare 1978).[8] Its popularity may have been due to the tangibility of the model compared to previous casework. This is clear from this officer's explanation for her involvement in the approach: she had been working with juveniles and their families so thought it a 'logical thing to do'. Her qualifying training had been 'very psychodynamic', and while this had instilled in her a professional attitude to work she had found the 'psychodynamic way of working difficult looking for a frame of reference'. As she put it: 'you can't just go in and ask Mrs. Jones if she's drinking heavily [....] you needed to be doing a lot more and I think it was from that point that I started my professional development'. She referred to the plethora of theories around in social work, and then described the effect upon her of training in family therapy:

> What these courses told me was that I wasn't scratching the top of it. I would use the framework as a frame of reference for work that I was doing with people, but what seemed clear to me especially as the course went on was that I would have to be doing much more practice and be supervised much more in the method if I was to employ it as a tool that I was using [...] the training taught you something about *why* they did things that they did at the Institute; it showed you *how* they did it because you could see live interviews [...] you were able to dip your toe in and have a go and try some of the methods out in role-plays which I found very powerful.
>
> It was alongside the Nothing Works ideas as well running through this time period in the 80s, and I think underneath you were looking for something that did work [...] they seemed to have an effect on these intractable problems.

It was the particular focus of the courses that she went on and the versatility of the approach that appealed:

> the courses I went on stuck with the systemic approach and I could understand that. It could also be used in other ways [....] you could use it as a framework with an individual or with a group of people.

It is clear that it had an enduring impact on her work generally:

> So what I used to do, for example, if I couldn't [or] if I had a problem with a case and couldn't work out a way forward or whatever, try and sit down and work out on paper what might be happening and it also improved my interviewing technique because the whole idea was to use open questions, follow through and listening and feedback.

However, she was involved with colleagues in a much more organised way. They set up an informal group within the Service and acted as a resource to which colleagues could refer. The final extract from her interview provides a clear description of a structured way of working.

> We'd set up an interview [...] we'd spend a lot of time discussing how we were going to invite them, when, those kind of things. The whole process, we were aware the whole process needed to be done in a kind of systematic way [...] Once they came, we started off by using two people as interviewers, working together in the family. There was usually two of us outside the interview [...] there was a video link [...] the family would come in. We would make them discuss what information we had, identify information we needed to gather but also based on the information we had we would have a kind of hypothesis about what might happen, into trying to identify what areas might merit questioning. And so, that was how it then proceeded along those lines. I always felt when I asked a question like – something about somebody's mother or son or father or to check out information on a generalised basis, how much would come back just by asking that question. So what happened then was that the first few interviews were very much information gathering, questioning and particularly concentrating on how you asked the questions – asking people what they thought about the situation – 'What do you think so and so thought when your mother..', that kind of thing.
> Then following that session there would be a break when the worker would come out and talk about what their feelings were and what the consultants' feelings were, and then adjusting the hypothesis and seeing if there was anything at that stage they could tell the family that might help them to unlock whatever it was or work they needed to do in order to effect some change [...] that was the process. Sometimes they would be given a task, sometimes they would be sent away and we said we need to think more about this [...] there was never an explanation given about what was thought necessary. Except that sometimes that was what was done, explaining the thinking and the difficulties in coming to a conclusion, so, as an intervention [...] this seemed to cause change.

The Heimler Scale of Social Functioning

Experiences in Buchenwald, Auschwitz and other extermination camps moved Heimler (1975) to explore the anatomy of survival. Then, in work with the unemployed in London where he was employed as a psychiatric social worker, he tested his premise that if people turn their negative experiences in a positive direction they can move forward. In a five-year follow-up study he discerned a pattern – 'those who 'functioned' in society as against those who did not function had the common feature of a subjectively felt satisfaction that corresponded with their level of bearable frustration' (8). Subsequently, he focused on this balance and devised a scale designed to measure the interplay between the satisfaction and frustration an individual felt at any one moment. It categorizes five areas in which success and failure exemplify themselves – work and interests; financial security; friendships and social relationships; family life and sexuality. Similarly, there are five areas in which frustration rests, namely, blocking or paralysis of activity; depression; alienation or feelings of persecution, insomatic or psychosomatic symptoms and finally escape routes such as alcohol. The scoring of the scale produces a positive and a negative score. A methodological schema is outlined which draws on non-directive counselling techniques such as reflection and summarising, and is designed to encourage the subject through self-observation, to identify themes, engage in a dialogue with the worker and formulate an action plan.

Week long courses with follow-up were run by regional staff development units; support groups were set up and selected people were given advanced training. For a time it permeated practice across a whole range of Service activity and it is still practiced. The impact a method like this can have on an officer is clear in this following account by an officer who still incorporates the model in his practice at the end of the 20th century:

> The man himself had an enormous effect on me and he impressed many of the students who listened to him and I had heard a lot of people say this who have heard him speak I mean he is charismatic in some senses. He's an enigma but he presents, he tells a very good story and that in itself I found fascinating and I found the story he told captivating in terms of the work he was doing.

Subsequently, he became a trainer himself, and used the scale over a twenty-year period as the following example demonstrates:

> I remember one guy – this was a man who seemingly had fixations about things. He was quite meticulous about everything he did and had these routines that everything had to be done properly. I did a couple of scales with him and they showed enormous differences in scores and they were wildly different in terms of satisfaction and I can remember saying to him... because the first two were so widely different there was something wrong and I didn't know what it was. I did it again, there was a total swing back to the first, then I did a fourth, and it was a swing back to the second. So, I had two unbelievably good and two unbelievably bad and I sort of threw these in front of him because you used the scale tell him what the numbers are about. They know about it and you throw it at them and you are shocked – for god sake what's happening, you know, am I talking to the same guy? What's wrong? And he said it was raining that morning and I said talk about it and

he said, ' I woke up, opened my eyes oh feeling fine', until he gets out of bed and opens the curtains...it's raining and his mood changes and from that minute for the rest of the day he's as miserable as sin. And um I asked him what it was about and he wasn't all that sure, so I took him through a particular technique which was a reactive thing where I asked him to describe in detail as though it had just happened: 'Waking up, you know, you're in bed, close your eyes, sit back and you are comfy and all the rest; you just woke up and you have had this feeling of everything being OK. Tell me, what does it feel like. Describe exactly what's happened. Do an action replay in your mind to describe what's happening'.

The man's mood darkened and the officer asked him to describe the first thing that came into his mind about childhood and it was his grandfather cursing the rain that was preventing them both from going to the allotment. The officer then described a specific technique in which he took the man back into childhood – a kind of role play in which the client is encouraged into a dialogue with his grandfather and himself.

He said, 'I said it doesn't matter gramps. We will go tomorrow.' And I then said to this guy, 'Does that child have anything to say to you?' 'No.' and he said he would say the same thing and I said, 'what do you mean?' 'It doesn't matter you can do it tomorrow.' So I said, 'What can you do tomorrow?' 'Go down the garden.' So I said, 'OK, we are back to the present, so what were you going to do this morning? 'Go down the garden', he said. And I said, 'Why?' 'Because I always go down the garden.' Why?' 'Because my grandfather always did.' 'Whose garden is it?' 'It was my grandfather's.' And I said, 'What's happening?' And he said, 'Oh my god, I have got to go down to the garden.' And he then goes on to talk....he says that he was into rituals, he was perpetuating the memory of his grandfather in looking after this bloody garden and he now starts to curse the garden and the little boy is saying you can do it tomorrow, and he starts to cry and he said he's right it doesn't matter and he said, 'Here's me destroying myself.'

Morley (1986), writing some twelve years after the approach had been introduced to the service acknowledges that it suffers from a lack of empirical testing.

For a time, the Service invested resources in the method,[9] but like other methods it passed out of vogue, only kept alive by single practitioners motivated by belief.[10]

Behaviour Modification

Farrington (1979), in his review of community-based behaviour modification work, first distinguishes between behaviour therapy based as it is on classical conditioning, and behaviour modification based on operant conditioning, It is the latter to which he devotes his attention, and he concludes that there are very few examples of empirically tested behaviour modification in the community.[11] He cites one example of a well constructed attempt to compare the effectiveness of a 'behaviourally oriented' probation technique with a more traditional one, which was undermined by officers not treating the juveniles in the experimental and control groups differently.

Hall (1974) comments on the growing body of published evidence of the effectiveness of behaviour modification, and stresses the need to assess its relevance to Britain. Then he provides an outline of the approach and its key principles. The approach, he explains, is premised on the idea 'that what people do is to a large extent governed by the consequences that follow what they do [and] rewards and incentives ("reinforcements") should be positive rather than negative, and at least initially should be as immediate as possible'. Furthermore, it stipulates that reinforcement must be relevant to the individual; and that people must be given credit or tokens for positive behaviour that can be repeated later (secondary conditioning) (46-7). Hall then stresses the importance of procedures that include observable, tangible, needs-related goals; and a well constructed and designed programme. In addition, he adds, there are three planning stages: 'first, a "behavioural analysis" of the particular problem area'; second, the identifying 'an effective reinforcer'; and third, linking the consequence to the behaviour or task undertaken (contingencies) (47).

Hall argues that such programmes have potential in the rehabilitation of offenders in Britain because 'they make it clear that deviant behaviour is the outcome, at least in part, of current experience[;] they emphasise that these consequences must be controlled and appropriate if behaviour is to change[;] they offer a framework within which the goals and aims of remedial and preventive work may be established[;] they point to the importance of consistency and a positive approach in rehabilitation, without having to resort to an escalating spiral of randomly applied painful punishment[;] and they rely on frontline staff for their application, not on the knowledge and skills of scarce highly-qualified staff' (49). Moreover, they confer a new role on the prison officer and residential care staff that offers more scope than that of custodian.

Remmington and Trusler (1981) lay down a three-point case for the use of behaviour modification in the probation service. First, it is founded on a 'behavioural, rather than a medical model of human action'; second, it has proven ability to help people with the kinds of problems faced by probation clients; and finally, it had been introduced successfully into the South West regional training programme (53). They elaborate on the theoretical core of the approach rooted as it is in social learning theory and the idea that human behaviour is not just a symptom of malfunction but an important factor in its own right. They identify four stages in the method: first, a detailed assessment of the client's behaviour; second, the setting of objectives; third, intervention 'based on principles deriving from operant conditioning, classical conditioning or social learning theory' (53); and finally, evaluation. Its relevance to probation is seen through the kinds of problems clinical psychologists have dealt with and are familiar to officers; they include impulsiveness, anxiety, poor self-control, depression and drug abuse.

They describe their work on short training courses in which they taught basic theory and skills. Although some officers were reluctant to give up the medical model, it was received with enthusiasm. Examples of the method used by the trained officers include a very heavy drinker reducing his drinking and thereby being reconciled to his family; a young recidivist who changed his anti-social behaviour to become a volunteer; and a lone parent who was taught to deal with her child's behaviour problems. One officer, trained by Remmington and Trustler explained to me what appealed to him about the approach that he had learned about from his own reading:

> I was quite impressed by it, in terms of its approach being quite scientific, trying to measure what you do and whether you are successful or not, in the simplest terms possible. And the evidence from America seemed more advanced than here, and it seemed to be showing that there was a way forward in terms of being successful and learning something, some clear techniques and trying to make a difference. [The work of Kasdin] was very impressive indeed, in terms of like, its kind of intellectual rigour, trying to explain the theory behind it all, but also the wealth of literature covered in there; all the surveys of effective work across a whole range of social problems. Whatever, you think of in terms of what might be problematic for people there was a kind of survey of all the relevant work that was done in that kind of approach. Trying to show you what works.

Later he became a trainer himself in what he described as the ABC approach – 'antecedents, behaviour and consequences'.

> Its essence was trying to work out the triggers in behavioural terms, not thinking, not cognitive, purely in behavioural terms [...] things don't just happen randomly. If you did that burglary at that particular time, or whatever, what was the build up, what did you do on that day? A step-by-step approach looking at what sparked off the behaviour, and then what were the consequences in terms of what reinforced it. Positive reinforcement of that behaviour. What negative reinforcement, trying to analyze it. a building block approach. And then looking to build in a way of combating that behaviour by how could you intervene at various points in the process, to break it down, looking for alternatives. Not only that but if you target alternative behaviour, you've got to build in an alternative reinforcer. You've got to find out what works for that individual. So, needing very skilful interviewing to get people to be honest enough to tell you exactly what they did, and then trying to get them to reveal hidden abilities and talents which they can build upon to do something instead. What I liked about the approach was, far from being coercive, which a lot of people thought was brainwashing. They didn't want any truck with it. Most of my colleagues here thought it was a Nazi approach...they used that phrase....but the actual way people used it was utterly different. You could find out from people about what their positive goals are, what their abilities, what their talents are, and try to build upon those, and don't be coercive. Always look for positive reinforcement, look for praise, look for good things which will help people change.

In *Probation* Aust (1987) provides another example of the application of the method, this time with a compulsive shoplifter. As well as her offending she also exhibited what he defines as problems such as 'excessive attention to neatness and tidiness' (145). The officer engaged the services of a clinical psychologist: the process entailed an assessment interview, which produced a detailed history and a family tree. At the next meeting the psychologist devised a programme involving covert sensitisation (the use of a recording of the client's imagined rehearsal of the shoplifting experience up to the point of arrest); the practicing of self-control techniques; and the creation of a task based programme by the client herself. Meetings with the psychologist were fortnightly, and the officer's role seems to have been that of encourager and a point of report back.

Task-Centred Casework

London's Impact Unit team had developed a number of different types of treatment but there was some concern over the fact that the work was protracted and spread too thinly over a range of problems (Dobson (1976). This is confirmed by the observation of one officer who was instrumental in the introduction of the model. He referred to the fact that it was the focus of a Cropwood conference in 1978, and that an important element of its appeal was that it represented a new 'theoretical model of change'. He delineated a number of factors in the decision that the Differential Treatment Unit team should embark on its own experiment: first, 'a political sub-text' related to the chief probation officer's commitment to the six-month probation order; second, dissatisfaction with the findings of the IMPACT research; and third, the influence of the work of Reid and Shyne (1969), which showed that planned, short-term work increased the chances of success, that the improvements lasted, and that it was applicable to most situations.

The Service negotiated with three local courts to make one-year orders that would be brought back to them for a conditional discharge after six months. The work was framed within a contract containing specific objectives and limitations upon the service offered. Caseloads were limited to twelve, cases were discussed at the two, four and six month stages, and two officers were attached to each case, the second officer acting as shadow and consultant. Another former member of the original team recalled that with the assistance of Matilda Goldberg from the National Institute for Social Work (NISW) and knowledge gained from direct contact with the authors of the model, Reid and Epstein, they 'trained themselves as they were doing it'. She also recalled some resistance to the approach within the Service because it was 'a very open approach and involved shared work'. It appealed to her for a number of inter-connected reasons. First, because it 'treated the client as an entity who had some control [rather than] rummaging around patronising, [and she had] always liked to let the client speak'. Second, because she liked the idea of examining what she was doing as opposed to casework which was 'like a Ruben's picture, all inspiration and nothing else'. Third, because the 'client was more centre stage'. Fourth, because the approach recognized that change was difficult. Finally, because the work was short and focused – as she put it 'get in and get out and leave people to lead their lives'. She also thought that the work was 'quite confrontational [...] and because you [were] supposed to know what you [were] doing all the time, the work was quite intense – you couldn't sustain old-style reporting'. She recalled particular success in joint work with a 'borderline mentally subnormal multi-offender'; and although unable to remember specific detail, she stated that they had used a Task-Centred approach with the family (mum, dad, two sisters and another brother) as a unit.

Echoes of these recollections are evident in Dobson's (1976) description of increased effort from both officer and client and a greater sense of purpose; and officers becoming more 'active and confronting' (106). He confirms that at the end of supervision a review reinforced the client's achievements, and that the experience of working in this way forced officers to confront their need to be long-term carers, listen to clients more and increase the adequacy of their assessments.

The problems targeted (such as interpersonal conflict, role performance, social transition, insufficient resources and emotional stress) were similar to those focused on in traditional casework but the emphasis on client choice and mutual agreement, and the structure within which they were addressed was different (Reid and Epstein 1972). There was tangibility about a prescribed process of review of possible problem areas, agreement on the problem to be addressed, agreement on action within a specified time-period and achievable intervention. What is more, there was concreteness about the role of the worker that included the facilitation of problem exploration, structuring the 'treatment relationship' and encouraging achievement. As Vaisey (1976) puts it '[t]he Task Centred method provides a disciplined structure whereby the worker can as near as possible rely on the method to ensure that he keeps a clear focused progress going' (110). Helpfully, he provides some insight into the actual work (and its value laden theories) through some case examples.

The first, Mrs. M aged 34 and recently separated from her violent husband is described as having difficulty in coping with her four children and problems of inadequacy. She is beset by 'inadequacy, hopelessness, chaos and mess – destructive feelings towards men and last but not least considerable debts and financial problems'. The problem area she chose was her "inadequate role performance as a mother and provider for her children'; and the task set was more effective budgeting through lists of expenditure and negotiation by her for free school meals and buses. The order is reported to have ended with her feeling increased self-worth, diminished depression, debts reduced and the children happier. Interestingly, the officer expressed his frustration about never having 'used his personality in a therapeutic way' (p. 111).

Although the team challenged him on this point, therapy was not eschewed, for Vaisey contends that it is the client's resistance to task that 'provides the therapeutic aspect of the model' (111). The second case is best told largely in the language used by the writer. She is Claire, a woman in her mid twenties, intelligent with a three-year-old son, and cohabiting with a violent man. Her task was to leave him, or in casework terms, to make a 'social transition'; however, weeks went by and she never attempted to leave. 'He [the probation officer] finally confronted her with his frustrated feelings of anger at the way she seemed to obtain satisfaction from being stubbornly extremely passive to all suggestions. He said, 'I wonder if your husband gets angry in the same way.' At this, she broke down in tears and a powerful catharsis followed whereby she spoke of tremendous feelings of guilt and inadequacy and a need to keep herself in a destructively dependent role. She then said, 'I suppose that if I really want to leave Michael I must firstly change my attitude towards myself' (112). A new task was set with the focus on saying 'no' to her partner and meaning it. The example is interesting more for what it reveals about the officer's lack of understanding of power relationships, and the fact that the Service had yet to be exposed to feminist critiques.

The application of the model had been subjected to evaluation in three studies. Although they were small (the biggest involving twenty cases) and the results somewhat unspecific and merely encouraging (in the biggest study 85 percent of the clients showed some improvement), it remains a very significant contribution to evidence-based practice because of the reflective nature of the researchers approach (Reid and Epstein 1972). Moreover, it stimulated the setting up of a research project with the National Institute of Social Work in order to refine the model with appropriate matching. In reporting on this, Goldberg and Stanley (1979) draw on the fact that Martinson (1974) amidst his generally pessimistic findings suggested a possible link between casework and individual counselling and reduction of offending when it solved immediate problems high on the offender's priority list. They further point out that in the IMPACT experiment there was sometimes a tenuous link between key problems, for instance unemployment, and help given. In contrast, there was a much greater focus on problems related to money, work and accommodation in the Task Centred Casework project. However, just as it was in the IMPACT experiment so too in this project more effectiveness was associated with clients with low criminal profiles and high problems.

They report that the approach is amenable to evaluation because of its explicitness, and that it included many tasks both practical and psychological; for instance, regaining self-respect, marital problems and 'working at behaviour, enhancing understanding [and] improving communication' (73). The focus was on getting a job, learning to read and write, finding lodgings but also on insight giving, social skills training, role-play and role rehearsal. Indeed, in one of the cases referred to by Dobson sculpting and communication exercises were also used. The authors conclude that '[t]he task-centred model can accommodate many approaches, from behavioural ones to those which aim at enhancing awareness of one's own and other people's behaviour, as long as both client and social worker have a specific aim in mind'; moreover, it 'demystifies social work' (73).

The commitment to the model went wider than London. Waters (1976) takes up the cudgels for Task-Centred work, advocating its use at the report stage, in prison, and in marital and groupwork, although he gives no examples of its use. The Sheffield special projects team (Harman 1978) undertook short-term work but this time it was with people awaiting trial or sentence at the Crown Court with the aim of making a positive impact on the defendant's situation in order to influence the subsequent sentencing decision.[12]

Neuro-Linguistic Programming (NLP)

The extent of the use of this method is difficult to work out but it is worth some consideration because of its direct application of theory to practice. Anderson (1981) first trails it in a short piece on non-verbal communication in which he draws on Bateson's analogic communication used in his Brief Therapy model; the basic premise being that verbal communication is distorted by our attributions and interpretations, and that analogic communication is in contrast totally honest. Later, he outlines his use of NLP (Anderson 1985 and 1986).

> Neuro-Linguistic Programming, as the name implies, is a model about how our brains work (Neuro); about how language interacts with the brain (Linguistic); and about how to use what we know about these to systematically get the results we want for ourselves and our clients (Programming).' (Dilts 1983 quoted in Anderson 1985: 7).

As an officer explained to me, John Grinder, a linguist, and Richard Bandler, a psychologist, developed the approach:

> [T]hey started to think about therapy and what was wrong with it and why it didn't work. They began to look around and worked out fairly quickly as anybody could that there were probably only half a dozen successful therapists anywhere in the world and most of them were in the States which made them readily available. So using the sort of disciplinary approach that mathematicians and linguists use they decided to have a really close look at what these successful therapist actually do regardless of what the sort of psycho theology is behind their therapy, have a look at what they actually do, what they say to people, how they move when they touch people, what goes on and they started to look very closely at that and were surprised to find out that however hugely different the psycho theologies were whether you were a family therapist or whatever – primal scream whatever – the people that are successful do exactly the same things. They say the same sort of things in the same sort of tone of voice. They make the same sort of movements in the same sort of time and you could actually still that down almost to the point you call train chimps to do successful therapy and that's the essence.

Anderson (1985) describes its application to five areas: management; court and community; social inquiry reports; assessment; and problem solving with clients. The officer, like officers using other models, tried it first having read about the approach and then went on courses run by trainers from America and Holland. He and a colleague reinforced their enthusiasm for the approach and introduced it to other members of their team. They learned and worked together. He described the effect of the approach with a prisoner's wife who was agoraphobic:

> [W]e went to see her and we did the NLP technique for phobias, and we did actually, with me doing the work and taking the book home because that's one we had never tried before. We couldn't remember a lot of it. When we

went back to see for a second interview at her home – she is very agoraphobic, she couldn't get out of the house, she couldn't even walk down to the corner shop. She tried that about a year before with one of her kids in the past down half way down the street, that's how agoraphobic she was and when we went back to see her the second time she was out. We said, 'great, finished, the work's done.' What was interesting was that she came in to see us a number of times over a period of several years after that, never ever acknowledged what had happened [...] but something like two or three years later her husband was sent to prison again and got transferred to Dartmoor, and she actually came into the office and said even with all your magic you will never get me down to Dartmoor! And that's all we needed to know really so that was one that's very dramatic and very quick.

This officer fully believed in the efficacy of the approach and practised it over a number of years. To some extent he was supported by his agency, particularly through training opportunities and time to undertake a personal fellowship but like most of these new innovations its survival appears to have depended on the individual enthusiasm, commitment and energy of the individual believer.

Transactional Analysis

TA, as it is called, straddles both individual work and groupwork,[13] and is interesting as a model because it involves teaching theory to probationers so that they can apply it themselves to their problems; and, like NLP, involves officers being trained specifically as therapists. Possibly the earliest reference to its use in probation in this country is made by Midgley (1981) who clearly believed that he was introducing it to the readership of *Probation Journal*, having himself attended what is called an *official 101* course run by a member of the International Transactional Analysis Association. He provides a short summary of the main tenets of the theory, in particular the three ego states – parent, adult and child – and in discussing their complexity (for instance, the parent state can be critical as well as nurturing), he claims that the ideas are not abstract 'like those of psychoanalysis, they are manifest realities which can be observed and recognised' (10).[14] His work, which is premised on the theory that the origins of offenders' problems are found in behaviour that is adapted to survive the constraints of childhood (the 'Adaptive Child'), is dependant on the successful negotiation and completion of contracts with his probationers.

Some ten years later, White (1992) provides an interesting example of the application of the approach to sex offenders. He determined to develop a theoretical framework that he could apply to sex offenders while he was undergoing 'clinical training' in the model. Based on his experience as well as his training, he judged that there were three deficits in the ego states of sex offenders: a parent state that lacked the capacity to provide nurturing, positive self-feedback; an adult that was ignorant of basic knowledge about sex; and, a child that lacked the ability to empathize with the feelings of others. He explains these deficits by reference to the idea of the scripts that offenders have incorporated into their thinking and behaviour from the messages of significant adults in their childhood. In his work with perpetrators he uses contracts; then looks at contaminated thinking that might hinder progress; and in an effort to explore the roots of the behaviour and thinking with the offender, uses, for example, a script questionnaire and guided fantasies, or regression work – '[t]aking the person back to childhood in a semi-trance and assisting them in meeting important figures in their lives to ask for views on sexual behaviour' (39). White warns his colleagues that the work is complex and should only be undertaken by those who have had lengthy training.

That process of selection and the structure of training (and growing up professionally) are described by a former officer as follows:

> I did two years in London, and I have since done a third year although at that time it is funded over three years. Initially I went on a weekend course called a 101 course and that's the initiation if you like into TA, and once you have got that you have done the course and done a little exam afterwards. You can then, it qualifies you to, go and train. So I went up for an interview with somebody called […] who was very well known in her field for psychotherapy counselling. She had recently come over from […], and the institute was run by four […]. It was different again, and it struck me that it was so different from the university training that I had had previously in that it was in a large house and it was, you know, flowers everywhere and it was very, very comfortable and cosy and nurturing. I guess in a way that I had not experienced in training or work, certainly.

The basis of the approach is drawn from the psychological theory of Eric Burn but this informant explained how she reconciled the use of therapy to her belief that socio-economic problems were factors in the reasons for people's offending, and then how she worked:

> It was confirming what I felt about where people had come from and the environment they were brought up in. Because, I mean, at the end of the day how come some people live on low money and they don't offend and other people have the propensity to offend all the time, to be extremely violent and so on. But my life experience and my job was teaching me that, and the therapy was simply supporting that and the two blended very well. Where they had come from and the history and how you could backtrack through generations and see how […] one family ended up here and another family ended up here.

> This guy who offended with cars motorcars for years and years and years. One of the main things for him was that his mother had died when he was in custody as a teenager and we did a lot of work around that. He was a very, very silent person. At one point I used to sit in another office and he used to telephone me because he wouldn't talk to me but he had been into it since he was about 10 and I guess he was twenty seven/twenty eight, nice guy. Very, very quiet. Wouldn't say, speak to anybody. Had never got close to anyone. He was very shut off, so I knew at that stage that perhaps what would be helpful to him would be to begin to open up and to be able to be socially

more acceptable which he could do. He looked the part but he just wasn't able to really, so he would go off and drive as an escape and I thought that if he could learn to communicate more he may not need to rush off and do that.

In a direct reference to TA theory and drawing on another model she described how she aimed to strengthen his *adult* by using a social skills training approach:

I think I probably did use social skills but within the framework of building the adult so that he could function better and have more options and indeed he went the longest I think during 'that time that he had gone without offending because he was here for a year and I don't think he was…well he certainly was getting caught which was something. At a later time probably after about 6/8 months we moved into working on his mother. I don't quite know how we got there but it was after quite a time when he trusted me enough to do that and he became very, very upset and tearful about it and he had never done that so he was like a walking unexploded bomb in a sense because he had been so close to his mum and this death had been such a tragedy. It was very cruel. I mean I think that's…about nurturing and respect to let a young kid at 15 not go to the funeral it's so cruel and awful so we did quite a lot of thinking and work around that and probably at that time I might even have been seeing him twice a week because he was in quite a vulnerable stage then and part of his offending was about keeping up the hard protective layer and of course what I was asking him to do, you know – back down – and that's not a very safe place to be. So again the re-parenting bit would say, well you know you see somebody more when they are in they earlier stage and if they want to give them the protection that they need. We say the 3 Ps, potency, protection, permission, and I think to be potent ourselves is very important but to offer the protection is also very important.

For her there was a direct connection between the application of the model and methods with the successful outcome of his subsequent job, settled relationships and independence from her. Such confidence is a consistent feature of each of the models of change referred to in this chapter but how far is it justified and what in general does it imply about the development of practice during this period in the Service's history? What do the examples outlined in this chapter tell us about practice during casework's period of uncertainty? How different, if at all, is it to casework premised as it was on the treatment model?

The search for an answer to those questions begins unavoidably with the commonalities. Although some of the effects of a *Non-Treatment Paradigm* are evident, like casework this practice is encompassed within the treatment model. It also retains a focus on changing the individual rather than their environment, and where there is reference to that environment it is usually in terms of what individuals can do to alter the nature of their interaction with it. Furthermore, it bestows expertise status on the officer as the expert guide and in this sense is as entwined with the quest for *scientific* solutions to crime related problems and the accompanying professional standing as the practice of casework. Moreover, like casework it is drawn from the realms of social work and psychology rather than work with offenders. However, there is a point at which it parts company with what might be called its helper cousin.

The distinction that Reid and Epstein (1972) make in their description of Task-Centred Casework between a model – 'a coherent set of directives which state how a given kind of treatment is to be carried out' – and a theory – 'a set of assumptions and hypotheses which provide a rationale for the treatment model' – is a useful starting point for a consideration of the differences (7). Both casework and these new variants have a theoretical rationale and they have guidelines for implementation; although, as we have seen, casework has flowed in many different directions. However, the models within which these examples functioned have a greater apparent coherence and tangibility than the perhaps more obscure casework model and its exploration of the unconscious. Each has a clear framework such as that provided by the Heimler Scale or the time limit of Task-Centred work. That transparency, therefore, may have proved attractive to practitioners. Compared to sometimes esoteric, long-term casework, practice activity that is goal oriented, focused on problem-solving and very specific behaviour, set within time limits and founded on success must have been very appealing. In this sense they can be seen to prefigure some of the elements of the forthcoming shift to evidence-based programmes. By the time that these new approaches were being undertaken casework itself had been subject to evaluation and there are indications (albeit to a varying degree) of a growing commitment to evaluation. This is particularly true of Task-Centred Casework, and it is from this that the most promising indicators of a more reflective approach can be discerned.

One of the directives that create space between casework and these new models is that of collaboration. Although the worker remains the guiding expert each model proffers some expertise to the client and either implies or makes explicit that the change effort should be based on agreement, greater transparency and the combined efforts of both worker and client. In Task-Centred Casework particularly this prefigured one of the elements of the *Non-Treatment Paradigm* of Bottoms and McWilliams.

Finally, several of these experiments in method (TCC being a notable exception) expose a frailty in practice that was to persist until the Home Office's *Effective Practice Initiative*, namely a lack of institutionalized support from the organization. They remained largely idiosyncratic and dependent on the energy and commitment of the particular practitioner-believer. Consequently, they either survived as the particular modus operandi of that practitioner or subsequently fizzled out to be replaced by the next new methodological toy. Moreover, they represent the last throes of probation officer autonomy as the Service moved to a position of greater accountability. That process, as the next chapter argues, brought many of the conflicts characteristic of practice through its history to a head.

Notes

[1] The practice of draining large amounts of blood from the body to relieve 'overexcited tissues'.

[2] Interestingly, this is close to the 'unfettered discretionary control' alluded to in the Cullen v Rodgers judgement relating to practice in Day Centres some years later.

[3] In a contribution to *Probation Journal*, a probation officer questioned the medical model and put forward the work of Gibbons in California in which the researchers developed 15 criminogenic types and matched them to treatment, as an exemplar for UK practitioners. Coates, L. V. (1974) 'Reflections on a Differential Treatment Plan', *Probation Journal*, 21, 1, 11-15.

[4] Hunt quotes a letter from an 18 year old in Borstal in which he admits that he needed a 'good hiding' and that Borstal was 'just as good as one' (246).

[5] The idea had a particular influence on induction groups.

[6] It is difficult to find specific examples of the application of pure system theory to practice although it had a generalized influence on practice strategies such as the use of contracts.

[7] See Raynor and Vanstone (2002) for a summary of the paradigm, and Raynor and Vanstone (1994a) for a revised paradigm.

[8] These approaches were influenced by the work of Waldren-Skinner, S. (1979).

[9] For instance in the South Wales and South West regional training area a support group for practitioners ran for several years.

[10] See Hudson 1988 for a theoretical explanation for this phenomenon.

[11] For an example described by a social work practitioner see Hudson, B. L. (1976) 'The haunted bedroom – a case study in behaviour modification', *Social Work* Today, 8, 10, 14-5. For the linking of the theory to social work see Jehu, D. (1967) *Learning Theory and Social Work*. London: Routledge and Kegan Paul.

[12] For a pragmatic argument for short-term work see Clulow, C. (1974) 'Time: a Solution for the Piecemeal Operative?', *Probation Journal*, 21, 2, 50-56.

[13] See J. Hill, S. Thomas and M. Vanstone (1993), *Opening doors with offenders: groupwork in a probation day centre,* in A. Brown and B. Caddick, *Groupwork Practice in Probation,* Whiting and Birch for an example of its application in groups.

[14] The theory is drawn from, among others the work of Berne.

Chapter 7

The Rise to Dominance of Evidence-Based Practice

For three-quarters of its 20th century history, practice steered probation service policy. However, during the final quarter (characterized as it was by an overt political agenda) there was a fundamental readjustment that resulted in practice being driven by increasingly centralized policy. As this history has shown, political agendas of one kind and another have been ever present on the stage. The political forces of the late 19th century which shaped the early structure of probation were motivated by concerns about moral degeneracy and dangerousness but also faith in the efficacy of officers; whereas those of the late 20th century were motivated by similar concerns expressed in terms of risk and public protection but scepticism about that efficacy. That scepticism was the fuel of a process of centralization enacted alongside age old, familiar conflicts such as the psychology of the individual versus the environment, help versus control, and treatment versus practical help. That process took place within a harsher political climate, and as this chapter shows involved mixed fortunes for advocates of officer autonomy, anti-discriminatory practice, the addressing of socio-economic problems and evidence-based programmes. During the final phase of autonomy, the end of which began with the Statement of National Objectives and Priorities (SNOP) (Home Office 1984), an eclectic range of practices flourished. With hindsight the period covered in this chapter can be judged to be one in which important work with people suffering disproportionately from social and penal policies was eclipsed by the emerging concern with the efficacy of probation effort. This is not to suggest that such concern was unnecessary but rather to question the wisdom of the policies designed to pursue that concern. *What Works* (as the development of evidence-based practice has been termed) encompasses a considerable body of work, and is too big a subject to do justice to in the final part of this history.[1] It is not my intention, therefore, in these final chapters to give a full account but rather to pick out those features of current thinking and current controversies which demonstrate a continuity of themes from the past rather than the clean break that it sometimes assumed to be.

Sub-plots?

> I wonder how it is that folk undoubtedly good think that poor humanity can be warmed, feed (sic), and comforted with tracts, or be saved with goody stories.[2]

Thus warned Thomas Holmes in 1901 when placing emphasis on the material problems of those under his supervision. Some eighty years later, Walker and Beaumont (1981) expressing concern about the neglect of the poverty of probation clients, described the practice of probation officers as 'patching up work' bearing 'little resemblance to the careful, planned activity of the official accounts', and being more akin to 'a series of rushed and superficial routine meetings' (29). So, there we have it: all the writings of probation officers and their associates amount to mere rhetoric, a collective delusion sustained for a century. The truth is more complicated. Walker and Beaumont seem to base their assertions about the reality of probation practice primarily on an unpublished survey by one probation service and one paper in *Social Work Today* by Geoffrey Parkinson. The latter was a London probation officer who in 1970 said that he gave his clients money but who four years earlier was writing about psychological systems in which clients found themselves (Parkinson 1966). These reservations aside, they draw attention to the sub-text of probation practice discourse this chapter attempts to explore; first, by examining some research findings on what probation officers do, and second, by describing examples of practice focused on the socio-economic problems of probationers.

Davies (1974) seems to confirm the relative superficiality of probation supervision claimed by Walker and Beaumont. Based on the file records of 507 young male probationers, his study describes work undertaken in their social environment (by which he means in their homes) with girl friends, wives and peers, and focused on employment, material needs, health and leisure. The findings on home visits are based on a sub-sample of 176 cases split into two groups, one with the fewest environmental problems and the other with the most. The most common activity by officers in the visits is information seeking (72 and 79 percent respectively), followed by advice giving (30 and 48 percent), assessment (27 and 42 percent), and applying intensive treatment (8 and 11 percent). In approximately a quarter of both groups (22 and 25 percent respectively), home visiting was regular, and the work undertaken in those groups fell into three categories – supportive-interpretative, controlling and nominal role only. Those that fell into the first category, what Davies terms 'a "classic" casework or therapeutic approach' had an emphasis on providing insight and 'therapeutic interpretation of the parents' roles vis-à-vis the probationer' (14).[3]

In truth, there *was* work of a more in-depth kind but Davies' general conclusion about the content of home visits was that it consisted mainly of superficial and information orientated verbal exchange with little focus on practical or material help. The story is largely the same in the other areas: for example, in 88 and 90 percent of the cases respectively, involvement in the working environment and intervention in the material needs of probationers was little or non-existent. In addition, Davies judges that where there was intervention there was little discernable impact on offending. The practice surveyed was that of the mid 1960s, the era of casework, so it confirms perhaps that the psychology of the individual remained the subject of officers' interest in the minority of cases involving work of some significance (the very same element of probation practice subjected to criticism in Bottom and McWilliams' *Non-Treatment Paradigm*).

Willis (1980, 1983) tells a different story. He positions his research within the discourse about ineffectiveness of probation and low probation officer confidence in the probation order: as he puts it, officers have 'come to question the treatment or reformative ethic on which probation orders are founded' (1980: 7).[4] The research is based on a survey of the first six weeks supervision of thirty male probationers. The researcher sat in on two early interviews in each case and interviewed the probationer and the officer separately to gain a perception of their respective views of the transactions. He concluded that the probationers and the officers largely agreed about the main problems and described them in practical terms: '[c]onsistently, then, and from a variety of angles, officers and clients describe and endorse a help model of probation' (260). In effect, Willis argues that they were already operating the *Non-Treatment Paradigm*. The detail of his findings throws some interesting light on the nature of officer/client transactions.

It seems that officers and probationers were not concerned about the reasons for offending or preventing future offending; nor was there much emphasis on formal conditions: 'probation officers were largely unwilling to have clients come face to face with the social control or formal aspects of supervision' (267). Willis speculates that this might relate to a fear of jeopardizing casework. When offending was addressed, it seemed to be about re-assurance. Only five cases focused on the offence but even then, it appeared to be a process of finding an excuse rather than challenging it. The following provides some insight into how:

> P.O.   So, how come you've had all this lot of offences in a relatively short space of time?
> Cl.   Ever since I've had that car. ..Since I've had a car I've been in trouble [...] But, it's a good job, that's what I need. Everybody wants a good job don't they? [...] If I can take home about £50 a week then I'm in God's pocket. But you can't...not where I live.
> P.O.   So, your offences started, you reckon, when you became unemployed [...] Well, that's something we can try and do a bit about, isn't it. Let's see now. What's open to us? Let's see what we can do very easily [...] I don't think you're trying [...] Another condition of the order is that you try and get a job [...] You've got to try (51).

In contrast to the earlier findings of Davies, Willis found plenty of evidence of concern with practical help. For example, where the probationer was unemployed 75 percent had an emphasis on finding a job. Willis judges this a 'collaborative rather than a competitive view of probation' (274). Apart from its challenge to the *Non-Treatment Paradigm*, Willis' research suggests that some officers were intervening in the environment of probationers and were at least part of the way into the socialist model proposed by Walker and Beaumont.

Another survey of practice only a few years later reveals evidence of officers beginning to pay more attention to offending. Using a sample of 62 officers from five probation areas and covering the period 1987 to 1988, Boswell and her colleagues (1993) found that the most frequent purpose of intervention was the prevention of offending. What is more, top of the list of ideas and skills drawn on by officers was casework skills followed closely by those of groupwork. However, it is a form of casework somewhat wider than the psychodynamic model of the past, and encompassing enabling, befriending, respect and care for people and self-determination. As one officer put it, 'Most of the time, it's talking about normal things in their lives with your antennae up like a Dalek'. It suggests therefore, that despite a succession of obituaries, casework premised on help continued to be viewed by some officers as 'their most fundamental tool of intervention with their clients' (148).

Mair and May (1997) provide more detail about the nature of this casework. Covering the same period, interviews with 1,213 probationers show that 94 percent of them agreed the content of a supervision plan, and that officers '[were] focusing on the problems associated with offending' (36). Probationers report those interviews lasted from approximately a half an hour to a maximum of two hours (42 percent approximately a half an hour; 38 percent 30 minutes to an hour; and 8 percent one to two hours). Confirmation of the concentration on the offence comes from the topics covered in the last supervision session as itemised by probationers. They are, why the offence was committed 63 percent; employment and personal problems 56 percent; money and debts 54 percent; problems with families 53 percent; using spare time to keep out of trouble 53 percent; problems relating to where probationer lives 52 percent; how offences affect other people 42 percent; drugs 32 percent; alcohol 40 percent; and health 35 percent.

Although the concentration on the offence suggests a change in practice, in other respects the concerns of probation officers in the latter part of the 20th century have a familiar ring to them, and they suggest that probation officers continue to involve themselves in the daily problems of probationers whether or not it is called treatment. It therefore brings into question whether Walker and Beaumont's target was a reality or merely their construction. For them, 'the whole edifice of probation rests on these unsound foundations' (37), namely that care and control are compatible, that probation is in the interests of society, and that a consensus view of society predominates. To them crime is a social construct. That each of the foundations is open to question is clear but so is their generalist assertion about crime. Victims find no place in the book's index, and the impact of crime on others seems not to be their emphasis. Probation, they argue, is important not because of its practice but because it helps the penal system maintain a liberal appearance, it upholds the moral view that work and good behaviour serve the interests of society. New developments in practice merely continue the theme of treatment and are irrelevant to working class life; moreover, they involve intensive treatment, more control, stronger messages about conformity and diversion from prison. This kind of mainstream incorporation applies, in their view, to radical critiques as well, for even Bill Jordan 'ignores structural and political problems in his prescriptions' (106). They define six areas of probation practice as essential to the socialist approach: first, defensive work entailing diversion from custody, minimal breach and delaying fuel disconnections; second, helping on a practical (benefits and welfare rights) and emotional level (non-oppressive therapy); third, educational work, for example on literacy; fourth, developing useful services such as bed-sits, social clubs and bus services; fifth, community involvement to include discussion at a local level about concerns about crime; and finally, campaigning through the union and other pressure groups.

The logic of their position sits uncomfortably alongside the reality of the probation officer's role.[5] The probation service hardly seems to be an appropriate or strategically efficacious realm of revolution, and Walker and Beaumont were denied the benefit of the left realist adjustment (Young and Matthews 1992). The value of their contribution lies not in its critical theory, which is rather flawed but in the degree to which it highlights the importance of probation work on the contextual problems of probationers' lives. The practice they suggest seems little different to that discernible in work designed to influence the systems within which probationers live their lives. A full account of that is not attempted here; instead, some illustrative examples are described.

Many commentators have exposed the nature of discrimination against black women and men in the criminal justice system (Agozino 1997; Chesney-Lind 1997; Chiqwada-Bailey 1997; Denney 1992; Denney and Carrington 1981, 1984; Whitehouse, 1983; Willis, 1983), and some Services have initiated strategies to counter it.[6] One of the earliest efforts to highlight the implications of race for casework has not aged well (Walcott 1968):

> The poorer and less educated West Indian tends to see the probation officer or social worker whoever he may be, as an extension of the government – the all powerful. Their marital problems are often best handled in a fatherly but authoritative way. Clients think you have power and authority and many will accept a firm word and return to their marriage determined to make it work. Casework in depth with many of these clients is likely to be inappropriate (47).

Nevertheless, it represents a constructive attempt to address the issue of difference and enhance understanding of the needs of a minority group. By the 1980s greater understanding had led to the development of both policy and strategy;[7] for example the Handsworth Alternative Scheme, a probation linked project described by Denney (1992) which specifically liaised with training and employment projects run by black people. Also, in Bristol following the disturbances in St. Pauls the team adopted a 'community-based and detached' approach that involved 'the vast majority of the work being undertaken on the streets, in cafes and in pursuit of recreational activities' (Lawson 1984: 93).

Other policy developments at this time focused on the needs of other disadvantaged groups (Raynor and Vanstone 2002). Thus, the employment and training needs of women (Nottinghamshire Probation Service 1993); the welfare rights needs of the poor (Ward 1977; Broadbent 1989; Northumbria Probation Service 1994); and the accommodation needs of young people (Drakeford and Vanstone 1996) were given specific attention by some probation areas.[8]

A focus on the practical problems of offenders has always been a part of the work of probation officers: Willis' findings reveal practice redolent of the work of the missionaries and very first probation officers. What have been less prevalent are attempts to influence the systems surrounding the individual and to see them as appropriate targets of change.[9] It is that which distinguishes the examples referred to in this chapter, and they remain an important part of probation history outside of the mainstream of probation activity. However, it is apparent from a reading of the late 20th century history of probation that even these relatively rare attempts at such influence were pushed further to the margins of probation activity by the growing influence of groupwork programmes of one kind or another.

The Power of Groups

Chapter 5 described the beginning of a therapeutic use of groups in the 1940s and how this increased through the 1950s and 1960s. From the early 1970s this approach to working with probationers gained momentum, and included groups for parents (Stanley and McCarthy 1965); young people (Adams and Howlett 1972; Dobson 1975); young adult prisoners (Coker and Sands 1970); and adult probationers (Shaw and Crook 1977).[10] Whether officers were committed to groupwork and what kind of groupwork they should be implementing was the subject of debate at this time (Flegg 1972; Jones 1967; Palmer 1966; Parsloe 1972) but nevertheless by the mid 1970s a growing number of CQSW courses within which probation officers were trained, included some theoretical input on working with groups (Brown et al. 1982). By the end of that decade Brown (an influential figure in the groupwork scene in the South West and South Wales, if not nationally at that time) produced his short and accessible guide to such work (Brown 1979), and work with groups sustained by the enthusiasm of officers was a common feature of probation practice. The Berkeley Sex Offenders group provides an interesting example (Weaver and Fox 1984). Run by two officers for non-violent sex offenders who attended voluntarily, and supported by a consultant psychiatrist it focused on the daily problems encountered by the men; sex education; strategies for avoiding offending; and the use of techniques such as identification of goals and the setting of tasks. It is distinguished by the officer's commitment to evaluation over a ten year period which included a monitoring of reconvictions and self-reported change.

One officer, not involved with sex offenders but who began thinking about working with groups shortly after he qualified at the end of the 1960s, initially learned about groups through observation and his own reading rather than formal training. He described how he was stimulated into putting his thoughts into action:

> The final trigger as it were was going on [...] the old continuation courses that we used to run and Alan Brown who was a lecturer on the course in Bristol – on a probation course in Bristol – he was talking about groupwork and I said I had been thinking about groupwork and we went over a model with Alan. And I was going back later on and Alan was going to act as a consultant and also in that year Harvey Jones who was a psychotherapist who was working in all sorts of ways including groups was coming in to the probation service – quite a good innovation actually – and meeting with a

group of people to discuss their work and acting as a consultant and we would meet with him once a month. So I used Harvey and Alan as consultants for setting up a group.

Although he recalled some theoretical input relating to the work of Bion on a course he subsequently attended, his greater motivation was to do with what he saw as the artificiality of the one-to-one relationship and the potential of the group as a means of social change:

> The real thing that pushed me into groupwork and really thinking about it was it felt that just dealing with people one to one felt unreal and to try and sort of expand into reality. And besides organising things for people to go out and actually hit, you know, the society out there they have to hit, I thought well if I get a group of clients together that's more like reality. I actually thought of working with clients and non-clients as well and that's more like reality and people can actually interact um and that was my real motivation. As far as models was concerned, um I...as far as a theoretical model was concerned I didn't actually pick up a theoretical model but like this notion that I had a lot of clients who were very talkative and quite bright, said a lot of things and didn't really keep to them; and I thought, well if I keep reflecting things back at them they are not going to take it up from me. I had another group of clients which I found out had enormous potential but were almost monosyllabic. But there were other elements that made me think they were actually pretty bright. They just didn't want to communicate. I thought that if I put them together it bright draw out the ones to communicate and they in turn seemed by in large perhaps a bit more sensible to some of the others with the way that they sometimes put me in my place.

His description of how he approached the group exemplifies its experimental nature but also quite graphically how uncertain and anxiety-provoking it was for him as a relatively new probation officer, and moreover, how he grappled with aspects of theory:

> I would look at the model – the Bion model – looking and thinking what is going to happen. Will there be pairing? Will they try and solve this through just two people or a little group of people? Will they take flight and what's going to happen? My biggest fear, my biggest anxiety about it all was to have a group of people there not saying anything and what would I do and I was shit scared of that. There was that and the other bit was confidentiality and I thought 'oh that's linked, they are not going to want to say much in front of these other buggers' – and going back [to the]1970s very early 1970s we are talking about 1971 – and the topic which I had, to throw in the middle because it had all sorts of ramifications about authority, about attitudes to authority was football games and football hooliganism which was still top of the pile then as it's not top of the pile now. So I thought I had that one in reserve and I needn't have bothered. The confidentiality bit – they went, they all introduced themselves. I had to support them, you know, just create space so that everybody can have a go. They actually poured stuff out – incredible – forget confidentiality and the whole thing worked. It

actually worked – the objectives of helping people become more articulate and say what they wanted. Other people who were articulate became more realistic actually at the end of the day. You could see it working in front of you and I was taking this back to Harvey and saying what was happening and it took a total of ten meetings. I don't know why I said ten. I think it was probably too many actually and I thought I had too many in the group to start with. It went down until there was only two or three, and I was thinking, 'Oh God this is awful.' I was thinking of packing up and they actually persuaded me to keep the group going and they all came back – yeah the clients were supporting me to keep it going and the others. They said 'oh they will come back...good weather' they said, 'they will come back, don't worry. You will be all right keep it going, go on don't fall down now'.

As the final extracts show, the group discussion went beyond the superficial:

One of the agenda things that came out, I mean, as parents parenting and it was a really big thing for them about family life and the effect of family life and also then the expansion on that of community life. Quite a few of them come from outside, which is pretty common. They come from various places and even from away in different parts of the Country; and one of the things was to compare the benefits as individuals of living in a big town and the drawbacks in a small community because the people [from] a big community [...] thought small communities would be supportive. There was this myth you know that they would know more people and everything would be better and it wasn't like that. They found themselves ostracised, they were labelled, they were labelled as delinquents and they took flight into anonymity. The people in the town were looking for something else and looking for something in community and then again a community where you fitted in. If you can do something you can get some support from it but at the same time you weren't being labelled or stereotyped [...] The other one was growing up and how to actually stop offending and they set the agenda in the first meeting. That one about how to stop crime was the thing that really threw it all in, you know, right in the centre right from the start. And that was going to be my agenda as it were. I told them why I wanted them to come together [...] Part of the agenda for me was to look at that but they put it right at the top of the agenda because it was causing them the problems. But they did want to look at the underlined things and the family was the biggest one of the lot and relationships with the opposite sex [...].

Once they got in a group there was none of that and they all actually acknowledged, recognized and thought they were stupid and it was harming their lives and they wanted to improve their lives and that helped my individual case work particularly when I went in the prison [...] We worked on the discomfort, how comfortable it was to be an offender [...] One of the big things was losing relationships [...] and they just became honest with each other and dwelt on the discomfort. So my biggest thing then was to help them look at how they could overcome that discomfort; in other words how they could stop offending and the various factors that came into it.

Interesting though this account and the other examples of officers' initiatives in this area of work are they do not account for the rise in dominance of groupwork. It is more appropriately attributed to the history of day centres, the work of Priestley and McGuire, induction groups (Brown and Seymour 1984), and the development of cognitive-behavioural programmes which culminated in the *Effective Practice Initiative*.

In the Day Training Centre experiment (which spawned the use of day centres in probation) the freedom from the demands of traditional work allowed for experimentation in method and intensive work with heavily convicted people. For example, the London Centre's aims were:

> to provide, in a non-custodial setting, the opportunity for offenders who appear frequently before the courts, and who show difficulty in coping with the complexities and demands of modern life, to examine their behaviour in the community and to become aware of its effects on others. To help such offenders learn how to satisfy their needs in ways that will not bring them into such continued conflict with the law, thus providing a greater protection for society through their rehabilitation (Inner London Probation Service, 1972).

Although it has been argued the centres can 'be seen as positively assisting the transition of the ideology of rehabilitation from the closed institution to the semi-institution' (Vanstone 1993), their most enduring influence has been to entrench groupwork in official policy. However, the impact of this influence was strengthened by the popularity among officers of the approaches to groupwork promulgated by Priestley and McGuire, first Social Skills and Personal Problem Solving, and second, offending behaviour (Priestley et al. 1978; McGuire and Priestley 1985). Their contribution has not been viewed entirely in a positive light. For instance, Senior (1991) argues that it led to a focus on task rather than process so that 'the groupworker had to have a stock of exercises on the shelf, get them down and do them' (p. 287). However, their short courses stimulated officers to set up groups focused on problems such as unemployment, alcohol and drug dependence and rights. One officer went on one of the early regional training courses in 1980. She described the structure and what she recalled about the theoretical content:

> The original one was a week. I think we had two planning days beforehand because – that's right – they wanted us to see if we could do some work in between. So we had a planning day in Bristol when they basically explained what we were hoping to do and give us the opportunity to give some input into the programme as well. So they were sort of teaching by example in that sense, if you like, in terms of getting us to own what was in it, which appealed as well. The second course I did about two or three years later and that was in two parts and that was three days and then there was a break whilst we went away and actually we spent the first three days planning the

programme that we were going to run and then going off and doing it and then coming back and feeding back about how it had gone or not gone.

The principle of voluntarism, equality, getting the client to identify the problem not sort of saying this is what it is, what are you going to do about it, which certainly appealed to me and made a lot of sense. The client owning what they wanted to work on and doing it at their pace; and then having established [and] assessed what the issue was then setting our own objectives and then working through it. I mean my other abiding memory of the first course was just rip it off which also appealed – if it works, you know. Fine what might work for one may not work for another, so in terms of method suck it and see almost is the thing and that I thought was great. I mean it freed me and I thought well you can be fairly imaginative about this and I think for a lot of the clients that used bits of the social skills programme particularly the job search it was good for them as well and they would actually come in and say, 'oh this is good, how about doing this' which meant that they really did have quite a big stake in it. They did own what was happening rather than it being something that was imposed upon them. So that's the most important thing – the voluntarism and the sort of feeling that they actually owned what was happening. I can't remember what else now. I seemed to remember at the time that they were saying that there wasn't just one sort of philosophical or theoretical base to it, that they had taken in sort of thinking about what was needed. They had taken bits from everywhere. I mean there was some cognitive behavioural therapy type bits and there was this bit and that bit from – I can't remember what all the sources were now but.

The officer described how she set up a six week, one session a week job search group after a period in which she did a lot of individual work in helping male probationers with such things as form-filling and using the telephone:

They were called 'want to work groups', which makes me cringe now but it seemed again it was to do with the era you know in the early 1980s that seemed a quite acceptable sort of catchy title. I ran job search programmes in the office for the whole of the office, I mean anyone could refer anyone for about 2 years, I suppose, in 81/82.

It was basically following the sort of process of assessment and objectives. So, the first couple of weeks there were lots of…I mean the first week was the sort of fun week really because usually it varied. I think if I remember rightly the maximum I ever had was 8 because most of the time I was working on my own and occasionally with a colleague but normally I was on my own. So the first week was all sorts of warm up games and people just feeling more comfortable about being in a group of people and scene setting. Perhaps just getting people to pair up and talk to one another about their experiences of looking for work and jobs that they had had or what they liked to do in sort of a fantasy thing – you know – what if, type things; and then moving on from that getting them to do some sort of paper and pencil exercise about what sort of job they would like, what they felt they were good at.

Those were the experiences that they had in a very sort of rough and ready way and then continuing that for the second week. I am just trying to remember what else. There was quite a lot about setting objectives so that sort of went on right the way through almost the whole programme really and I kept reviewing it every week as people would change; but by about half way through they certainly would have got them really to think quite long and hard about the sorts of jobs that they were going to go for and what would stop me getting this, what would make it easier for me – so that they were in a position to highlight the areas that they would want to work on and each programme was I think probably slightly different because of that.

I mean, certainly the sorts of common things that came out that they wanted to practice – writing letters and CVs almost every course. I don't think there was one course where we didn't do a lot of that. Role playing interviews, telephone calls, what to tell and the sort of problem areas – what do you tell a prospective employer about your background particularly your offending and how would you put that across in a more positive way and that sort of thing; and trying by the sort of last two weeks then to get them to be in a position perhaps to try some of the skills out so at least they ended on a positive note.

It may not have been as much as getting a job although quite a few of them actually did succeed fairly shortly afterwards in finding work but it was to do with at least practising some of the skills. So at the end when sort of feeding back and evaluating how it had been for them that they had you know all of them were sort of saying quite positive things about themselves and that they had achieved at least one thing. They did practise phoning up. I mean we had a whole battery of friendly employers in those days. How times have changed. On one course I had actually an employer, somebody from Panasonic had just started in Cardiff and they actually came in and did some mock interviews which was very helpful. It seems an awful long time ago now.

The Offending Behaviour model emanated from Priestley and McGuire's concern that insufficient attention was being paid to the offence in probation practice; moreover, it was the first attempt in the United Kingdom to respond to the critiques by Palmer (1975) and Blackburn (1980) of the 'Nothing Works' message (Vanstone 2000). Accordingly the methods promoted were supported by a wide range of empirical evidence of effectiveness, and put into action throughout the probation service (see, for example, Davies and Lister 1992; Singer 1991). Combined, the two models had a considerable influence on the future direction of evidence-based practice (Vanstone 2000).

Such a claim cannot be made for induction groups but their significance lies in how they shaped thinking about the management of probationers' needs. In Bristol, for example, Sutton (date unspecified) created a team structure in which all new probationers went into an induction group premised on the notion of 'self-location', and then (on the basis of a contract) entered into a range of other programmes focused on criminogenic need[11] such as one-to-one supervision, social skills groups, activity clubs, alcohol groups, day centres and family therapy. In a sense it was an attempt to introduce systems theory into supervision, and it was developed in various forms in other parts of the country (Millard 1989; Preston West Team 1977; Stanley 1982).

In addition groups have been used to combat the disadvantages and discrimination referred to above, for example, the Black Offender Initiative established in North London (Jenkins and Lawrence, 1992). This was a programme based on research into the needs and experiences of Black probation clients by Geoffrey Pearson and Duncan Lawrence of Goldsmiths' College, and designed to empower black clients while at the same time challenge their offending. It was pioneering in a number of ways but in particular because it was planned with the involvement of Black probation staff who were trained to run the programme. In Mid Glamorgan female officers planned and established the Miskin group for women aged 17 to 57 to counter the dominance of male oriented practice work (Jones et al.1993). Run exclusively by women for women it provided a programme within which women could focus on their own needs but it also challenged their offending. (Similar work was undertaken in Bristol by Mistry1993). The final example of groupwork used in this way involved the challenging of some of the causes of discrimination. Benstead et al. (1994) set up an all male group in order to engage with male identity and help the men make sense of how versions of masculinity contributed to both their offending behaviour and their attitudes to others.

Several of the initiatives outlined above, in their different ways can be seen to be precursors to the *Effective Practice Initiative* introduced in Home Office Circular 35/1998, and in this sense have contributed to its dominance. However, by far the single most influential factor on that initiative has been cognitive-behavioural programmes (see Antonowicz and Ross 1994; Hedderman and Sugg 1997; McGuire 1995; McGuire and Priestley 1995; Rowson and McGuire 1992; Underdown 1998; Vanstone 2000; Vennard et al. 1997). Pioneered in Canada (Ross and Fabiano 1985) and subsequently in the United Kingdom (Raynor and Vanstone 1996; Raynor and Vanstone 1997), it was supported by a considerable body of research (Andrews et al. 1990; Goldblatt and Lewis 1998; Lipsey 1995; Losel 1995; Macdonald 1993; McIvor 1990; McClaren 1992; Petersilia 1990; Trotter 1993). Criticisms of the model have focused on its neglect of social and cultural contexts (Neary 1992; Pitts 1992) and its limitations as a one track approach (Farrell 2003, 2003a). Indeed the controversy surrounding the influence of this approach should not be underestimated, and it is quite feasible that this influence will diminish under the leadership of the National Offender Management service. Nevertheless it remains true that more than anything else it has posited groupwork programmes at the centre of the probation service's efforts to reduce offending, 'and contributed significantly to increased governance of the nature and direction of Service policy and of offenders themselves' (Vanstone 2004a: 195). Robinson (2000) has elucidated the machinations of power and control in the increased governance of probation policy and practice. Undoubtedly these have shaped those in positive ways; in particular, by establishing the importance of empiricism but they are in danger of marginalising the needs of offenders. Powis and Walmsley (2000), for instance, have highlighted the continuing needs of offenders from ethnic minority groups. Work on those needs and on other issues such as poverty and unemployment (as described above) is in danger of being expunged from the lexicon of probation practice, and the challenge for future policy and practice is to integrate such work into an evidence-based approach.

Notes

[1] Readers interested in a general account of its development can do no better than McGuire (1995); and for alternative perspectives, Farrell (2003, 2003a) and Gorman (2001).

[2] From Thomas Holmes, Pictures and Problems from London Police Courts. 1900 Nelson Edition, p. 43.

[3] He defines classic casework as 'the use of relatively intensive, interpretive and therapeutic techniques' 134).

[4] While Willis is right to point to the decline in recommendations for probation, it is possible the decline might have been more to do with a policy switch to diversion from custody than such a loss of faith.

[5] For four retrospective critiques see Probation Journal (1991), 38, 3, 144-9.

[6] For example, the Black Offender Initiative set up by the Inner London Service to meet the unmet needs of black probationers (Jenkins and Lawrence 1992); and the Miskin group for women set up by the Mid Glamorgan Service (Jones et al. 1993).

[7] During the 1980s and 1990s the *Probation Journal* is dominated by the subject of anti-discrimination, and although this might reflect editorial policy more than the reality of practice it does show that the issue was an important part of the visible professional discourse of the period.

[8] The Berkshire Probation Service Offender Accommodation Strategy documents of 1990-1993 and 1993-6 show a strategic approach by management. For more detail on these various initiatives see Drakeford and Vanstone (1996).

[9] A model for future work can be seen in the Turas motoring offences project in West Belfast where an unemployment rate of 80 per cent on the local housing estates demanded that the work was undertaken within the contexts of the social consequences of government policy, and the social and cultural realities of young people's lives (Chapman 1995).

[10] For detail readers need to go to the articles themselves but for a summary see Vanstone (2003).

[11] A term not yet in the vocabulary of probation officers, however, typically, Sutton was one of the first managers to establish such need as essential to community supervision.

Chapter 8

Conclusion: Back to Where we Started

Despite these examples of initiatives driven by the determination of some local Services to deal with the structural problems faced by probationers, throughout the history of the Service such work has been the exception rather than the rule. Influencing the individual has been the main focus, and in the last fifteen years of the twentieth century this has been reinforced by central government inspired agenda of management characterized by what some have called 'managerialism' (May 1991; McWilliams 1987). From the publication of the Statement of National Objectives and Priorities (Home Office 1984) to National Standards (Home Office 1992, 1995), the *Effective Practice Initiative*, and the Carter Review (Carter 2003) the world of the practitioner has become increasingly prescribed and rule-bound. That world has become positioned in what some have contentiously described as an actuarial society (Feeley and Simon 1992). Whether that judgement is accurate or not, it is incontrovertible that at the end of the century officers perform their duties in a policy context of risk assessment, effectiveness evaluation and increased accountability. Moreover, it is a policy context of increasing uncertainty, and change is currently so rapid that it is beyond the scope of this study to elaborate the perceptions, beliefs and methodology of officers at the conclusion of the century. However, one survey undertaken in the early 1990s at least gives us a clue.

Sandham (no date) surveyed the skills and theoretical models used by 47 officers in Warwickshire. Officers reported the use of a number of theoretical models. They were, cognitive behavioural 62 percent; task centred 62 percent; crisis intervention 53 percent; counselling 51 percent; social skills training 30 percent; family work/therapy 17 percent; psychodynamic social work 17 percent; feminist social work 15 percent; systemic social work 13 percent; community social work 9 percent; transactional analysis 4 percent; and radical Marxist social work 0 percent. So, as Sandham reports, '[w]hilst over half of all staff were regularly using all of the first four approaches, frequency declines very rapidly thereafter with 29 percent of staff regularly using social skills training, 17 percent using psycho-dynamic social work and none regularly using Radical/Marxist social work' (5). Referring to the *What Works* research findings, he concludes that these 'results seem encouraging for both staff and management' (5). In addition he surveyed the focus of work, and officers reported regular work in the following proportions: acohol misuse 72 percent; dangerousness 72 percent; accommodation 68 percent; drug misuse 68 percent; anger 66 percent; violent offending 66 percent; victim awareness 62 percent; property offending 60 percent; debt 57 percent; employment 57 percent; family relationship problems 49 percent; lack of social skills 47 percent; marital/relationship problems 40 percent; child welfare issues 36 percent; sex offending 26 percent; self harm 23 percent; mental disorder 21 percent; literacy 11 percent; reparation 6 percent; disability and illness 4 percent; and victim support 4 percent; (p. 8). This is reproduced in full because as a litany of work (with some exceptions such as victim support) it would not look out of place in Gamon's study at the beginning of the 19th century. Moreover, several studies (for example, Hil 1986; Pritchard et al. 1994; Willis 1986) have shown that probationers value tangible help with the pressing problems of daily survival, and Sandham's survey (like those of Mair, May, and Willis referred to earlier) suggests that officers respond particularly to those they believe to be linked to offending. Perhaps this was also true of their early 20th century counterparts. However, even if we are back to where we started as far as the subject matter of supervision and the focus on influencing individuals who value tangible help is concerned, the practice described in the previous chapter alone suggests that the theory and methods of many modern officers is more diverse than that of their forbears. So what are the implications of this for the probation service in the 21st century?

This book has described a history of rhetoric and discourse about a variety of attempts by practitioners to resolve similar and recurrent problems. As indicated in the introduction, inevitably it is a history of what they say they did rather than what they actually did. Can, therefore, a close connection between what people say and do be assumed? To the extent that the data on which the book is based has been drawn from a variety of sources, it can be argued perhaps that the closest approximation to the actual practice of probation officers possible in a retrospective analysis has been reached. Indeed, the various accounts appear to have produced a realistic picture revealing as they do practice on a continuum from the mundane and routine to theoretically informed practice of some sophistication. However, as in all research, it is important to retain a healthy scepticism, and as the words of one officer in a letter to me about work in the 1960s suggest, the capacity of each individual practitioner to subvert the expectations of the organization within which they work should not be underestimated:

> One has to work in the times one lives in and under the rules of the day or, at least, to appear to do so in order to obtain credibility. The conforming may, however, be modified on a day-to-day basis. This was especially so regarding the conventional approach to probation of the time. This was the age of seeking to understand the client's history and developing a 'therapeutic' response. It was this kind of approach that we had in training – to diagnose the problem (deep seated) and which we were meant to unravel. All this was to be encapsulated in the client records.
>
> This approach was in the style of psychoanalysis which, as I noted earlier, critically (sic) received by students at Rainer House and this was even more obvious in practice – 'I haven't time to practise 'casework' was the cry. Records, however, were often couched in the terms 'required' and I was a past-master at the inclusion of anything that seemed to satisfy those who read such things [...] I was quite happy to evoke Oedipus, sibling rivalry or grandparent indulging as I was to go to court in a suit! Father-son conflicts as a source of criminality features regularly but what I was really interested in was the future – what was the client going to do about their problems and their criminality and how could I help? Ho what a tangled web we weave!

Amidst the cynicism, however, there is evidence that the work of probation officers may well be more scientifically informed. Perhaps now we can endorse unequivocally McWilliams' theory that the social diagnosticians have prevailed. That said, the cognitive-behavioural specialists on the new Pathfinder projects retain a commonality with Nelson and Batchelor; the success of their work *does* depend on the principles underpinning effective practice but it depends also on the ability to engage the individual in a relationship founded on concreteness, empathy and commitment. Inherent in the sceptical voice of the final contributor to this history is an implicit message about the importance of that relationship. As he puts it, 'I think one of the most important things is having a point of contact which embodies stability and interest in them'. Does this, then, encapsulate the core of probation, and if so, has anything else changed? This history provides an affirmative answer to both these questions but what else have we learned?

Although the concept of probation developed as a result of reformist concerns about the impact of a harsh criminal justice system on the poor, it was moulded by political elites who were concerned about maintaining social order (Vanstone 2004). Constantly through its history it has been the focus of sometimes opposing humanitarian, scientific,[1] social and political pressures, and in the sense that it has fulfilled a State function of controlling offenders it has been bound up inextricably with governance and the application of power. Moreover, it has taken place against a backdrop of a process of professionalization, and what the rhetoric of practitioners through their stories has confirmed is that the drive for professionalism has been as potent a force as any other motivation. Each of these elements has interrelated in a complex and not always easily understood way; and at different moments in the history of probation each will have been the more dominant force. There is a danger, therefore, that a relatively short concluding discussion will imply a coherent and accessible structure to their relationship. Hopefully when set against the detail of the history that danger will be averted.

In addition, the history has demonstrated that probation practice from its early missionary to its legislative role has survived largely because of faith: faith that it was justified morally, helpful, welcomed by its recipients and effective in reducing offending. From the confidence inherent in Frederic Rainer's letter to the endorsement of the Morison Committee (1962) it has apparently existed in a benign political and social climate as a humanizing element of the process of dispensing justice. However, the missionaries, and later, probation officers were not always welcomed in the courts; their continued presence has been the result of a continuous process of negotiating a role that might be perceived as useful. It has undergone a number of transformations: from helping the courts separate the deserving from the undeserving through moral exhortations to pseudo-scientific assessment of those who could appropriately be helped in the community and those who could not; and from distinguishing between those who might be helped to stop offending (and those who were too intransigent) to separating the low risk from the high risk. Those changes have been made the Service vulnerable to diverse influences, including Christianity, eugenics, mental hygiene and psychoanalysis. For instance, chapter three argued that both the missionaries and the first probation officers were conduits for the concerns of powerful elites about the threat posed to social order by the degenerate poor. Moreover, it has been characterised by a quest by some for the cloak of respectability bestowed by science, and latterly also by anti-oppressive practice; while at the same time some have persevered with what might be seen as commonsense, practical help, and a small core have endeavoured to change the environment of those they supervised. Not until the last quarter of the 20th century was the efficacy of all this effort tested empirically.

Ironically, perhaps, that empiricism served to revive the core polemics of probation philosophy: care versus control, treatment versus collaborative change effort, and individualism versus radicalism (Vanstone 2004). *What Works* has been embroiled in conflicts always inherent in the probation project; it has been welcomed by some as an important step towards a professional knowledge base that can inform effective help but criticised by others as a revival of treatment. As argued at the beginning of this chapter, what the broad survey of practice rhetoric has shown, however, is that the most consistent factor amidst the conflict and change has been a focus on the individual as the main target of influence. The primary subject of both probation practice and discourse has been the individual offender; and that individual offender has been the object of help conditional upon submission to official authority and control. Probation at the beginning of the 21st century remains as entwined in political and societal concerns about social order as it was when Hill promoted the use of recognizance for juvenile offenders, and perhaps this is why politicians have put so much effort into changing probation rather than into changing prisons, or fines, or judges – it has had to be brought into line. Furthermore, we have seen that it has been subject to a gendered construction of what that social order should be like. Offending women, like their male counterparts, have been viewed as abnormal but their abnormality has been defined in terms of the roles and expectations of women in society generally (Heidensohn 1987; Worrall 1990). The modern female offender may indeed be viewed no differently from the inebriate women confined in institutions at the beginning of the 20th century. Moreover, probation has been tailored mainly to the needs of the majority male group (Rumgay 1996), and the shift to high risk groups has exacerbated the difficulty of providing an effective service for women, a fact emphasized by the exceptional nature, for instance, of the Miskin model referred to in chapter seven.

Perhaps the single most powerful stimulator of the changes referred to above has been the drive for professional status. This history has unearthed evidence of this from the writings of people from within the Service and those close to it even before probation was placed on the statute book; and much of it influenced considerably by American practice. It has been interesting to find that that drive has been characterized largely by a preference for non-verifiable theory, from psychoanalysis to neuro-linguistic programming. An explanation for this might be that the non-verifiable nature of such theories has provided protection for an organization with only a tenuous hold on professional status; itself a reason perhaps for a further feature of probation, namely its lack of self-confidence. For however confident the individual contributions of the many contributions surveyed in this work have been, the Service as a whole has always lived its life in the shadow of the other professions within the criminal justice system.

Mathieson (1975) proposed that in the 1970s there were three schools of thought, 'the traditional punitively-motivated, the psychoanalytical/treatment, and the sociological/political' (p. 38). Some ten years later, both Senior (1984) and Raynor (1985) argued that in the 1980s and 1990s there were six models of probation practice, namely rehabilitation, surveillance (or control), sentenced to social work, separatist, personalist (or non-treatment) and socialist (or radical). This history has exposed an even wider range of models employed in the practise of community supervision, and perhaps provided a rationale for the Service to examine critically its thinking about what rehabilitation actually means.[2]

The whole project began with a Christian model premised on the notion that offenders could be changed by homilies and exhortation, and combined with the rehabilitative model it straddled the first half century of the Service's life. Only late in the 20th century did Service personnel begin to devote their attention to the disproportionate impact of the criminal justice system upon particular groups such as Black men and women (and women generally) and the systems impinging on offenders' lives. Even then those issues remained relatively marginal to Service concerns, and what has been termed *new rehabilitation* has had a more tangible impact on the traditional approach to community supervision. In the age of the community rehabilitation order the effective improvement of the problem-solving skills of individual offenders in order to reduce the risk that they pose to others in the community is now the dominant objective of practice, but that still leaves room for a focus on the wider context of people's offending.

There are reasons to be both hopeful and pessimistic for the future. Some ninety years ago Thomas Holmes declared confidently that probation officers knew as much about crime, its causes and treatment as any of the scientists; and he did so relatively safe from contradiction. In the light of the first intimations of a commitment to evidence-based practice and the imminent absorption into the National Offender Management Service (with prisons), the current challenge for the Service is that it can begin to assert that kind of confidence. It needs to enter the new organization as a strong partner bringing with it a knowledge base drawn from informed practice and self-critical evaluation. Only in that way can it retain its unique identity within a partnership likely to be dominated by its prisons component. It does not have a monopoly of values of fairness and social justice but it does have an important history of providing the criminal justice system with a perspective about offenders based on those values. It must be remembered however that it has a history of involvement in social control and a susceptibility to political persuasiveness of one kind or another. Of course it cannot avoid complying with the policy directions of its political paymasters but without retaining a clear sense of its value base it may be simply enveloped in the policies and values of its larger partner. The single most positive feature of the Carter Review (2003) is its commitment to reducing the prison population and widening the contribution of community supervision; probation *might* yet be able to exploit that commitment to further the contribution of social justice to criminal justice.

Undoubtedly the Service exists in a much more challenging climate and therefore it needs at least some of Holmes' self-belief. A commitment to effectiveness in its fullest sense provides the opportunity of drawing on the strength of its experience and tradition of working with offenders in the community in order to assert itself in the new Service. It does know how to 'manage' offenders in the community *but* by offering tangible help to deal with problems associated with offending rather than unthinking control. It can choose, therefore, to build upon that knowledge through a genuine commitment to learning.

Within the new partnership it can devote itself to a positive contribution to Carter's (2003) avowed aim of reducing the prison population while at the same time demonstrating that the implementation of social justice has to be demonstrably effective in order for criminal justice to be achieved. To do this it has to promulgate a dual strategy of influencing both individuals and systems underpinned by an interest in the efficacy of that strategy; and to this end the Service can exploit its unique historical role within the criminal justice system. At this pivotal time in the Service's history there is a genuine concern that its humanitarian base may be fatally undermined. It may happen (and there are transparent reasons for such pessimism) but there is less chance of this if the Service recognizes that humanitarianism alone is not enough, and that just as it was in the formative years it is a part of the political and social world. The difference is that the current political and social world demands tangibly beneficial outcomes from the Service's work. More than anything else this means contributing to the reduction of harm to both the individual offender and the wider community caused by offending. The survival of the humanitarian aspect of supervising offenders in the community depends on it.

Notes

[1] This is not to imply that scientific action cannot be humanitarian but rather to draw a distinction between practice that was guided simply by a desire 'to do good' and practice that was informed by theory and research evidence.

[2] See appendix 5.

APPENDICES

APPENDICES

Appendix 1

The Police Court Mission Training Scheme (Taken from The Probation Handbook, Le Mesurier 1935)

This is on somewhat different lines from that of the Home Office, detailed above, as it is designed to enable candidates to attend whilst carrying on their existing occupation. It involves attendance at lectures and classes lasting about two hours on one evening a week during three terms each year, and the full diploma course covers four years. Written work in accordance with the regulations must be done weekly to the satisfaction of the lecturer, and at the end of each session the student is required to pass the usual examinations.

The scheme is conducted by the London University Extension and Tutorial Classes Council. The diploma of the University of London is awarded to successful students, and they receive in addition the Police Court Mission Diploma. The scheme is designed for persons who are not intending to graduate, and there is no need to have matriculated. It does not include provision for training in the practical side of probation work, but is designed to improve educational qualifications. The course of study includes Social Economics, Problems of Poverty, the Psychology of Criminal Tendencies, and Criminal Law and Administration.

Appendix 2

The Content of an Ideal Court Report (taken from Leeson, C. (1914) *The Probation System*, London: P.S. King and Son, Pages 72-5)

RECORD:

Court: Previous convictions: offences (times summarily arrested, times summoned): penalties (fine or gaol: if fined, did he pay, or go to gaol in default?). Previously on probation? (Give approximate dates.)
Home: Previous offences condoned? (Give their nature, and length of time ago.)

OFFENCE:

Nature and Circumstances: co-defendants (if any) with their records (the purpose of this is to show whether the present offender was made a 'tool' of by some older or more hardened criminal). If the offender be a child, was any adult, parent or other, contributory to his delinquency? If so, how did the child come to know the adult?

HABITS:

How does the offender spend his leisure? Amusements, sports, reading (member of library?), music-halls (of what type), picture-house, public-houses, coffee-houses?

Associates: Have companions appeared in court? Does offender belong to a 'gang' or a boys' or social club, or settlement? If the offender be a girl or youth, does she or he keep company with opposite sex? Do they frequent public-houses together, or other places where liquor is sold?

Tobacco, drink, drugs (if the offender is adult, has he ever received treatment for drink or drug habit?).

Gambling (horse-racing, football-coupon betting, sweepstakes, pitch-and-toss, banker, etc.).

Sex habits: masturbation, immorality, prostitution?
Will-power, easily led? (Does offender make companions of persons younger than

himself?) Self-control (hasty or even temper?).

Selfish, honest, conscientious, social, secretive, irritable, vain, affectionate, vicious, untruthful, energetic or lazy, careful or careless, untidy, disobedient, mischievous (if a child).

If offender is a child, has he ever absconded from, or been driven from, his parents' home, or slept out? (If so, give approximate dates.)

PHYSICAL AND MENTAL CONDITION:

Heredity: Epilepsy, feeble- or weak- mindedness, insanity, chronic alcoholism?
Health: General condition and appearance, particularly in relation to employment?
Physical defects: Eyes, ears, nose, throat, teeth (adenoids, enlarged tonsils, etc.).
Diseases: Skin, venereal, tuberculosis (if a child, small-pox, diphtheria, scarlet fever, mumps, measles, whooping cough?).

Temporary ailments, permanent impairments? Mental development and condition.

HOME:

Parents: Living together or separated ? If offender is a child, does he live with his parents; if not, with whom? If offender is an adult, is he married, single, separated; living with family, with whom else; or alone, or in lodging-house?

Father: Occupation, wages. Ever deserted or failed to support family? Stepfather? Father (or stepfather) ever convicted ? Has he proper control over children?

Mother: Does she go out to work? If so, are children in proper care; for how many hours daily are they without proper care? Stepmother? Mother (or stepmother) ever convicted? Has she proper control over children?

Children: Legitimate or illegitimate? Number, ages, occupations. Are they living at home, or married; or in industrial or reformatory schools, or charitable homes, or asylums? Have any of the children been convicted?

Financial Condition of Home: Money going into it: from father, mother, children, lodgers, other sources; charitable aid.

Type of Dwelling: If in a court-yard, whether closed or open to street? If a flat, what floor? Number of rooms, rent (weekly), number of persons in house; lodgers, their occupations (whether convicted thieves or prostitutes?). If offender is a child, with whom does he share his bedroom? Sanitation and general appearance of home (bearing in mind its financial condition and the type of dwelling), moral condition of home. Character of neighbourhood. How long at this address? Previous addresses (with dates).

EDUCATION:

School: standard, attendance, conduct, scholarship. Favourite studies?

EMPLOYMENT:

Trade or customary employment, occupation now followed?

Employer (with address), how long there, wages? Ever worked for this employer before ?
Previous employers, how long with each, how long unemployed between each engagement, how did he secure a livelihood during these intervals?

If offender is a child, is he, or has he been, a street-trader? Hours of work, and whether in addition to school attendance.

RELIGIOUS OR SOCIAL ORGANISATIONS:

Faith: Church or other institution attended. If not at present attending anywhere, place last attended, how long ago, why attendance ceased. Pastor or other person to whom offender is known. If offender is a child what Sunday school, name and address of teacher? Member of boys' Club or settlement? Boy scouts?

The information furnished by the preliminary inquiry should be sufficient to answer three principal questions:
(a) Do the offender's character and antecedents show him unmistakably and fixedly depraved, or do they indicate but a tendency to depravity?
(b) Does the offender, having regard to his disposition and to the surroundings in which he lives, afford reasonable promise of becoming law-abiding?
(c) If, owing to his present disposition or his present surroundings, or to other circumstances, this cannot reasonably be hoped of him, can such changes be effected through the agency of probation, as to make it reasonably probable that he will become law-abiding?

The Home Office Training Course for Probation Officers (taken from The Handbook of Probation, Le Mesurier 1935)

This scheme was started in 1930 to provide facilities by which men and women of the right personality, and anxious to become probation officers, could fit themselves for the work. Experience had shown the difficulty of filling vacancies for full-time probation officers, owing to the absence of candidates with any practical knowledge of the work. This difficulty was particularly noticeable in the case of places-and they are the majority-where there is only one full-time probation officer. The object of the scheme was two-fold-not only to give practical training in actual Court work, but also to provide facilities for further education to those candidates of suitable personality whose advantages in that respect had been limited. In the summer of each year four or five men and one or two women between the ages of 24 and 30 are selected for training. An advertisement is inserted in trading daily newspapers both in London and the Provinces, inviting applications for training. A 'short list' is prepared of likely applicants, and the candidates are chosen from this list by a small committee of selection appointed for the purpose by the Secretary of State.

Candidates are interviewed in London, but in the last two years, interviews have also been arranged in Manchester, to reduce the cost of travelling expenses, which fall on the candidates. Selected candidates who have had a university education or have already obtained a diploma in Social Science from one of the universities, receive training in practical probation work for not more than a year under the supervision of a senior probation officer. Those who have no such educational qualifications divide their period of training equally between practical probation work and the university studies prescribed for students seeking a diploma in Social Science. The latter candidates are expected to obtain the university diploma at the end of their training period, which is normally completed in two years. Up to the present candidates have been trained in London and Essex, Liverpool, Birmingham, Manchester and Sheffield, where adequate facilities exist both for practical probation training and for university education in social subjects.

Selected candidates are appointed assistant probation officers at the centre where they are trained, and give such assistance as they are able in the practical work. The senior probation officers under whom they are placed are asked to take special care to give them opportunities of gaining as much experience as possible in making reports to the Court, and in actual supervision of persons placed on probation.

As a part of a candidate's training, visits are arranged to prisons, Borstal institutions, Home Office schools of different types, remand homes, probation homes, probation hostels, boys' and girls' clubs, etc. The education facilities vary according to the university attended. In London candidates attend the courses prescribed by the London School of Economics.

Candidates receive during their training period an annual salary of £150, and the fees for any university course which they are required to take are paid for them. The cost is paid by the local authority, subject to a fifty per cent Government grant.

Upon selection, candidates are required to give an undertaking that at the end of the period of training they will accept any vacancy for a full-time probation officer which may be offered to them in any part of England or Wales.

Up to the present six selections have been made, and thirty-one candidates (twenty-five men and six women) have been accepted for training under the scheme. Seven men and five women have completed their training and received full-time appointments, one man has withdrawn, and the training of five men has been terminated because they failed to pass their examination or seemed unlikely to fit themselves for the work. The remaining thirteen candidates (twelve men and one woman) are still in training.

Appendix 4

Examples of the Curricula of the University of London Diploma Syllabus 1948 (A Summary) Supplied by a Former Officer

Criminology (Herbert Mannheim)

1. Crime: its legal, moral and social significance in primitive and modern civilizations.
2. Physical factors: anthropological and biological theories.
3. Social factors (1): crime and social order, the family, broken homes.
4. Social factors (2): Housing, delinquency areas. Town and country. Education. Crowds and gangs.
5. Social factors (3): the economic structure. Poverty, wealth and unemployment.
6. Social factors (4): problems of leisure. Alcohol, gambling, cinema, prostitution.
7. Selected aspects of previous lectures.
8. Penal philosophy and psychology.
9. Penal history and the beginnings of the present prison system.
10. Prison and prison after-care.
11. Borstals and Approved Schools.
12. Probation. Capital punishment.
13. Juvenile and adult courts.
14. Reconsideration.

Social Psychology (Dr. N. Elias - examiner, Cyril Burt)

1. The field of social psychology: the study of man, the scientific approach.
2. Some biological conditions of social and mental life.
3. Patterns of evolution.
4. Basic social experiences of children: biological maturation, social training, feeding and weaning.
5. Development of mental functions by social experience in childhood.
6. Normal mental adaption to social life: conflicts as levers of personality development. Mental maturity.

7. Types of mental and social maladjustment (1): psychoses, neuroses.
8. Types of mental and social maladjustment (2): suicide.
9. Types of mental and social maladjustment (3): delinquency.
10. Man in society (1): crowd psychology, social and environmental factors.
11. Man in society (2): Recent advances in the study of groups.
12. Man in society (3): concept of instinct, social conditioned emotions, fantasy thinking and reality thinking.
13. Early stages of social development (1): survey of social patterns.
14. Early stages of social development (2): survey of mental patterns.
15. Medieval stages of social and mental development: from tribal communities to centralized state.
16. Social and psychological problems of western society (1): characteristics of the nation state, violence, class, increased productivity.
17. Social and psychological problems of western society (2): conditions of life in a mass society.
18. The civilising process.
19. Patterns of family life.
20. Problems of social differentiation: division of labour, psychological characteristics of different social strata.
21. National consciousness and national characteristics.
22. Psychological problems of internal relations: good and bad nations.
23. Understanding people: reconstructing past situations - the essentials of a case history - the interview, methods of advice, mental guidance.
24. Understanding oneself: self awareness, mental health as a condition for helping others.

The Psychology of Delinquency (Kenneth Soddy, M. D., D. P. M)

1. The place of delinquency in the community: popular attitudes and the scientific approach to delinquency. Moral responsibility and culpability. Faulty relationships between individual and society, the result of powerful forces. The interaction of heredity, individual life experience and social forces. Delinquency and the development of the child.
2. Emotional development in early infancy.
3. Emotional development of the pre-school child.
4. Development in later adolescence and childhood.
5. Mental mechanisms: conscious and unconscious factors. Growth a continuous process of maturation and modification of instinctive forces. Inborn types, extroverted and introverted reaction patterns.
6. Delinquency related to the earliest period of infancy: interference with primary relationship formation by early separations of mother and child.
7. Aggression and delinquency: disturbances related to the era of weaning, toilet training and early essays in parental discipline.

8. Abnormality of character development: intra-family relationships and neurotic failure of conflicts, bad family influences, rebellion, neurotic 'wickedness'.
9. Problems related to later childhood: unhealthy reactions, the gang, sex differences in delinquency.
10. Problem families and the subnormal group of the population: delinquency and the lowest socio-economic level of the population. The cumulative effect of poor heredity, personal inferiority and social handicap.
11. Preventive measures: eugenic measures and attention to mental hygiene. Sociological measures, alleviation of bad conditions, vocational guidance and occupational welfare, youth clubs.
12. Remedial measures; the relevance of punishment. The law, medicine and psychology. The need for greater knowledge.

Social Structure and Social Conditions in England (B. C. Adams)

1. The growth of modern England: the industrial revolution.
2. The population: growth and changes since 1801.
3. The economic structure: import and exports, economic organisations, trade unions, industrial and political power.
4. National income and taxation.
5. Poverty: as a historical problem, attitudes and surveys, relief and social security.
6. Wages and standard of living: measurement, family budget.
7. Employment and conditions of work: unequal distribution of unemployment, remedial measures.
8. Occupations and professions: distribution of population, vocational guidance and training.
9. Health and health services.
10. Housing and Town and Country Planning.
11. The State and the child: the modern attitude to child welfare, education system.
12. The cultural background: leisure and adult education.
13. The machinery of administration: the growth of State social services.
14. The nature of society: man as a social animal, the influence of the environment on social development.
15. The sustaining forces of society: tradition, religion, order and law.

Social Philosophy (Ivor Lerclerc)

1. Introductory: the scope of social philosophy.
2. The Greek background.
3. Missing
4. Missing
5. Plato: the Laws.
6. Aristotle: Politics (1).

7. Aristotle: Politics (2).
8. Aristotle: Politics (3).
9. Transition of Medievalism.
10. St. Augustine.
11. St. Thomas Aquinas.
12. Thomas Hobbes.
13. John Locke.
14. The Utilitarians.
15. Rousseau.
16. Theory of State.
17. Democratic and Authoritarian States.
18. Individual, Societies, and Community.
19. Justice? Rights and Duties.

Appendix 5

Models of Probation Practice

Model	Characteristics	Protagonists	Examples
Redemptive/ Christian	Exhortation and pledges	Bachelor, Holmes and Nelson	
Rehabilitation	Treatment and Diagnosis	M. Monger Foren and Bailey	1950s and 1960s practice
Surveillance and Control	Conditions Discipline Containment Punishment	M. Davies W.A. Griffiths	Kent Control Unit Electronic Tagging Tracking
Sentenced to Social Work	Primary and Secondary Contracts Shop window: offers of help Control and help	M. Bryant et al	Hampshire Probation Service
Separatism	No supervision Voluntary Social Work Unconditional Help	R.Harris	None
Non-Treatment or Personalist	Client-centred Respect for persons Choices under constraint Unconditional Help	Bottoms and M.C. Williams B. Hugman	Induction Groups Day Training Centres
Radicalism or Socialism	Few conditions Voluntarism Help Structural change	Walker and Beaumont	Voluntary Day Centres Detached Probation Unit
Anti-oppressive	Focus on particular problems of black people and women	D. Denney L. Gelsthorpe P. Carlen	Black Probationers Support Unit Women offenders Outreach project

Systems Intervention (1)	Reduction of Harm Cautioning Diversion from custody Bail Information	H. Thomas D. Thorpe P. Raynor A. Rutherford	Alternatives to custody Northampton Juvenile Bureau
Systems intervention (2)	Collaboration with probationer Focus on offending within socio-economic context	Drakeford and Vanstone	Northumbrian Anti-poverty Strategy
New Rehabilitation	Help consistent with reduction of harm and relevant to criminogenic need Dialogue and Negotiation	Raynor and Vanstone Priestley and McGuire G. McIvor	STOP Offending Behaviour programmes Anger Management Pontypridd Probation experiment

NB. As stated in the main text this is developed from the work of Paul Senior and Peter Raynor

Bibliography

Adams, C. and Howlett, J. (1972) 'Working with clients in the group setting or diversionary therapy', *Probation Journal*, 18, 2, 54-6.

Addison, W. (1969) 'The probation officer's place in the penal system', *Probation*, 15, 2, 51-3.

Agozino, B. (1997) Black Women and the Criminal Justice System, Aldershot: Ashgate.

Ainley, M. (1979) *An Exploration of the Place of Post-Qualifying Training Opportunities Within Avon Probation and After-Care Service and an Evaluation of the Impact of Courses Attended upon Officers' Subsequent Work*. Personal Social Services Fellowship, Bristol University.

Alban Atkins, Right Reverend. (1941) 'Problems of moral conduct as related to current trends', *Probation*, 4, 5, 64-6.

Anderson, B. (1981) 'The intuitive response', *Probation Journal*, 28, 2, 56-8.

Anderson, B. (1985) *The Application of Neuro-Linguistic Programming to the Work of the Probation Service*. Personal Social Services Fellowship, University of Bristol.

Anderson, B. (1986) 'Using NLP to achieve change', *Probation Journal*, 33, 1, 22-3.

Andrews, D.D., Zinger, I., Hoge, R.D., Bonta, J., Gendreau, P. and Cullen, F.T. (1990) 'Does correctional treatment work? A clinically relevant and psychologically informed meta-analysis', *Criminology*, 28, 369-404.

Anonymous (1858) *Letter Concerning The Labors Of Mr. John Augustus, The Well-Known Philanthropist. From One Who Knows Him*. Boston: Published For Private Circulation.

Anonymous (1956) 'Generic training for social work', *Probation*, 8, 4, 49-51.

Antonowicz, D. and Ross, R. (1994) 'Essential components of successful rehabilitation programs for offenders', *International Journal of Offender Therapy and Comparative Criminology*, 38, 97-104.

Ashley, P.D. (1962) 'Group work in the probation setting', *Probation*, 10, 1, 6-8.

Ashley, P.D. (1965) 'The development of a mixed group', *Probation*, 11, 3, 94-9.

Augustus, J. (1852) *A Report of the Labors of John Augustus, for the Last Ten Years, in Aid of the Unfortunate: Containing a Description of his Method of Operation: Striking Incidents, and Observation upon the Improvement of some of Our City Institutions, with a View to the Benefit of the Prisoner and Society*. Boston: Wright & Hasty, Printers. Reprinted as John Augustus, First Probation Officer by the National Probation Association in 1939.

Aust, A. (1987) 'Gaining control of compulsive shop theft', *Probation Journal*, 34, 4, 145-6.

Aylwin, G.D.L. (1961) 'Personality in probation work', *Probation*, 9, 12, 178-9.

Ayscough, H.H. (1923) *When Mercy Seasons Justice. A Short History of the Works of the Church of England in the Police Courts*. The Church of England Temperance Society.

Ayscough, H.H. (1929) *The Probation of Offenders*. London: William John Hewitt.

Baker, T.L. (1988) *Doing Social Research*, New York: McGraw-Hill.

Barr, H. (1966) *A Survey of Group Work in the Probation Service*. HORS 9 London: HMSO.

Barrow, J.P. (1923) 'A forward movement: its importance and value', *National Association of Probation Officers*, 20, 447-8.

Barton Hall, M. (1934) 'Psychological causes of delinquency', *Probation*, 1, 21, 308-30.

Bartrip, P.W.J. (1975) *The career of Matthew Davenport Hill with special reference to his place in penal and educational reform movements in Mid-Nineteenth Century England.* Phd Thesis, University of Wales, Cardiff.

Bean, P. (1976) *Rehabilitation and Deviance.* London: Routledge and Kegan Paul.

Benstead, J., Wall, R. and Forbes, C. (1994) ' Cyberpunks, Ronnie Biggs and the culture of masculinity: getting men thinking', *Probation Journal*, 41, 1, 18-22.

Biestek, F.P. (1961) *The Casework Relationship.* London: Allen and Unwin.

Bilston, W.G. (1961) 'Group therapy in a probation setting', *Probation*, 9, 150-51.

Bissell, D. (1962) 'Group work in the probation setting', *British Journal Of Criminology*, 2, 3, 229-50.

Bissell, D. (1964) 'Group work in the probation setting', *Probation*, 10, 12, 178-81.

Blackburn, R. (1980) 'Still not working? A look at recent outcomes in offender rehabilitation', Paper presented at the Scottish Branch of the British Psychological Society Conference on Deviance, University of Stirling.

Bochel, D. (1976) *Probation and After-care: Its Development in England & Wales.* Edinburgh: Scottish Academic Press.

Boswell, G., Davies, M. and Wright, A. (1993) *Contemporary Probation Practice.* Aldershot: Avebury.

Bottoms, A. and Stelman, A. (1988) *Social Inqiry Reports. A Framework for Practice.* Aldershot: Wildwood House.

Bottoms, A.E. and McWilliams, W. (1979) 'A non-treatment paradigm for probation practice', *British Journal of Social Work*, 9, 159-202.

Bowpitt, G. (1998) 'Evangelical Christianity, secular humanism, and the genesis of British social work', *British Journal of Social Work*, 28, 675-93.

Braithwaite, R.M. (1969) 'The search for a primary task', *Probation Journal*, 15, 1, 57-60.

Broadbent, A. (1989) 'Poor clients: what can I do?', *Probation Journal*, 36, 151-4.

Brody, S.R. (1976) *The Effectiveness of Sentencing.* London: HMSO.

Brown, A. (1979) *Groupwork.* London: Heinemann Educational.

Brown, A., Caddick, B., Gardner, M. and Sleeman, S. (1982) 'Towards a British model of groupwork', British Journal of Social Work, 12, 587-603.

Brown, A. and Seymour, B. (eds) (1984) *Intake Groups for Clients: A Probation Innovation.* University of Bristol.

Brown, J.M. and McCulloch, J.W. (1969) 'Reading habits of probation officers', *Probation Journal*, 15, 1, 13-17.

Brown, W. (1934) 'Psychology and the offender', *Probation*, 1, 18, 275-6.

Brownlee, I. (1998) *Community Punishment. A Critical Introduction.* Harlow: Longman.

Bryant, M., Coker, J., Estlea, B., Himmel., S. and Knapp, T. (1978) 'Sentenced to social work', *Probation Journal*, 38, 123-6.

Bunning, M.R. (1975) 'The Summit Club', *Probation*, 22, 1. 22-5.

Burns, Dr. (1930) 'The psychology of the criminal', *Probation*, 1, 3, 38-40.

Burns, Dr. C.L.C. (1930) 'Points in the study and treatment of the young probationer', *Probation*, 1, 4, 52-3.

Burns, Dr. C.L.C. (1931) 'Investigations. report of a debate at the annual conference of the National Association of Probation Officers', *Probation*, 1, 9, 133-4.

Carey, Mrs. (1924) 'A probation officer's point of view', *Howard Journal of Criminal Justice*, 1, 3, 108-111.

Carpenter, M. and Gibbens, F. (1973) 'Combined operations (Intermediate Treatment)', *Probation*, 20, 3. 84-7.

Carr, J. (1913) 'Probation and its relationship with other agencies', *National Association of Probation Officers*, 3, 28-34.

Carroll, D. (1952) 'Personal relationships in the rehabilitation of persons on probation', in *European Seminar on Probation*. United Nations.

Carter, P. (2003) *Managing Offenders and Reducing Crime. A New Approach.* London: Home Office.

Cary, Mrs. (1913) 'The value of the probation system as applied to women', *National Association of Probation Officers*, 3, 14-15.

Cary, Mrs. (1915) 'Social clubs for probationers; their needs and objects', *National Association of Probation Officers*, 6, 102-3.

Chapman, C. (1926) *The Poor Man's Court of Justice: Twenty Five Years As A Metropolitan Magistrate.* London: Hodder and Stoughton.

Chapman, T. (1995) 'Creating a culture of change: A case study of a car crime project in Belfast', in McGuire, J. (ed.) (1995) *What Works: Reducing Offending.* Chichester: Wiley.

Cheetham, J., Fuller, R., McIvor, G. and Petch, A. (1992) *Evaluating Social Work Effectiveness.* Buckingham: Open University Press.

Chesney-Lind, M. (1997) *The Female Offender. Girls, Women and Crime.* London: Sage.

Chesterton, Mrs. Cecil. (1928) Women of the Underworld. London: Stanley Paul and Co. Ltd.

Chinn, H. (1916) 'Probation work among children', *National Association of Probation Officers*, 7, 123-5.

Chinn, H. (1920) 'Probation officers and their work', *National Association of Probation Officers*, 13, 248-9.

Chinn, H. (1926) 'One aspect of the problem of adolescence', *National Association of Probation Officers*, 25, 600-603.

Chinn, H. (1930) 'A comparative study of probation in America', *Probation*, 1, 4, 56-9.

Chinn, H. (1931) 'Home visiting', *Probation*, 1, 6, 84-5.

Chinn, H. (1931a) 'Investigations. Report of a debate at the annual conference of the National Association of Probation Officers', *Probation*, 1, 9, 131-2.

Chinn, H. (1932) 'Investigations by the probation officer', *Probation*, 1, 13, 199-200.

Chiqwada-Bailey, R. (1997) *Black Women's Experiences of the Criminal Justice System.* Winchester: Waterside Press.

Church of England Temperance Chronicle (1873) Canon Ellison's Sermon at St. Pauls 1st May.

Church of England Temperance Society (1885) Minutes of the Executive of the Church of England Temperance Society.

Church of England Temperance Society (1889) Minutes of the Council of Church of England Temperance Society.

Church of England Temperance Society (1922) *Sixty Years Old. A Short History of a Great Work 1862-1922.* Westminster: Church of England Temperance Society.

Chute, C.L. (1933) 'The Development of probation in the United States', in Glueck, S. (ed.) *Probation and Criminal Justice. Essays in Honor of Herbert. C. Parsons.* New York: The Macmillan Company.

Chute, C.L. (1939) *Preface to John Augustus (1852) A Report of the Labors of John Augustus, for the Last Ten Years, in Aid of the Unfortunate: Containing a Description of his Method of Operation: Striking Incidents, and Observation upon the Improvement of some of Our City Institutions, with a View to the Benefit of the Prisoner and Society.* Boston: Wright & Hasty, Printers. Reprinted as John Augustus, First Probation Officer by the National Probation Association in 1939.

Chute, C.L. and Bell, M. (1956) *Crimes, Courts and Probation.* New York: The Macmillan Company.

Clarke Hall, W. (1912) How to Deal with Juvenile Female Vice. A paper read at the Conference of the Association Of Lady Visitors to Prisons 7th May 1912. Notes on Work amongst the Fallen and Cautionary List, No. 113, London October 1912.

Clarke Hall, W. (1929) 'The training and appointment of probation officers', *Probation*, 1, 1, 7-8.

Clarke Hall, W. (1931) 'Investigations. Report of a debate at the annual conference of the National Association of Probation Officers', *Probation*, 1, 9, 131-3.

Clarke Hall, W. (1933) 'The extent of probation in England', in Glueck, S. (ed.) *Probation and Criminal Justice. Essays in Honor of Herbert. C. Parsons.* New York: The Macmillan Company.

Clement Brown, S. (1934) 'Is delinquency an individual or a family problem', *Probation*, 1, 19, 297-300.

Clift, C.E. (1931) 'Investigations. Report of a debate at the annual conference of the National Association of Probation Officers', *Probation*, 1, 9, 135.

Clulow, C. (1974) 'Time: a Solution for the Piecemeal Operative?', *Probation Journal*, 21, 2, 50-6.

Coates, L.V. (1974) 'Reflections on a Differential Treatment Plan', *Probation Journal*, 21, 1, 11-15.

Coker, J.D. and Sands, D. (1970) 'The use of small groups in prison', *Probation*, 16, 1, 71-5.

Cooper, E. (1987) 'Probation practice in the criminal and civil courts', in Harding, J. (ed.) *Probation and the Community. A practice and policy reader.* London and New York: Tavistock Publications.

Corden, J. (1980) 'Contracts in social work practice', *British Journal of Social Work*, 10, 143-61.

Cottam, J. C. H. (1943) 'Causes and treatment of delinquency', *Probation*, 4, 6, 71-3.

Cox, E.W. (1877) *The Principles of Punishment as Applied in the Administration of the Criminal Law byJudges and Magistrates.* London: Law Times Office.

Crabb, W. C. (1915) 'Probation officers and probationers: Their relation towards each other', *National Association of Probation Officers*, 6, 98-100.

Creighton-Miller, H. (1929) 'The unconscious motive of the juvenile delinquent', *Probation*, 1, 1, 12-14.

Creighton-Miller, H. (1931) 'The probationer and the social contract', *Probation*, 1, 7, 99-100.

Croker-King, E. (1915) 'Juvenile probation', *National Association of Probation Officers*, 5, 66-7.

Dark, S. (1939) *IN AS MUCH....Christianity in the Police Courts*. London: Student Christian Movement Press.

Davies, H. and Lister, M. (1992) *Evaluation of Offending Behaviour Groups*. Birmingham: West Midlands Probation Service.

Davies, M. (1974) *Social Work in the Environment. A Study of One Aspect of Probation Practice*. HORS 21. London: HMSO.

Dawtry, F. (1958) 'Whither probation', *British Journal of Delinquency*, VIII, 3, 180-87.

de B. Hubert, W. H. (1935) 'Nervous illness and delinquency', *Probation*, 1, 23, 363-6.

de Constobadie, F. (1930) 'Problems of probation and missionary work', *Probation*, 1, 3, 42-4.

Deering, J., Thurston, R. and Vanstone, M. (1996) 'Individual supervision and reconviction: an experimental programme in Pontypridd', *Probation Journal*, 43, 70-76.

Denney, D. (1992) *Racism and Anti-Racism in Probation*. London: Routledge.

Denney, D. and Carrington, B. (1981) 'Young Rastifarians and the probation service', *Probation Journal*, 28, 4, 111-17.

Dilts, R. (1983) *Applications of Neuro-Linguistic Programming*. Meta Publications.

Dobson, G. (1975) 'Team work before groupwork', *Probation Journal*, 22, 1, 17-22.

Dobson, G. (1976) 'The Differential Treatment Unit: Part 1', *Probation Journal*, 23, 4, 105-8.

Drakeford, M. and Vanstone, M. (eds) (1996) *Beyond Offending Behaviour*. Aldershot: Arena.

Du Cane, E. F. (1885) *The Punishment and Prevention of Crime*. London: Macmillan.

Durbin, R. J. (1982) 'A barge experiment', *Probation Journal*, 29, 2, 51-3.

Ellis, H. (1910) *The Criminal*. Fourth Edition. London: Blackwood, Scott and Company.

Ellison, M. (1934) *Sparks beneath the Ashes. Experiences of a London Probation Officer*. London: John Murray.

Farrall, S. (2003) 'J'accuse: Probation evaluation research epistemologies. Part one: The critique', *Criminal Justice*, 3, 2, 161-79.

Farrall, S. (2003a) 'J'accuse: Probation evaluation research epistemologies. Part two: This time its personal and social factors', *Criminal Justice*, 3, 3, 249-68.

Farrimond, R.H. (1960) 'Casework', *Probation*, 9, 8, 120.

Farrimond, R.H. (1965) 'Casework', *Probation*, 11, 1, 9-11.

Farrington, D.P. (1979) 'Delinquent behaviour modification in the natural environment', *British Journal of Ciminology*, 19, 4, 353-72.

Feeley, M. and Simon, J. (1992) 'The new penology: notes on the emerging strategy of corrections and its implications', *Criminology*, 30, 449-74.

Feldman, Dr. I. (1931) 'Some problems of the normal adolescent', *Probation*, 1, 9, 134-5.

Felton, F. (1967) 'Compulsion and casework', *Probation Journal*, 13, 1, 13-14.

Fenner, F. (1856) *Raising The Veil; Or, Scenes In The Courts*. Boston: James French & Company.

Ferris, R.H. (1933) 'The Case History in Probation', in Glueck, S. (ed.) *Probation and Criminal Justice. Essays in Honor of Herbert. C. Parsons*. New York: The Macmillan Company.

182   *Supervising Offenders in the Community*

Fielding, N. (No date) *The Training of Probation Officers*. Occasional Paper No. 2.
Sociology Department, University of Surrey.
Fishwick, C. (1969) 'Pointers for probation', *Probation*, 15, 1, 54-7.
Flather, Miss. (1898) 'Changed aspects and present needs of rescue work', *Notes on work
amongst the fallen and the cautionary list*. London July 1898 Annual Conference.
Flegg, J. (1972) 'But probation officers do run groups', *Probation*, 18, 2, 56-8.
Fletcher-Cooke, C. (1962) 'The Morison Report and after', *Probation*, 10, 2, 24-9.
Flexner, B. and Baldwin, R.N. (1916) *Juvenile Courts and Probation*. New York: Century Co.
Folkard, M. S., Fowles, A.J., McWilliams, B.C., Smith, D.D., Smith, D.E. and Walmsley,
G.R. (1974) *IMPACT. Intensive Matched Probation and After-Care Treatment. Volume
1. The design of the probation experiment and an interim evaluation*. HORS 24 London:
HMSO.
Folkard, M.S., Smith, D.E. and Smith, D.D. (1976) *IMPACT. Intensive Matched Probation
and After-Care Treatment. Volume 11. The results of the experiment*. HORS 36 London:
HMSO.
Folkard, S., Lyon, K., Carver, M.M. and O'Leary, E. (1966) *Probation Research. A
Preliminary Report*. HORS 7 London: HMSO.
Forder, R.A. (1960) 'Casework', *Probation*, 9, 8, 120.
Foren, R. and Bailey, R. (1968) *Authority in Social Casework*. Oxford: Pergamon Press.
Forster, N. (1994) 'The analysis of company documentation', in Cassell, C. and Symon, G.
(eds) *Qualitative Methods in Organizational Research*. London: Sage.
Foucault, M. (1977) *Discipline and Punish. The Birth of the Prison*. London: Penguin
Books.
France, S. (1917) ' "Crime" and "Criminals" ', *National Association of Probation Officers*,
8, 150-52.
Francis, J.R. (1932) 'Constructive probation work', *Probation*, 1, 11, 168-9.
Frayne, L. (1968) 'Supervision in social casework', *Probation*, 14, 3, 84-8.
Freeguard, M. (1964) 'Five girls against Authority', *New Society*, 18-20.
Fry, M. (1952) 'The scope for the use for probation', in *European Seminar on Probation*.
United Nations.
Galton, F. (1909) *Essays in Eugenics*. London: The Eugenics Education Society.
Gamon, H. R. P. (1907) *The London Police Court. Today and Tomorrow*. London: J. M.
Dent.
Garland, D. (1985) Punishment and Welfare: A History of Penal Strategies. Aldershot:
Gower.
Garland, D. (1990) *Punishment and Modern Society*. Oxford: Clarendon.
Garrett, A. C. (1961) 'Casework', *Probation*, 9, 9, 134.
Glueck, B. (1933) 'Analytical psychiatry and criminology', in Glueck, S. (ed.) *Probation
and Criminal Justice. Essays in Honor of Herbert. C. Parsons*. New York: The
Macmillan Company.
Glueck, S. (ed.) (1933) *Probation and Criminal Justice. Essays in Honor of Herbert. C.
Parsons*. New York: The Macmillan Company.
Glueck, S. (1933a) 'The significance and promise of probation', in Glueck, S. (ed.)
Probation and Criminal Justice. Essays in Honor of Herbert. C. Parsons. New York:
The Macmillan Company.

Glueck, S. (1939) *Introduction to John Augustus (1852) A Report of the Labors of John Augustus, for the Last Ten Years, in Aid of the Unfortunate: Containing a Description of his Method of Operation: Striking Incidents, and Observation upon the Improvement of some of Our City Institutions, with a View to the Benefit of the Prisoner and Society.* Boston: Wright & Hasty, Printers. Reprinted as John Augustus, First Probation Officer by the National Probation Association in 1939.

Goldberg, E.M. and Stanley, S.J. (1979) 'A Task Centred approach to probation', in King, J. (ed.) *Pressures and Change in the Probation Service.* Cropwood Conference series 11.

Goldblatt, P. and Lewis, C. (1998) *Reducing Offending: an assessment of research evidence on ways of dealing with offending behaviour,* HORS 187, London: Home Office.

Golding, R.R.W. (1959) 'A probation technique', *Probation,* 11, 1, 9-11.

Goldstone, H. (1932) 'Economic causes of crime', *Probation,* 1, 12, 185-6.

Goring, C. (1919) *The English Convict.* Abridged Edition. London: HMSO.

Gorman, K. (2001) 'Cognitive Behaviourism and the Holy Grail', *Probation Journal,* 48, 1, 3-9.

Goslin, J. (1964) 'The Great Deception', Probation, 10, 11, 168-70.

Grinnell, F.W. (1917) 'Probation as an orthodox common law practice in Massachusetts prior to the statutory system', *Massachusetts Law Review* 2, 591-639.

Grinnell, F.W. (1941) 'The common law history of probation. An illustration of the "equitable" growth of criminal law', *Journal of Criminal Law and Criminology,* XXXII, 1, 70-91.

Gwym, S.A. (1941) 'Causes of delinquency', *Probation,* 3, 16, 226-7.

Hadfield, Dr. J.A. (1933) 'Probation in the scheme of national mental welfare', *Probation,* 1, 17, 267-8.

Haines, J. (1967) 'Satisfaction in probation work', *Probation,* 13, 3, 75-80.

Hall, J. (1974) 'Penal institutions and behaviour modification', *Probation Journal,* 21, 2, 46-50.

Hamblin Smith, M. (1931) 'The Birmingham scheme – a review', *Howard Journal,* 1, 1, 81-5.

Hankinson, I. and Stephens, D. (1984) 'A barge experiment', *Probation Journal,* 31, 1, 25-8.

Hansard 5th May 1886. *Probation of First Offenders Bill.* Second Reading. House of Commons.

Hansard 8th May 1907. *Probation of Offenders Bill.* Order for Second Reading. House of Commons.

Hardiker, P. (1977) 'Social work ideologies in the probation service', *British Journal of Social Work,* 7, 2, 13-54.

Harding, J. (1971) 'Barge cruising: an experiment in group work', *Probation,* 17, 3, 45-7.

Harman, J. (1978) 'Crisis Intervention (a form of diversion)', *Probation Journal,* 25, 4, 115-21.

Harris, J. (1937) *A Sheaf of Memories.* Lowestoft: M. F. Robinson and Co. Ltd.

Harris, R.J. (1980) 'A changing service: the case for separating care and control in probation practice', *British Journal of Social Work,* 10 (2), 163-84.

Harris, S.W. (1937) *Probation and Other Social Work of the Courts.* The Third Clarke Hall Lecture delivered in the Hall of Gray's Inn London on 27th January, 1937. Rochester: Stanhope Press.

Harrison, B. (1971) *Drink and the Victorians*. The Temperance Question in England 1815-72. London: Faber and Faber.

Hawkins, E. (1952) 'Some thoughts on the principles of group reporting', *Probation*, 6, 16, 184-5.

Hedderman, C. and Sugg, D. (1997) *The Influence of Cognitive-Behavioural Approaches: a Survey of Probation Programmes*, Part 2, HORS 171, London: Home Office.

Heidensohn, F. (1987) *Women and Crime*. Basingstoke: Macmillan.

Heimler, E. (1975), *Survival in Society*. London: Weidenfield and Nicolson.

Helmsley, Mr. (1915) 'Juvenile crime: some causes and remedies', *National Association of Probation Officers*, 6, 100-102.

Hemsley, Mrs. (1920) 'Probation from a women's outlook', *National Association of Probation Officers*, 12, 221-2.

Hil, R. (1986) 'Centre 81: clients' and officers' views on the Southampton day centre', in Pointing, J. (ed.) *Alternatives to Custody*. Oxford: Blackwell.

Hill, J., Thomas, S. and Vanstone, M. (1993) 'Opening doors with offenders: groupwork in a probation day centre', in A. Brown and B. Caddick, *Groupwork Practice in Probation*. London: Whiting and Birch.

Hill, M.D. (1857) *Suggestions for the Repression of Crime Contained in Charges Delivered to the Grand Juries of Birmingham Supported by Additional Facts and Arguments: Together with Articles from Reviews and Newspapers Controverting or Advocating the Conclusions of the Author*. London: John. W. Parker and Son.

Hodson, C.B.S. (1932) 'Biological aspects of crime', *Probation*, 10, 151-2.

Holden, G.E. (1960) 'The role of the caseworker', *Probation*, 9, 8, 119-20.

Holmes, R. (1915) *My Police Court Friends with the Colours*. Edinburgh and London: William Blackwood and Sons.

Holmes, R. (1923) *Them That Fall*. Edinburgh and London: William Blackwood and Sons.

Holmes, T. (1902) *Pictures and Problems from London Police Courts*. London: Edward Arnold.

Holmes, T. (1908) *Known to the Police*. London: Edward Arnold.

Holmes, T. (1912) *Psychology and Crime*. London: J. M. Dent and Sons Ltd.

Home Office (1909) *Report of the Departmental Committee on the Probation of Offenders Act*. London: HMSO.

Home Office (1922) *Report of the Departmental Committee on the Training, Appointment and Payment of Probation Officers*. London: HMSO.

Home Office (1932) *Report of the Departmental Committee on Persistent Offenders*. London: HMSO.

Home Office (1962) *Report of the Departmental Committee on the work Probation Service*. Cmnd. 1650. London: HMSO.

Home Office (1966) *Report on the work of the Probation and After-Care Department 1962 to 1965*. Cmnd. 3107 London: HMSO.

Home Office (1970) *Report of the Advisory Council on the Penal System. Non-Custodial and Semi-Custodial Penalties*. London: HMSO.

Home Office (1984) *Probation Service in England and Wales: Statement of National Objectives and Priorities*. London: Home Office.

Home Office (1992) *National Standards for the Supervision of Offenders in the Community*. London: Home Office.

Home Office (1995) *National Standards for the Supervision of Offenders in the Community*.London: Home Office.

Home Office (1998) *Effective Practice Initiative. National Implementation Plan for the Supervision of Offenders*. Circular 35, London: HMSO.

Hopkins, P (1939) Psychology and the social worker', *Probation*, 3, 4, 53-55 and 64.

House of Lords Debates 5th August 1907. House of Lords.

Hubert, A. (1917) Untitled paper given to the annual conference of NAPO, *National Association of Probation Officers*, 8, 152-3.

Hudson, B. (1996) *Understanding Justice: An introduction to the ideas, perspectives and controversies in modern penal theory*. Buckingham: Open University Press.

Hudson, B.L. (1988) 'Social skills training in practice', *Probation* Journal. 35, 3, 85-91.

Hudson, B.L. (1976) 'The haunted bedroom - a case study in behaviour modification', *Social Work* Today, 8, 10, 14-15.

Hughes, E.P. (1903) *The Probation System of America*. London: The Howard Association.

Hugman, B. (1980) 'Radical practice in probation', in Brake, M. and Bailey, R. (eds) *Radical Social Work and Practice*. London: Edward Arnold.

Hunt, A.W. (1964) 'Enforcement in probation casework', *Howard Journal*, 4, 3, 239-52.

Hunt, A.W. (1966) 'Enforcement in probation casework', in Younghusband, E. (ed.) *New Developments in Casework. Readings in Social Work.* Volume 11. London: George Allen and Unwin Ltd.

Hunt, D.E. (1972) 'Probation Forum. Why probation officers don't run groups', *Probation*, 18, 2, 59-60.

Ignatieff, M. (1978) *A Just Measure of Pain. The Penitentiary in the Industrial Revolution 1750-1850*. New York: Pantheon Books.

Inner London Probation Service (1972*) Proposal paper for the establishment of a day training centre within the area*. Inner London Probation Service.

Ireland, M. and Dawes, J. (1975) 'Working with the client in his family', *Probation Journal*, 22, 4, 113-16.

Jarvis, F. (1972) *Advise, Assist and Befriend: A History of the Probation and After-Care Service*. London: NAPO.

Jarvis, F. (1972a) *Friend at Court. A Career in Probation and After-Care*. Reading: Educational Explorers.

Jehu, D. (1967) *Learning Theory and Social Work*. London: Routledge and Kegan Paul.

Jenkins, J. and Lawrence, D. (1992) *Black Groups Initiative Review*, unpublished paper, Inner London Probation Service.

Johnson, A. (ed.) (1928) *Dictionary of American Biography*. London: Oxford University Press.

Johnson, F.R. (1928a) *Probation for Juveniles and Adults. A Study of Principles and Methods*. New York: Century Co.

Jones, D.A. (1967) 'Group work – in search of a model', *Probation*, 13, 2, 44-6.

Jones, H. (1962) 'The group approach to treatment', *Howard Journal*, XI, 1, 58-63.

Jones, H. (1965) 'Groupwork. Some general considerations', *Probation*, 11, 3, 91-4.

Jones, M., Mordecai, M., Rutter, F. and Thomas, L. (1993) 'A Miskin model of groupwork with women offenders', in Brown, A. and Caddick, B. (eds) *Groupwork with Offenders*. London: Whiting and Birch.

Kay, R. (no date) *The Rainer Foundation*. London: Rainer Foundation.

Keidan, H. (1963) 'A multi-purpose service', *Probation*, 10, 5, 70-72.

Kennedy, J.E.R. (1941) 'Mother and child', *Probation*, 3, 16, 225-6.

Kenyon, Mrs. (1921) 'How to help girls in a Manufacturing Town', *National Association of Probation Officers*, 16, 317-18.

King, J. (1969) *The Probation and After-Care Service*. Third Edition. London: Butterworth

Kydd, J.A. (1936) 'Probation and social economics', *Probation*, 2, 3, 41-3.

Lacey, M. (1984) 'Intermediate Treatment: a theory for practice', *Probation Journal*, 31, 3, 104-7.

Landers, J.J. (1957) 'Group therapy in H M Prison, Wormwood Scrubs', *Howard Journal*, Vol. IX, 4, 328-42.

Lawson, J. (1984) 'Probation in St. Pauls. Teamwork in a multi-racial, inner city area', *Probation Journal*, 31, 3, 93-5.

Le Mesurier, L. (1931) *Boys in Trouble. A study of Adolescent Crime and its Treatment*. London: John Murray.

Le Mesurier, L. (1935) *A Handbook of Probation*. London: National Association of Probation Officers.

Leeson, C. (1914) *The Probation System*. London: P.S. King and Son.

Leeves, R.E. (1963) 'The principles of probation', *Probation*, 10, 5, 68-70.

Leeves, R.E. (1965) 'Casework in probation', *Probation*, 11, 2, 65-6.

Leeves, R.E. (1972) 'New form of intensive supervision', *Probation*, 18, 2, 48-51.

Leycester King, J. (1939) 'Personality relations in probation work', *Probation*, 3, 7, 99-100 and 111.

Lickorish, J.R. (1965) 'The offender and the psychologist', *Probation*, 11, 2, 67-8.

Lipsey, M. (1995) 'What do we learn from 400 research studies on the effectiveness of treatment with juvenile delinquents?', in McGuire, J. (ed.) (1995) *What Works: Reducing Offending*. Chichester: Wiley.

Lipton, D., Martinson, R. and Wilks, J. (1975) *The Effectiveness of Correctional Treatment*. New York: Praeger.

Losel, F. (1995) 'The efficacy of correctional treatment: a review and synthesis of meta-evaluations', in McGuire, J. (ed.) (1995) *What Works: Reducing Offending*. Chichester: Wiley.

Loughlin, J. (1915) 'Juvenile Crime and Some of the Causes', *National Association of Probation Officers*, 6, 109-11.

Macadam, E. (1925) *The Equipment of the Social Worker*. London: George Allen & Unwin Ltd.

MacDonald, G. (1993) 'Developing empirically-based practice in probation', *British Journal of Social Work*, 24, 405-27.

Macrae, F.J. (1958) 'The English probation training system', *British Journal of Delinquency*, VIII, 3, 210-15.

Mair, G. (1988) *Probation Day Centres*. Home Office Research and Planning Unit, London: HMSO.

Mair, G. (1997) 'Community penalties and probation', in Maguire, M., Morgan, R. and Reiner, R. (eds) *The Oxford Handbook of Criminology*, Second Edition. Oxford: Clarendon Press.

Mair, G. and May, C. (1997) Offenders on Probation. HORS 167. London: HMSO.

Martinson, R. (1974), 'What works? Questions and answers about prison reform', *The Public Interest*, Spring No.5: 22-54.

Mathieson, D. (1975) 'Conflict and change in probation', *Probation Journal*, 22, 2, 36-41.

May, T. (1991) *Probation: Politics, Policy and Practice*. Buckingham: Open University Press.

May, T. (1991a) 'Under siege: probation in a changing environment', in Reiner, R. and Cross, M. (eds) *Beyond Law and Order*. London: Macmillan.

May, T. (1993) *Social Research. Issues, Methods and Process*. Buckingham: Open University Press.

May, T. (1994) Probation and community sanctions, in Maguire, M., Morgan, R. and Reiner, R. (eds) *The Oxford Handbook of Criminology*, Second Edition. Oxford: Clarendon Press.

Mayling, G.H. (1933) 'Probation officers' investigations', *Probation*, 1, 14, 217-19.

McCullough, M.K. (1962) 'The practice of groupwork in a hostel', *Probation*, 10, 3, 36-7.

McCullough, M.K. (1963) 'Groupwork in probation', *New Society*, 21, 9-11.

McCullough, M.K. and Ely, P. (1968) *Social Work with Groups*. London: Routledge and Kegan Paul.

McGuire, J. and Priestley, P. (1985) *Offending Behaviour: skills and stratagems for going straight*. London: Batsford.

McGuire, J. and Priestley, P. (1995) 'Reviewing "what works": past, present and future', in McGuire, J. (ed.) (1995) *What Works: Reducing Offending*. Chichester: Wiley.

McIvor, G. (1990) *Sanctions for Serious or Persistent Offenders*. Stirling: Social Work Research Centre.

McConville, S. (1995) 'The Victorian prison: England, 1865-1965', in Morris, N. and Rothman, D. J. (eds) *The Oxford History of the English Prison. The practice of Punishment in Western Society*. Oxford: Oxford University Press.

McWilliams, W. (1983) 'The Mission to the English police courts 1876-1936,' *Howard Journal Of Criminal Justice*, 22, 129-47.

McWilliams, W. (1985) 'The Mission transformed: professionalism of probation between the wars,' *Howard Journal Of Criminal Justice*, 24, 257-74.

McWilliams, W. (1986) 'The English probation system and the diagnostic ideal,' *Howard Journal Of Criminal Justice*, 25, 241-60.

McWilliams, W. (1987) 'Probation, pragmatism and policy,' *Howard Journal Of Criminal Justice*, 26, 97-121.

Membury, S.J. (1922) 'Brothers, we are builders of men', *National Association of Probation Officers*, 17, 345-6.

Millard, D. (1989), 'Looking backwards to the future', *Probation Journal*, 36 (1), 18-21.

Minn, W.G. (1950) 'Probation work', in Morris, C. (ed.) *Social Casework in Great Britain*. London: Faber and Faber.

Mistry, T. (1993) Establishing a feminist model of groupwork in the probation service in Brown, A. and Caddick, B. (eds) *Groupwork with Offenders*. London: Whiting and Birch.

Moreland, D.W. (1941) 'John Augustus and his successors', *National Association Yearbook*, 1-23.

Morley, H. (1986) 'Heimler's Human Social Functioning', *Probation Journal*, 33, 4, 140-42.

Morris, P. (1966) 'Trends in the probation and after-care service', *Probation*, 12, 3, 84-91.

Muirhead, J.H. (1914) *Introduction to C. Leeson. The Probation System*. London: P.S. King and Son.

Murch, M. (1969) 'Seebohm: a painful dilemma for probation', *Probation*, 15, 1, 18-23.

Musgrove, R. (1923) 'The probation officer's influence', *National Association of Probation Officers*, 20, 434-5.

NADPAS (1956) Handbook of the National Association of Discharged Prisoners' Societies. London: NADPAS.

NAPO (1925) 'East End boys' hostel. Problem of adolescents', *National Association of Probation Officers*, 23, 547-8.

NAPO (1956) 'Casework supervision in the probation service', *Probation*, 8, 7, 97-100.

Neary, M. (1992) 'Robert Ross, probation and the problem of rationality', unpublished paper distributed at the 'What Works' conference, Salford University.

Newburn, T. (1995) *Crime and Criminal Justice Policy*. Harlow: Longman.

Newton, G. (1956) 'Trends in probation training', *British Journal of Delinquency*, VII, 2, 123-35.

Norris, A.H. (1934) 'The problem of the mentally defective child or young person', *Probation*, 1, 20, 308-9.

Northumbria Probation Service (1994) *Survey of Probation Practice on Poverty Issues*. Northumbria Probation Service.

NPCM (1950) *Annual Report*. National Police Court Mission.

OEDIPUS (1956) 'How deep is your casework', *Probation*, 8, 1, 10-12.

Osler, A. (1995) *Introduction to the Probation Service*. Winchester: Waterside Press.

Page, M. (1992) *Crime Fighters of London. A History of the Origins and Development of the London Probation Service 1876-1965*. London: Inner London Probation Service Development Trust.

Paine, E.C. (1931) 'Investigations. Report of a debate at the annual conference of the National Association of Probation Officers', *Probation*, 1, 9, 134-5.

Palin, J. (1915) 'Homes, rescue and prevention, in connection with probation work', *National Association of Probation Officers*, 6, 88-9.

Palmer, D.S. (1966) 'Group work in probation', *Probation*, 12, 1, 18-20.

Palmer, T. (1975) 'Martinson revisited', *Journal of Research in Crime and Delinquency*, 12, 133-52.

Parker, K. and Bilston, W.G. (1959) 'Belmont: a therapeutic opportunity', *Probation*, 9, 3, 36-7.

Parkinson, G. (1965) 'Casework and the persistent offender', *Probation*, 11, 1, 11-17.

Parkinson, G. (1966) 'Passivity and delinquency', *Probation*, 12, 2, 59-65.

Parris, K.C. (1968) 'Casework in a probation setting', *Probation*, 14, 2, 36-40.

Parsloe, P. (1972) 'Why don't probation officers run client groups?', *Probation*, 18, 1, 4-8.

Paskell, W. (1952) 'Probation casework: basic principles and methods', in European Seminar on Probation. United Nations.

Pearce, W.H. (1951) 'Probationers in camp', *Probation*, 6, 2, 15-16.

Pearson, G. (1983) *Hooligan. A History of Respectable Fears*. London: Macmillan.

Pease, K. (1999) 'The probation career of Al Truism', *Howard Journal of Criminal Justice*, 38, 1, 2-16.

Percival, F.W. (1941) 'The problem of juvenile delinquency', *Probation*, 3, 16, 227-8.

Perry, F. G. (1974) *Information for the Court. A New Look at Social Inquiry Reports.* Cambridge: University of Cambridge Institute of Criminology.

Petersilia, J. (1990) 'Conditions that permit intensive supervision programmes to survive', *Crime and Delinquency*, 36, 126-45.

Pickersgill-Cunliffe, Miss. (1913) Opinions and Hints on Rescue Work. Notes on work amongst the fallen and the cautionary list. London April 1913 Annual Conference.

Pincus, A. and Minahan, A. (1973) Social *Work Practice: Model and Method.* Itasca: F.E. Peacock.

Pitts, J. (1992) 'The end of an era', *Howard Journal Of Criminal Justice*, 31, 133-49.

Potter, J. Hasloch (1927) *IN AS MUCH. The Story of the Police Court Mission 1876-1926.* London: Williams and Northgate Ltd.

Potts, W.A. (1903) *The problem of the morally defect. A paper read at the recent Conference on the Care of the Feeble-minded at the Guildhall.* Notes on work Amongst the Fallen and Cautionary List.

Potts, W.A. (1928) 'The medical aspects of delinquency', *National Association of Probation Officers*, 8, 671-3.

Poulton, F. (1925) 'The spiritual factor in probation work', *National Association of Probation Officers*, 23, 546-7.

Pratt, A.B. (1925) 'Work with the delinquent outside of an institution', *National Association Of Probation Officers*, 23, 548-9.

Pratt, E.G. and Ratcliffe, S. (1954) 'Arethusa Camp. Notes and criticisms', *British Journal of Delinquency*, VI, 1, 53-61.

Pratt, J. (2000) 'Emotive and ostentatious punishment. Its decline and resurgence in modern society', *Punishment and Society*, 2, 4, 417-39.

Pratt, J. (2000a) 'The return of the wheelbarrow men: or, the arrival of postmodern penality', *British Journal of Criminology*, 40, 127-45.

Preston West Team (1977) 'Putting the sacred cows out to grass', *Probation Journal*, 24, 3, 92-6.

Priestley, P. (1985) *Victorian Prison Lives. English Prison Biography 1830-1914.* London: Methuen.

Priestley, P., McGuire, J., Flegg, D., Hemsley, V. and Welham, D. (1978) *Social Skills and Personal Problem Solving. A Handbook of Methods.* London: Tavistock.

Pritchard, C., Ford, P. and Cox, M. (1994) *Consumer opinions of the probation service: advice, assistance, befriending and reduction of crime.* Dorset Probation Service.

Probation Forum (1960) 'Responses to Golding', *Probation*, 9, 5, 68-70.

Radzinowicz, l. (ed.) (1958) *The Results of probation. A report of the Cambridge Department of Criminal Science.* London: Macmillan and Company Ltd.

Raeburn, W. (1958) 'Probation was made for man', *British Journal of Delinquency*, VIII, 3, 162-79.

Rainer Foundation (no date) *Advertisement for the Rainer Foundation.* Rainer Foundation Archive.

Ralli, N. (1941) 'Delinquency: how to tackle it', *Probation*, 3, 16, 229-30.

Rankin, C. (1921) 'The problem of the difficult case', *National Association of Probation Officers*, 16, 321-3.

Rawlings, P. (1999) *Crime and Power. A History of Criminal Justice 1688-1998.* London: Longmans.

190 *Supervising Offenders in the Community*

Raynor, P. (1985) *Social Work, Justice and Control.*, Oxford; Blackwell.

Raynor, P. (1988) *Probation as an Alternative to Custody.* Aldershot, Avebury.

Raynor, P. and Vanstone, M. (1994) 'Probation, Practice Effectiveness and the Non-Treatment Paradigm, *British Journal of Social Work*, 24, 387-404.

Raynor, P. and Vanstone, M. (1997) *Straight Thinking On Probation (STOP): The Mid Glamorgan Experiment. Probation Studies Unit.* Report No. 4. University of Oxford Centre For Criminological Research.

Raynor, P. and Vanstone, M. (2002) *Understanding Community Penalties; Probation, Change and Social Context.* Buckingham: Open University Press.

Rees, J.R. (1932) 'Psychological causes of crime', *Probation*, 1, 12, 183-4.

Reid, W.J. and Epstein, L. (1972) *Task-Centred Casework.* New York: Columbia University Press.

Reid, W.J. and Shyne, A. (1969) *Brief and Extended Casework.* New York: Columbia University Press.

Remmington, B. and Trusler, P. (1981) 'Behavioural methods for the probation service', *Probation Journal*, 28, 2, 52-5.

Report: Annual Report of the Howard Association, 1867.

Report: Annual Report of the Howard Association, 1868.

Report: Annual Report of the Howard Association, 1873.

Report: Annual Report of the Howard Association, 1874.

Report: Annual Report of the Howard Association, 1878.

Report: Annual Report of the Howard Association, 1881.

Report: Annual Report of the Howard Association, 1882.

Report: Annual Report of the Howard Association, 1883.

Report: Annual Report of the Howard Association, 1884.

Report: Annual Report of the Howard Association, 1896.

Report: Annual Report of the Howard Association, 1898.

Report: Annual Report of the Howard Association, 1901.

Report: Annual Report of the Howard Association, 1902.

Report: Annual Report of the Howard Association, 1903.

Report: Annual Report of the Howard Association, 1904.

Report: Annual Report of the Howard Association, 1905.

Report: Annual Report of the Howard Association, 1906.

Report: *Juvenile Offenders.* A Report based on an inquiry instituted by the Committee of the Howard Association. 1898a.

Report: The Third Annual Report of the London Diocesan Branch of the Church of England Temperance Society. 1895.

Report: The Ninth Annual Report of the London Diocesan Branch of the Church of England Temperance Society. 1901

Report: The Thirteenth Annual Report of the London Diocesan Branch of the Church of England Temperance Society. 1905

Report: *The Problem of the Feeble-Minded.* An Abstract of the Report of the Royal Commission on the Care and Control of the Feeble-Minded. 1909. London: P. S. King and Son.

Rimmer, J. (1995) 'How social workers and probation officers in England conceived their roles and responsibilities in the 1930s and 1940s', in Schwieson, J and Pettit, P. (eds) *Aspects of the History of British Social Work*. University of Reading.

Rose, A.G. (1947) 'What kind of probation officers do we need', *Probation*, 5, 12, 166-7.

Rose, G. (1961) *The Struggle for Penal Reform. The Howard League and its Predecessors*. London: Stevens and Sons Ltd.

Rose, N. (1985) *The Psychological Complex. Psychology, politics and society in England, 1869-1939*. London: Routledge and Kegan Paul.

Rose, N. (1996) 'Psychiatry as a political science: advanced liberalism and the administration of risk', *History of the Human Sciences*, 9, 2, 1-23.

Ross, R.R. and Fabiano, E.A. (1985) *Time to Think: a cognitive model of delinquency prevention and offender rehabilitation*. Johnson City, Tennessee: Institute of Social Sciences and Arts.

Ross, R.R. and Ross, R.D. (eds) (1995) *Thinking Straight*. Ottawa: AIR Training and Publications.

Ross, R.R., Fabiano, E.A. and Ewles, C.D. (1988) 'Reasoning and Rehabilitation', *International Journal of Offender Therapy and Comparative Criminology*, 32, 29-35.

Ross, R.R., Fabiano, E.A. and Ross, R.D. (1986) *Reasoning and Rehabilitation: a handbook for teaching cognitive skills*. Ottawa: University of Ottawa.

Rowntree, M. (1971) 'An introduction to intermediate treatment', *Probation*, 17, 1, 18-20.

Rowson, B. and McGuire, J. (eds). (1992) *What Works; effective methods to reduce offending*. Conference Proceedings 18th-19th April 1991.

Rumgay, J. (1996) 'Women offenders: towards needs-based policy', *Vista*, 2, 2, 104-15.

Russell, R. (1923) 'An Introduction to the Study of Psychology', *National Association of Probation Officers*, 19, 409-10.

Rutherford, A. (1986) *Growing Out of Crime*. Harmondsworth: Penguin.

Saleilles,R. (1911) *The Individualization of Punishment*. Translated from the second French edition by Rachel Szold Jastrow. London: William Heineman.

Sanders, H. (1961) 'A Time of re-birth', *Probation*, 9, 10, 141-4.

Sanders, H. (1962) 'A Turning point – in which direction', *Probation*, 10, 2, 21-4.

Sandham, J. (no date) *A Skills Audit for Warwickshire Probation Service*. Unpublished paper.

Schmideberg, M. (1965) 'Psychotherapy of offenders: its rationale and implications for general psychotherapy', *Probation*, 11, 1, 4-9.

Schmideberg, M. (1965a) 'Casework and the persistent offender', *Probation*, 11, 2, 66-7.

Senior, P. (1984) 'The probation order: vehicle of social work or social control?', *Probation Journal*, 31, 2, 64-70.

Senior, P. (1991) 'Groupwork in the probation service: care or control in the 1990s', *Groupwork*, 4, 3, 284-95.

Shaw, R. and Crook, H. (1977) 'Group techniques', *Probation*, 24, 2, 61-5.

Singer, L.R. (1991) 'A non-punitive paradigm for probation practice: some sobering thoughts', *British Journal of Social Work*, 21, 611-26.

Smith, H. (1922) 'The drunken offender and probation', *National Association of Probation Officers*, 18, 383-5.

Sohn, L. (1952) 'Group therapy for young delinquents', British Journal of Delinquency, 3,

20-33.

Sprott, W.J.H. (1931) 'Psychology and moral education', *Probation*, 1, 8, 123-4.

Stanley, A.R. (1982), 'A new structure for intake and allocation in a field probation unit', *British Journal of Social Work*, 12, 5, 487-506.

Stanley, R. and McCarthy, J. (1965) 'Working with parents', *Probation*, 11, 3, 99-101.

Stanton, W. (1925) 'The probation officer: a product of the new era', *National Association of Probation Officers*, 22, 499-501.

Stead, B.M. (1922) 'A personal survey of the probation system as applied to young women and girls', *National Association of Probation Officers*, 18, 374-5.

Stedman Jones, G. (1971) *Outcast London. A Study in the Relationship between Classes in Victorian Society*. Oxford: Clarendon Press.

Suttie, Dr. I.D. (1930) 'Normal offenders', *Probation,* 1, 5, 69-70.

Suttie, Dr. I.D. (1933) 'Mental and social health', Probation, 1, 15, 229-30.

Sutton, D. (no date) *A New Approach to Probation Supervision*. Unpublished paper.

Talbot, N.S. (1934) 'Influence and the probation officer', *Probation*, 1, 18, 273-4.

Tallack, W. (1871) Humanity and Humanitarianism. The Question of Criminal Lunacy and Capital Punishment. London: F. B. Kitto.

Tallack, W. (1872) *Defects in the Criminal Administration and Penal Legislation of Great Britain and Ireland. With Remedial Suggestions*. London: F. B. Kitto.

Tallack, W. (1984) *Penological and Preventative Principles*. New York and London: Garland Publishing, Inc. Original publication 1889 London: Wertheimer, Lea and Co.

Taylor, D. (1998) *Crime, Policing and Punishment in England, 1750-1914*. New York: St. Martin's Press.

Thompson, L. and Clare, R. (1978) 'Family therapy in probation', *Probation Journal*, 25, 3, 79-83.

Thompson, P. (1978) *The Voice of the Past. Oral History*. Oxford: Oxford University Press.

Thornborough, M.M. (1960) 'What are we doing and why?', *Probation*, 9, 6, 89-90.

Thornborough, P. (1974) 'Impact in Inner London', *Probation Journal*, 21, 2, 42-4.

Timasheff, N.S. (1941) *One Hundred Years of Probation 1841-1941 Part One. Probation in the United States, England and the Commonwealth of Nations*. New York: Fordham University Press.

Timasheff, N.S. (1941a) *Probation in Contemporary law. A Centennial Survey*. New York: Fordham University Press.

Timasheff, N.S. (1943) *One Hundred Years of Probation 1841-1941 Part Two. Probation in Continental Europe, Latin America, Asia, and Africa.*. New York: Fordham University Press.

Timasheff, N.S. (1949) *Probation in the Light of Criminal Statistics*. New York: Fordham University Press.

Totman, Miss (1897) Homes for Girls. Notes on work amongst the fallen and the cautionary list. No 35 London June 1897 Annual Conference.

Trotter, C. (1993) The Supervision of Offenders – *What Works?* A Study Undertaken in Community Based Corrections, Victoria. Social Work Department, Monash University and the Victoria Department of Justice, Melbourne.

Trought, Mr. (1925) 'Probation work as a profession', *National Association of Probation Officers*, 22, 509-10.

Tyrer, A.E. (1936) 'A probation officer at work', *Probation*, 2, 4, 57-8.

Underdown, A. (1998) *Strategies for Effective Supervision: Report of the HMIP What Works Project*. London: Home Office.

Vaisey, R. (1976) 'The Differential Treatment Unit: Part 2', *Probation Journal*, 23, 4, 108-11.

Vanstone, M. (1985) 'Moving away from help?: Policy and practice in probation day centres', *Howard Journal of Criminal Justice*, 24, 1, 20-28.

Vanstone, M. (2000) 'Cognitive-behavioural work with offenders in the UK: a history of influential endeavour', *Howard Journal of Criminal Justice*, 39, 2, 171-83.

Vanstone, M. (2003) 'A History of the Use of Groups in Probation Work: Part One – from 'Clubbing the Unclubbables' to Therapeutic Intervention', *Howard Journal*, 42, 1, 69-86.

Vanstone, M. (2004) 'Mission Control: The Origins and Early History of Probation', *Probation Journal*, 51, 1, 34-47.

Vanstone, M. (2004a) 'A history of the use of groups in probation work: part two - from negotiated treatment to evidenced-based practice in an accountable service', *Howard Journal*, 43, 2, 180-202.

Vass, A.A. (1990) *Alternatives to Prison: Punishment, Custody and The Community*. London, Sage Publications.

Vass, A.A. and Weston, A. (1990), 'Probation Day Centres as an alternative to custody: a "Trojan Horse" examined', *British Journal of Criminology*, 30: 189-206.

Vennard, J., Sugg, D. and Hedderman, C. (1997) *The use of cognitive-behavioural approaches with offenders: messages from research Part 1*. HORS 171, London: Home Office.

Vigor, J.A. (1945) 'First impressions of juvenile delinquency', *Probation*, 4, 10, 113-15.

Voelcker, M. (1969) 'Hafod Meurig: an experiment in 'Intermediate Treatment'', *Probation*, 15, 1, 8-12.

Walcott, R. (1968) 'The West Indian in the British casework setting', *Probation*, 14, 2, 45-7.

Waldren-Skinner, S. (1979) *Family Therapy: the Treatment of Natural Systems*. Routledge and Kegan Paul.

Walker, M. and Beaumont, B. (1981) *Probation Work: Critical Theory and Practice*. Oxford. Blackwell.

Walker, P. and Morley, R.E. (1954) 'A barge experiment', *Probation*, 7, 6, 63-4.

Ward, K. (1979) 'Fuel debts and the probation service', *Probation Journal*, 26, 4, 110-14.

Warner, Miss. (1929) 'The technique of probation', *Probation*, 1, 1, 10-11.

Waterhouse, J. (1983) 'The effectiveness of probation supervision', in Lishman, J. (ed.) *Social Work with Adult Offenders*. Research Highlights Number 5. University of Aberdeen.

Waters, R.W. (1976) 'The value of short-term work', *Probation Journal*, 23, 1, 17-20.

Way, T. (1932) 'Relaxations of standards of ordered life', *Probation*, 1, 12, 187-8.

Waycott, J.A. (1961) 'Probation officers and group therapy', *Probation*, 9, 11, 166-7.

Weaver, C. and Fox, C. (1984) 'Berkeley sex offenders group: a seven year evaluation', *Probation Journal*, 31, 143-6.

Weiss, H. (1933) 'The social worker's technique', in Glueck, S. (ed.) (1933) *Probation and Criminal Justice. Essays in honor of Herbert. C. Parsons*. New York: The Macmillan Company.

White, C. (1992) 'A TA approach to child sex abusers', *Probation Journal*, 39, 1, 36-40.

White, S. (1978) 'The nineteenth century origins of Pre-Sentence Reports', *Australian and New Zealand Journal of Criminology*, 11, 157-78.

White, S. (1979) 'Howard Vincent and the development of probation in Australia, New Zealand and the United Kingdom', *Historical Studies*, 18, 73, 598-617.

Whitehouse, P. (1983) 'Race, bias and social enquiry reports', *Probation Journal*, 30, 2, 43-9.

Whitfield, D. (1998) *Introduction to the Probation Service*. Second Edition. Winchester: Waterside Press.

Wilkins, L.T. (1958) 'A small comparative study of the results of probation', *British Journal of Delinquency*, VIII, 3, 201-7.

Willis, A. (1980) *Young Men on Probation. A Survey of the Probation Experience of Young Adult Male Offenders and their Supervising Officers*. Unpublished Monograph.

Willis, A. (1983) 'The balance between care and control in probation: a research note', *British Journal of Social Work*, 13, 339-46.

Willis, A. (1986), 'Help and control in probation: an empirical assessment of probation practice', in Pointing, J. (ed.) *Alternatives to Custody*. Oxford: Blackwell.

Wood, C. J. and Shember, A. J. (1973) 'A new role for the probation service', *Probation*, 19, 1, 18-21.

Wootton, B. (1959) *Social Science and Pathology*. London: George Allen & Unwin Ltd.

Worrall, A. (1990) *Offending Women: Female Lawbreakers and the Criminal Justice System*. London: Routledge.

Young, J. and Matthews, R. (eds) (1992) *Rethinking Criminology: The Realist Debate*. London: Sage.

Young, P. (1976) 'A sociological analysis of the early history of probation', *British Journal of Law and Society*, 3, 44-58.

Younghusband, E. (1952) 'Probation personnel', in European Seminar on Probation. United Nations.

Index